Domestic Arrangements

Medieval & Renaissance Literary Studies

Domestic Arrangements *in* Early Modern England

edited by
Kari Boyd McBride

Duquesne University Press
Pittsburgh, Pennsylvania

Published in the United States of America by

Duquesne University Press
600 Forbes Avenue
Pittsburgh, Pennsylvania 15282

Library of Congress Cataloging-in-Publication Data

Domestic arrangements in early modern England / edited by Kari Boyd McBride.
p. cm. — (Medieval & Renaissance literary studies)
Includes bibliographical references and index.
ISBN 0-8207-0324-9 (hardcover : alk. paper)
1. English literature — Early modern, 1500–1700 — History and criticism. 2. Manners and customs in literature. 3. Literature and society — England — History — 16th century. 4. Literature and society — England — History — 17th century. 5. Domestic relations in literature. 6. Parent and child in literature. 7. Married people in literature. 8. Marriage in literature. 9. Family in literature. 10. Home in literature. I. McBride, Kari Boyd. II. Medieval and Renaissance literary studies.
PR428.M35 D66 2002
820.9′355—dc21

2001007740

∞ Printed on acid-free paper.

Contents

Acknowledgments

The idea for this collection was born of a Modern Language Association Conference special session that I chaired on "Domestic Arrangements in Early Modern England" in Toronto in December 1997. The call for papers elicited such a varied range of excellent proposals that I almost immediately conceived the idea of turning the rubric for the conference session into a much larger project, which now is brought to light here. Many of those who had initially sent abstracts for the conference were willing to work together on a book, and a handful of others who had heard about the project through the academic grapevine added their contributions to the mix. My first thanks, then, go to those who found the concept of "domestic arrangements" inspiring and who stayed the course through the vicissitudes of publication. I also want to thank the editors and readers at Duquesne, in particular, the meticulous copyeditor who read our manuscripts. John T. Shawcross read an earlier version of this collection, and I thank him for his encouragement and wise counsel. Thanks go also to the Women's Studies Department of the University of Arizona, which has supported my work on this and all projects.

Some of the material in the Introduction is taken from my *Country House Discourse in Early Modern England* (Ashgate, 2001). A portion of Susan Staub's essay here appeared as "Matchlesse Monsters of the Female Sex" in *Renaissance Papers* (1995). And Heather Dubrow's essay includes material published elsewhere (in her "'I fear there will a worse come in his place,'" in *Maternal Measures*, ed. Naomi J. Miller and Naomi Yavneh [Ashgate, 2000], and *Shakespeare and Domestic Loss* [Cambridge, 1999].) Thanks to Ashgate Press, Cambridge University Press, and the Southeastern Renaissance Conference for their permission to reprint.

Introduction

The Politics of Domestic Arrangements

Kari Boyd McBride

The last decade of the twentieth century witnessed an explosion of interdisciplinary work on issues surrounding "domesticity" in early modern England, understood not merely as a trope for articulating political authority that might then have consequences in the patriarchal household but as a sphere of lived experience that both incorporates and inflects the structures of society as a whole. In Susan Dwyer Amussen's words, "the family and the state were inextricably intertwined in the minds of English women and men of the sixteenth and seventeenth centuries"; as a consequence, "we cannot understand politics (as conventionally defined) without understanding the politics of the family."[1] Amussen articulates a theory of scholarly inquiry that now practically goes without saying but that represents a culmination of nearly a century of work by social, cultural and literary historians and feminist scholars of many fields to rethink both research methodology and its proper objects of study. The innovations of the *annales* school of history paved the way for the kinds of studies — particular, localized and interdisciplinary; concerned with the disposition of space, with material culture and with everyday life — that we now take for granted. Beginning in the late 1920s, Marc Bloch and other pioneers revolutionized scholarly inquiry when they borrowed social science methods and methodologies for the toolbox of history, rejected the almost exclusive focus on "high politics" that had previously characterized historical work, and privileged the local, the social and the cultural in their research.[2] When feminist historians and literary scholars began the recuperative work that characterized second wave academic feminism in the 1970s, searching for the detritus of women's lives in archives and cataloging long-forgotten pamphlets, poems, books and diaries written by women, there was some precedent for this difficult task in the work of those earlier historians of home, village and countryside. In addition, those early scholars of women's history learned from feminism to listen for the silences as well as the voices in the records of the past and to read against the grain, and they remapped the landscape of historical and literary scholarship in a brief span of a few decades.[3]

Their work has intersected with trends in the theory and practice of literary study to produce the kinds of essays represented in this book, which show little regard for traditional divisions between literature, history and sociology. The fundamental insights of materialist theories of history (especially those indebted to Marxism) and of (post)structuralism — often working in tandem — have remade the ways we think about disciplinarity in general and about traditional academic fields (in which, nonetheless, most of us continue to be trained), presenting new objects for study and providing new lenses for the study of those objects, from cultural materialism in its various incarnations to postcolonial and queer theories. Those scholars trained primarily in literature have been perhaps the most willing to poach from other fields, theories, and methodologies (though they have not always been welcome transgressors of disciplinary boundaries), but the fruits of those thefts have been rich and bountiful, enlivening the study of literature, history, archeology and art, to name only a few topoi of inquiry.

The study of family life and domestic space has a particular history of its own, a thread running through the larger fabric of this history. Early inquiries by Alice Clark, Gladys Scott Thomson, Ruth Kelso, John Summerson and Philippe Ariès and, later, by Lawrence Stone, Alan Macfarlane and Mark Girouard attempted to define how and when a private or domestic sphere emerged in the architecture and social commentary of the early modern world (and, indeed, saw the construction of private space as a defining feature of what we might call "modern" in any sense). At the same time, such scholars began to break down the boundaries between public and private in our thinking about the past, in the process enlarging the scope of historical inquiry to include women and children as well as adult men. And, though her work is difficult to situate generically among these studies, surely Virginia Woolf has had an abiding influence on how we think about gender, work and domesticity.[4] The work of all these scholars formed the foundation for studies in the 1980s, many of which focused on the consequences of domesticity for women and men, for their identity within the family and within the *polis*.[5] In tandem with current trends in feminist theory, more recent studies have focused on women's resistance to repressive doctrine of the era and have widened the scope of earlier studies.[6] In addition, feminist scholars have articulated a productive critique of new historicism, a critique suggesting that the wider range of texts and sources acknowledged by those practitioners be used to engage a wider range of early modern cultural artifacts rather than merely reinscribing the hegemony of the male, the canonical and the political, as has often been the case. Jean E. Howard and Patricia Fumerton are especially insightful in their assessment of the limitations of new historicism while promoting what Fumerton calls "a new new historicism" that attends to the material and the everyday (categories that have traditionally been associated with women).[7] In this vein, noting the tendency for early work on domesticity to focus almost entirely on the gentry (that is, on a white, landed class), many scholars have expanded the sphere of inquiry to middle class, working class, and peasant households (including Carole Shammas) and to include race as a category of analysis (notably, Kim F. Hall).[8] Others have looked to previously unexamined documents to discern contemporary attitudes about women and their proper place (for example, Joy Wiltenburg's study of street literature, continued in this collection by Susan Staub), while others have applied feminist theories to particular households (as has Alice T. Friedman) or have challenged the long-accepted conclusions about domesticity and the family (as James Schultz, in his reassessment of Ariès's arguments).[9] Queer theory has challenged many assumptions about gender roles and relationships, particularly in recent studies of transvestism and the English stage; such work has profound implications for how we think about domesticity.[10] Scholarly interest in the meaning and implications of domesticity continues to rise, as evidenced by continuing work on the subject by Heather Dubrow (whose work is represented in this volume), Margaret Ezell, Patricia Parker, Diane Purkiss, Lorna Hutson, Susan Amussen, Lena Cowen Orlin and Richard Helgerson.[11] These trends in scholarship make possible the range of inquiry represented here, where studies of domestic space and its representation in literature repeatedly explode the boundaries of the household and the family unit.

As a prelude to the studies that follow in this collection, I want to sketch here some broad outlines of "domestic arrangements" that early modern England inherited from a mythologized vision of an ideal past, an ideal that had currency as a traditional touchstone even as the country became decreasingly rural and agrarian and increasingly urban and mercantile.[12] Perhaps because of the rapid changes in social, economic and political life (the pace of which contemporaries noted with some alarm), the late medieval country estate remained the symbol of good housekeeping: a moral economy wherein all classes and all peoples lived in right relationship with each other and with the rest of creation — in Andrew McRae's words, "a static, hierarchical socioeconomic structure . . . which gives to every individual an immutable social and geographic place and fixes all within a network of duties and responsibilities. . . . The landlord stands at the centre of this structure as a paternal figure: a steward of the land and its dependants rather than an owner with absolute proprietorial rights. Under him the manor operates with the goal of a comfortable self-sufficiency."[13] This ideal grew in significance during the protracted evolution of the sixteenth and seventeenth centuries from manorialism in its various manifestations to the agrarian capitalism that ultimately came to define the rural landscape, from the medieval ideal of the "three orders" to a society dominated both economically and politically by the middle class. This particular domestic ideal centered on the aristocracy, the landed class for whom, in Michael Bush's words, "the estate was not simply a source of income but also an expression of lordship, a means of local influence and a mark of social position."[14] However, during the course of the sixteenth and seventeenth centuries, many factors impinged on this static definition of lordship, undermining what had seemed a natural and divinely ordained social structure built on the trinity of birth, land and wealth.

These disruptions to order — the agrarian revolution, a rising population, inflation, an active land market, the rise of the middle class, nascent capitalism, exploration and colonization, the woman controversy, the emergence of alternative religious, social and political perspectives and subjectivities — forced both a renewed articulation of traditional justifications for privilege and, at the same time, an accommodation of newness: new titles, new families, new expressions of power, new "domestic arrangements." There was no abrupt or absolute change from earlier discussions; rather, traditional apologies and critiques began to be merged with discussions of class relationships, gender relationships and gender roles — the social forms and practices regulated within the domestic sphere.

Gender was an integral — and often invisible — feature of political and social power throughout this period. I do not mean merely the positioning of particular women within households, but rather the way in which authority was understood to be fundamentally and ontologically male. That is, the exercise of power depended on a distinction between masculinity and femininity or, more accurately perhaps, on the control of everything associated with the feminine by those who claimed the fullness of masculine privilege. Good husbandry, then, was revealed fundamentally in the management of a wife; indeed, as Lorna Hutson has suggested, "supervision of wife and household" are inseparable from each other and are "synechdoches" for noble praxis: husbandry is "a form of cultural production which enables the government of peoples."[15] And the virtuous wife was central to the well-ordered household, her virtue both dependent on and significant of her husband's particularly noble virility. So Hutson has illustrated the repeated analogy in sixteenth century treatises between horse-breaking, tilling and the training of a wife.[16] The noble house — the *oikos* — may have been the proper sphere of gentlewomen, but its management — its *oikonomos* — was ultimately the concern of the noble man. Within this discourse of husbandry, then, the wife could never be more than *locum tenens* for her husband, to whom belonged the rights and responsibilities for the household's virtuous ordering. His legitimacy was most visible in the invisibility of his cloistered wife, his ventriloquized voice audible in her chaste silence.

These ideals of order that connected the domestic to the political, articulated from an aristocratic perspective and planted in the countryside, were challenged in some measure by emerging middle class, city-based values and a class system that was somewhat more "horizontal" than "vertical." Vertical alignment is based on a "great chain of being" or a "feudal" model, wherein one is allied up and down the social scale to members of other classes, and where one's own class status emerges significantly out of one's relationships within that hierarchy. So William McClung points to the Paston family who were "allied 'vertically' through a system of patronage and vassalage to greater and lesser families in Norfolk, London, and across the country." Horizontal models tended to define urban society, where even the domestic servants in middle class households would be of "middling sort" and might themselves move on to establish households and employ domestic labor.[17] In the vertical social model, the "value" of an aristocrat's retainers — both domestic servants and the larger network of beneficiaries of noble patronage — affected the "value" of the lord and defined noble status and legitimacy. The power and authority of a feudal lord had been constructed in great part by the power and authority of those who pledged homage and fealty to him. A portion of that aristocratic valence inhered in the actual ability of one's retainers to muster an armed host in time of war. But, even in its earliest expression, this definition of power was the result of a particular kind of conspicuous consumption wherein noble status was recognizable in the size and magnificence of one's retinue, the moveable court that bespoke nobility in both public and private spaces. In a kind of circular dynamic of power, a retainer's power was calculated by the authority of the one he served, whose authority in turn was the sum of the combined status of all his retainers.

"Domestic servant," of course, implies a wide range of economic and social status — in P. W. Fleming's assessment, "anyone employed for a wage, from the day labourer hired to gather the harvest home to the family retainer grown old in loyal service."[18] Those who conform to the modern notion of a "servant," that is, folk "hired by the year who lived in with their employers," accounted for perhaps 20 to 30 percent of the population at any one time at the beginning of this period. In addition, "most young people regardless of social standing spent some time in service" in noble or gentry households or apprenticed to trades.[19]

In the early sixteenth century, women of all social ranks were outnumbered in aristocratic houses by as much as 20 to one, and all of the servants in the aristocratic house, with few exceptions, were male, for service represented employment and preferment for men of all ranks until that medieval system began to be superseded by clientage and patronage. The only women in most country houses would have been the lord's wife and daughters, their gentlewomen companions, female "chamberers" (and some chamberers were male), nurses to the children, and laundresses. Sixteenth century courtesy books also discouraged the employment of women, and all household statutes of the period specified male servants.[20] Even those few women who inhabited the noble household were restricted in their access to many areas of the house, forming "an island of womanhood" in a "masculine world."[21] The gentlewomen were perhaps most restricted of all. Their lives in the country houses were "private and sheltered," says Alice T. Friedman, limited to "the great chamber, dining chamber, parlor, and nursery." She argues that, while women may have had more rooms available to them in the prodigy houses built under Elizabeth (as opposed to the medieval manor), they were more isolated within their assigned space.[22]

But during the period covered by this study, as agrarian capitalism, trade, mining and nascent manufacturing came to displace land rents as the primary source of wealth and power (if not as the symbol of noble status), the significance of service in a noble household and the composition of the staff gradually changed to accommodate the revolution. Ambitious commoners and gentlemen, who a century earlier would have attached themselves to a nobleman and his household, sought their fortune instead in London, where the rewards of the court were dispensed and the expeditions that heralded an emerging empire were launched. Kate Mertes notes that "[b]etween 1550 and 1600, one begins to note a general tendency for households to employ a greater percentage of women, whose roles could seldom have been more than wholly domestic. . . . Once a stubborn enclave of men devoted to the furtherance of their master's political authority, the group of household members had become by the later seventeenth century an almost entirely female and largely privately employed staff of servants. The household was as politically impotent as were the women who staffed it."[23] In the houses of the lesser rural gentry, women comprised the majority of the domestic servant staff by the mid-seventeenth century, but this fashion for female servants entered the great establishments slowly. The shift from the male- to the female-staffed household was protracted and resisted, particularly in the houses of the most powerful landowners, those who had the most at stake in maintaining neofeudal fictions about social and economic legitimacy, who looked to traditional definitions of nobility dependent on the status of one's staff — and male servants brought more social currency than females.

The tendency to employ women rather than men in household service can first be seen in towns, in evidence in some areas of England by the late middle ages. P. J. P. Goldberg speculates that this tendency was driven by the labor shortages of the late Middle Ages caused by the Black Death, which made all laborers scarce; women tended to fill the "niches created by the shortage of trained, that is, former servant, male labour." At the same time, no doubt in part as a result of these economic shifts, a fashion for female servants was developing in urban centers (York, Durham, Scarborough and northern commercial centers in addition to London), something that was seen as modern, particularly in contrast to the tradition of the male-dominated staff of rural establishments. The "labour-starved towns attracted workers of either sex, just as the established town-dwellers, the bourgeoisie, demanded female domestics to mark their status in society."[24] The mobility that was made possible by the plague, followed by economic opportunities that emerged in the resurgence that followed, allowed women not only to find wider employment in service, but, at least initially, to enter the margins of the merchant class. However, by the late fifteenth century, women's access to these commercial activities was circumscribed, due in part to economic recession. Those women who did remain employed in the market economy (that is, who were not living as servants within another's household) were limited to feminized trades like laundry or nursing (work that tended to re-domesticate them in any case), while in some areas they were explicitly "excluded from all craft activities." Many town women returned to service, primarily in mercantile households, while artisan households, employing apprentices, tended to be overwhelmingly male in composition. Thus, according to Goldberg, "female service became associated with non-productive functions and the advertisement of wealth and status, becoming in itself a low status occupation — a particular kind of conspicuous consumption."[25]

A case in point is the relegation of women to work that was, by circular definition, "unskilled" simply because it was done by women. Merry E. Wiesner explains that, "[d]uring the early modern period, gender . . . became an important factor in separating what was considered skilled from what was considered unskilled work. . . . During the sixteenth century, wherever the knitting frame was introduced, men began to argue that using it was so complicated that only men could possibly learn; the frame actually made knitting easier and much faster, but women were prohibited from using it anyway with the excuse that they were unskilled. They were relegated to knitting by hand, and had to sell their products more cheaply to compete with stockings made much more quickly by male frame-knitters."[26] Mary Prior contends that the concept of work itself was limited to what men did. She notes that, while "[w]ork was a necessity for nearly everyone" in this period, not all activity was actually classified as "work." "Whatever a man did . . . was work, and what a woman did was her duty." In a middle-class town household, then, "if, for instance, a man was a glover, his work was clearly defined, and whatever else had to be done to keep the home fires burning was his wife's duty. If he became ill and could do less and less, then she must do more and more, supervising the apprentices, seeing the orders were fulfilled; or even by some employment, like taking in washing, she must supplement a failing business."[27] But what she did was not work; rather, she remained a (house)wife, not a glover. Thus, urban women were repeatedly "domesticated" within emerging economic and social forms, either because their economic activity tended to be confined to the household or because they were limited to work as domestic servants.

When female domestic servants do appear in written sources, they are often figured stereotypically as sexualized and sexually available — available particularly if not exclusively to the male head of the household, a situation that, of course, had its counterpart in the real-life situations under which female domestic servants labored (as it were). The notion that female domestics were sexually available to the paterfamilias (and his sons) has a long lineage, perhaps most famous in the tradition of the *droit du seigneur*, the lord's ownership of everything on the estate and within the household and, thus, his right to sleep with a female servant before "granting" her to her servant husband. That kind of thinking, though certainly not law in sixteenth and seventeenth century England, still echoes through many texts. Ben Jonson's homage "To Penshurst" famously depicts the sexually available bodies of the tenant farmer's daughters as but another kind of offering to the lord of the estate:

> [A]ll come in, the farmer and the clown,
> And no one empty-handed, to salute
>   Thy lord and lady, though they have no suit.
> Some bring a capon, some a rural cake,
>   Some nuts, some apples; some that think they make
> The better cheeses, bring 'em; or else send
>   By their ripe daughters, whom they would commend
> This way to husbands; and whose baskets bear
>   An emblem of themselves, in plum or pear.[28]

The "ripe daughters" are commended to husbands by first being offered to Robert Sidney, Lord Lisle, an echo of the tradition that might once have been fully and carnally enacted on an estate. Private documents and the fiction of this period (and long after) are filled with accounts of the rape or seduction of servant girls by householders of all class status, from Samuel Pepys's confessions in his diary of his repeated (and repeatedly regretted) inability to keep his hands off the serving girls to the systematic rape of slave women by their masters.

In sum, domestic arrangements were (and are) complex, and they always provide a locus for the study of the larger culture. As Claire M. Busse notes in her contribution to this collection, for early modern authors the domestic sphere "served as an easily representable fictional space" where the conundrums of the larger world could be modeled and manipulated and so provides unique opportunities for localizing early modern thought and practice on a universe of topics. This rich gathering of studies illuminates the many ways in which the domestic space served as a stage for playing out the pressing questions that perplexed the writers and thinkers of early modern England — questions about family, certainly, but, even more significantly, questions about emerging political realities. While "home" may seem to invoke blood ties — the mother with a child at her breast or siblings at play — it is finally the bonds that replace blood that demand the mythos of domestic arrangements in all their variety — from the legal, social, economic and cultural ties of marriage, sealed by the exchange of women from man to man and house to house, to the relationships of stepparents and stepchildren, to the even more tenuous ties that bind class to class and citizen to citizen. The latter — "unnatural" and *unheimlich* alliances — demand a powerful mythology and an apparently secure context for their maintenance, perhaps particularly in times of change and even revolution. It is not surprising, then, that the house becomes a home for political engagement in the sixteenth and seventeenth centuries. As the site of prelapsarian memories of wholeness and atavistic bonds, the home seemed able to contain the most disturbing and threatening conflicts of the age, providing a safe place for testing and accommodating change. All legal obligations, social ties and economic relationships in flux could thus be imagined as, in some sense, domestic arrangements. At the same time, because the domestic sphere was continually charged with the burden of a wider political consequence, by theorists as divergent as James I, Margaret Cavendish, Ben Jonson and Aphra Behn, it would almost inevitably fail to accommodate and facilitate public intercourse. The bright light of inquiry could reveal the poverty of home and housewifery and the failures of parenting and of marriage. Rather than reiterating homely myths, such invocations could, instead, reveal the fractures and limitations of the domestic sphere and show it to be merely a piece of the larger culture rather than its touchstone and foundation. Finally, then, these essays reveal the fluidity of domestic metaphor and its limits, as the very discourses that seek to define public by private and public from private serve, instead, to blur the distinction and destroy the myth.

1 • "Those Whom God Hath Joined Together"
Bondage Metaphors and Marital Advice in Early Modern England

Sid Ray

"The institution of Matrimonie is an indissoluble bond and knot, whereby the husband and wife are fastened together by the ordinance of God."[1] So wrote Robert Cleaver in his marriage tract, *A Godlie Forme of Householde Government*. Printed in nine editions between 1598 and 1624, it included whole swaths of prose from Heinrich Bullinger's earlier tract, *The Christen State of Matrimonye*, which itself went to four editions. *A Godlie Forme* and similar treatises were easily disseminated propaganda written by Puritan ministers to instill and promote domestic orthodoxy.[2] Whether or not the messages were received as intended has been the subject of some debate.[3] This essay argues that marriage tract writers define and assign roles of authority and subordination using metaphors that subvert their purpose of codifying and maintaining household order. The proliferation of particular figures, such as "yokefellows," the "bond of matrimony," and "tying the knot," problematizes claims about authority and subordination because the varying meanings of such metaphors extend the parameters of authority and exaggerate the ways that subordination is to be maintained. They hyperbolize the degree of power invested on the side of male authority and overstate the subjection of wives, encouraging containment of them that goes beyond Puritan goals for standardizing behavior. When these metaphors appear in antimarriage tracts, what seem to be inherently stable and natural domestic hierarchies become disputable. The Puritan marriage tracts, therefore, may unwittingly have contributed to domestic strife in the early modern period. More compellingly, because household hierarchies were enlisted as a standard for structuring government, metaphors in Puritan marriage tracts left open important questions about the rights of people under an English monarch.

The marriage tracts are full of borrowed phrases and platitudinous claims. Kathleen Davies writes that "none of the authors propounds anything startlingly unexpected in the relationships between husbands and wives, parents and children or masters and servants."[4] Inspired by Aristotle's writings on the household, Saint Paul's letters in the New Testament, and Catholic and humanist marital advice, marriage tract writers were not constructing ideology as much as renovating and energizing it for applications appropriate to post-Reformation years when social hierarchies were challenged by urban migration, popular uprisings, food shortages, inflation, a rising middle class and a female monarch.[5] The attempt to maintain order through a meticulous delineation of marital duties reflects the need for social stability in troubled times, but the tract writers' shifty metaphors, belabored repetition of these metaphors, and reckless catachresis combine to weaken Puritan precepts.

Experts on rhetoric — Desiderius Erasmus, Henry Peacham, George Puttenham and Thomas Wilson — published treatises on the delights of figurative language, but they also advised using particular tropes with caution. Puttenham identifies the downside of metaphor: "As figures be the instruments of ornament in every language, so be they also in a sorte abuses or rather trespasses in speach, because they passe the ordinary limits of common utterance, and be occupied of purpose to deceive the eare and also the minde, drawing it from plainnesse and simplicitie to a certaine doublenesse, whereby our talke is the more guilefull and abusing, for what else is your *Metaphor* but an inversion of sense of transport?"[6] In Puttenham's logic, a metaphor occurs when the meaning of one word is displaced onto another, resulting in "a kinde of wresting of single words from his owne right signification, to another not so naturall, but yet of some affinitie or conveniencie with it" (189). Metaphor depends on two elements, the tenor and the vehicle, and thus it abuses "plainnesse and simplicitie" by incurring a certain "doublenesse," that itself creates other meanings (166). When certain types of metaphor are repeated in a way that recreates and amplifies the pressure of the doubleness, still other meanings are put into play. When this happens, the audience may interpret metaphors in ways the author did not intend.

By definition, then, metaphors complicate phrasing and clarity, but the tract writers were advised to use them by rhetoricians who claimed that figurative language makes plain prose more interesting to the bored or roving mind. Wilson's *Arte of Rhetorique* encourages preachers, especially, to strive for variety in their discourse: "Except menne finde delight, thei will not long abide: delight theim, and wynne them: werie theim, and you lose theim for ever. And that is the reason, that menne commonly tary at the ende of a merie plaie, and cannot abide the halfe hearyng of a sower checkyng Sermon. Therefore, even these auncient preachers must now and then plaie the fooles in the pulpite, to serve the fickle eares of their fleetyng audience."[7] Wilson later warns, however, that "there ought muche wareness to be used in chosyng of wordes translated [metaphors], that the same be not unlike that thing, whereunto it is applied, nor yet that the translation be uncomely or such as may give occasion of any uncleane meaning" (344). Just so, the duplicity of a metaphor can cause it to refer to objects or ideas that the writer may not have intended or anticipated. When, for example, marriage tract writers repetitively insist that marriage is a knot rather than a union, a bond rather than a covenant, they evoke the sense that marriage is a way of controlling behavior instead of promoting companionship and domestic harmony. Knots, after all, are deployed to contain things — to curtail movement, control actions and prevent people or objects from exceeding certain boundaries. One would imagine that authors attempting to codify marital roles would tread carefully on such unstable rhetorical ground, but the marriage tracts are nevertheless congested with confusing and provocative figures. Their writers ignore caveats against repetition and catachresis as well. Erasmus writes: "Nothing indeed keeps us from forming metaphors ourselves by reading and by observing the nature of all things, provided only that the metaphor be not harsh, or low, or more exaggerated than is proper, or mixed, or too frequent, especially in the same class."[8] Marriage tract writers do exactly what Erasmus warns against; they incorporate metaphors that are too "harsh," "more exaggerated than is proper," "mixed" and "too frequent." In their attempt at eloquence, they use language promiscuously, creating an overdetermined rhetoric that articulates diverse, often competing motivations or intentions. They imply that marriage is not only a figurative bond, or covenant, between two people, but also a literal form of bondage. Though the Puritan's domestic model was analogous in many ways to the structure of English monarchy — husband as head of the household commonwealth — the meanings implied by marital metaphors easily slip into harsh or improper registers, sometimes figuring the household as more of a fiefdom than a monarchy, and at other times figuring the household as church, as a farm, and even as a beehive. Such constructions had real consequences for the English people. If, as Lena Cowen Orlin argues, marital rhetoric was manipulated by the state to authorize nonstandard governmental practices — to increase the authority and wealth of the monarch, for example[9] — then evoking a variety of polities with which to compare household government would allow for reinterpreting the rights of the people in the larger public realm. The consequences of loose language were thus potentially great.

In a tract written to convince his female cousin to marry, Thomas Pritchard declares his intention to "set forthe the dignitie of honorable wedlocke, and holy Matrimonie."[10] Pritchard's intention accords with that of other Protestant marriage theorists of the sixteenth century, such as Thomas Becon and Henry Smith, who strive to counter the Catholic celebration of celibacy by praising marriage, or, as many of them call it, "wedlocke."[11] In *The Glasse of Godly Love,* which is appended to his commendation of marriage, Pritchard employs metaphors such as the "yoke of matrimony" to uphold the binding qualities of the nuptial contract. He claims that "one man and one woman are coupled and knit together in one flesh and body" under the rubric of "mutuall love," encouraging a perception of marriage as a blissful estate in which husband and wife execute mutual duties in Edenic concord. The spiritual tone changes abruptly, however, when Pritchard adds that the husband must generally "seeth and heareth" for his wife, while she "be discret, chaste, huswifely, shamefast, good, meeke, pacient, and sober . . . with a cumly gravitie and a sad behavior of a constant minde, true tongued, and of few words" (sigs. K2v–K4). With this secondary emphasis on hierarchy, the knitting metaphor connotes something more oppressive than unity. In this state of so-called mutual love, the writers' metaphors encourage the husband to act the role of jailer. Juan Luis Vives's *The Office and Duty of a Husband*, a humanist treatise, stresses the importance of surveillance in the husband's daily functions: "For the master and ruler of the house must know and understand that he is set as it were in a high tower, to behold and see who cometh into the house and to withstand all such things as may hurt the emoluments and commodities of the same or the good name and report of his wife." William Whately says that a husband should "stand as a watchman in a watch tower, to looke to every side, that no enemy doe surprise the same at unawares." To wives, he writes, "If God have made thine house thy dungeon, thine husband thy Jaylor; yet thou must not seeke to make an escape, till he deliver thee out that put thee in." Cleaver implies the same when he states that "the dutie of the husband is, to be entermedling: and the wife, to be solitaire and withdrawne." The distribution of duties between husbands and wives pits them against each other as censor and censored, and "wedlocke" begins to signify containment of the woman rather than connectedness between husband and wife.[12]

Besides employing an excessive number of metaphors that connote imprisonment, the tract writers also mix different types. Their catachresis creates overlapping meanings that add to the sense that marriage is, paradoxically, an institution of unity and discord. In *A Preparative to Marriage*, Henry Smith discusses marriage as occurring "when that knot is tyed," while in other places he notes that husbands are "fettered with their wives." David Clapham, who translates Cornelius Agrippa's *Commendation of Matrimony*, mixes three metaphors when he writes, "for god the maker of al thynges, wold this most holy bonde so to be knit with indissoluble glewe." Erasmus characterizes wedlock as a state wherein husbands "stick to" their wives, and William Heale calls marriage a "Gordian knot" and "the ring of union." In *Of Domesticall Duties*, William Gouge writes that a "man is glued to his wife," but adds that the couple is "tied" together, "joyned together," "linked together" and "knit together." Thomas Gataker writes in *A Good Wife Gods Gift* that "Man and Wife are as the stocke and hence, the one ingraffed into the other, and so fastened together, that they cannot be sundred"; Gataker follows the grafting and the stock metaphors by noting that a man is "glewed unto" or "cleaved" to his wife. Cleaver argues that the wife is "annexed and joyned" unto her husband, and Whately states that "if holy duties knit not, and rivet not your hearts together, they will soone bee severed."[13] The character of Abigail in Robert Snawsel's *A Looking Glasse for Maried Folkes* claims that the bonds of marriage "may not onely be termed hempen cords, but rather strong iron chaines to tie and bind not only you but every man to his wife, in the inseparable knot of love."[14] This sampling of the hundreds of mixed metaphors found in the marriage tracts registers the near obsessive repetition of various kinds of bondage metaphors, which provoke a distracting array of associations — "glued" and "annexed" imply home building; "rivets" connotes metalwork or architecture; "grafting" suggests biological or human surgery; the "stock" and "fetters" evoke punitive devices like the pillory; and the preoccupation with "knitting" brings a number of ideas into play — nautical knot tying, punitive knot tying, sewing, female conception, and even castration ("to knit" can mean to conceive, and conversely it can also mean to geld by tying up the scrotum). Instead of promoting marriage, these metaphors discourage it. Moreover, the allusion to myriad containment devices creates a problem of coherence, even within discrete tracts. Is marriage a bond, a knot or a lock? Are husband and wife linked together, tied together, grafted onto one another, glued together or knit? Are spouses equal in their mutual bond?

In contrast to treatises that defend the rights of wives, such as Daniel Tuvil's *Asylum Veneris* and pamphlets by Mathew Griffith and Mary Tattle-well, the Puritan marriage tracts do not advocate equality between the sexes, despite metaphors that imply spousal unity and the tract writers' use of the word "equality" when they mean mutuality. As L. T. Fitz writes, "Although it cannot be doubted that marital equality was an issue in the Renaissance, it is also clear that few people had traveled down the road towards this equality, and that few writers on matrimony wished them to."[15] Wives were believed to be their husbands' spiritual equals, though inferior to them in every other way. Thus they had mutual duties but no social equity.

William Gouge exemplifies the Puritan tract writers' belief in a hierarchy over and above this ideal of marital mutuality: "Nature hath placed an eminencie in the male over the female: so as they are linked together in one yoake, it is given by nature that he should governe, she obey" (*Of Domesticall Duties*, 270). Gouge's use of the yoking metaphor belies his otherwise emphatic demarcation of a hierarchy. A yoke demands that two individuals (usually animals) draw the same burden with equal amounts of effort. If one is stronger than the other, the labor becomes unbalanced. Indeed, yokefellows such as oxen work in a state of mutual and enforced submission to a higher authority, the plowman, but there is no hierarchy between the oxen themselves. Oxen are by definition castrated males, rendered so to maintain a balance of strength and to minimize fighting.[16] Taylor recognizes the importance of balance between yokefellows when he discusses marital mutuality: "Here is an equal yoke," he writes, "when both are like minded and draw one way . . . when both are fit and mutuall helpes, marriage becometh a sweete yoke" (*A Good Husband*, sig. B4v). But the relationship between husband and wife only resembles the relationship between animals yoked together in that they both must mutually submit to a higher authority, God as plowman. Nevertheless, the marriage theorists appropriate "yokefellows" as an expedient though deceptive term. Whately writes, "they must be partners in paines taking, as two oxen that draw in one yoke" (*A Bride-Bush*, sig. M3). The language of yoking, according to Henry Smith, derives from the New Testament and Saint Paul's epistles: "That other word in the 2 Cor. 6:14 is Yoke, there mariage is called a Yoke. *Paule* saith, *Be not unequally yoked.* If Mariage be a yoke, then they which drawe in it must be fit, like two Oxen which draw the yoke together, or els all the burden will lie upon one" (*Preparative*, 34). The pastoral connotations of "yokefellows" encourage readers to view marriage as an ideal estate wherein men and women have mutual duties, but the pastoral metaphor contradicts the assiduous delineation of a hierarchy. William Perkins writes in *Christian Economy* that "a couple is that whereby two persons standing in mutual relation to each other are combined together as it were in one. And of the two, the one is always higher and beareth rule, the other is lower and yieldeth subjection."[17] Perkins reveals the opposing impulses that motivate the tract writers' proliferation of bondage rhetoric. On the one hand, bondage connotes the mutual linking of man and wife — they are mutually and harmoniously bound together in marriage as yokefellows or, in another simile, "like two owers [oars] in a boat" (Smith, *Preparative*, 66). Such associations would make the marriage contract distinct from an employment indenture between master and apprentice who are not so linked. On the other hand, bondage metaphors connote a hierarchy in which the woman is in an inferior position, meaning that she is bound or eternally indentured to her husband. In this context and according to the wife's vows in *The Book of Common Prayer*, she, like a servant, has to obey her master. Evidently, there are contradictory pressures operating. One demands mutuality between husbands and wives, which is never satisfactorily defined; the other demands male dominance, which seems always to resound clearly.

The opposing claims of mutuality and dominance frustrate a clear understanding of the husband and wife relationship.

While men and women did not expect to be equals in marriage, mutuality implies a reciprocity beneficial to both parties. But the privileges reserved for husbands — the right to legal recourse, control of the couple's "mutual" property, and the freedom to leave the house and express opinions — have no reciprocal element to them. Catherine Belsey observes, for example, that in *A Godlie Forme of Household Government* "the husband's responsibilities occupy 29 pages, and the wife's, with some repetition, rather less than two."[18] Unlike mutual covenants between laborer and employer or apprentice and master, in which the obligation was truly mutual — the laborer received wages, the apprentice an education — the marriage contract confers little on the wife, except, perhaps, protection. Although the wife nominally holds a position superior to male servants, she has fewer liberties than they. Whately and Smith define the wife as a "deputy," which implies that she can act for the husband in his absence.[19] But even under those circumstances, she still cannot invest or dispose of their property, travel alone or sue in the courts. In reality, her position is more akin to that of a feudal villein than that of a deputy. Indeed, with so much stress on the eternal "bond" between husbands and wives through knitting, tying and other bondage metaphors, readers might assume that wives, like villeins, were legally enslaved and subject to the absolute power of their lord. Cleaver makes this insinuation a bold statement: "Therefore the husband without any exception, is master over all the house, and hath as touching his familie more authority then a king in his kingdome" (*A Godlie Forme*, sig. M8). Thus the claim to mutuality, which is sometimes worded as "equality," dishonestly elevates the woman and, even more dangerous to early modern order, belies claims about the domestic hierarchy and its chain of command. In the context of their mutual relationship, husband and wife govern the children and servants together as partners; but in the context of their hierarchical relationship, husbands govern their wives. As Cleaver says, "There is one rule to governe the wife by, another for the children, another for the servants" (sig. B3), but there is no coherently defined system of governance.

Although, as Orlin, in *Private Matters*, claims, "it was necessarily impossible for [tract writers] to anticipate and categorize every quotidian instance of overlapping and conflicting responsibilities" (102) codifying roles is one of the goals of these marriage tracts. The doubleness of the metaphors that describe marital duties and proper behavior clearly adds to the problem of coherence. The question of wife beating is one issue that remains contentious and is further complicated by the pressure of bondage metaphors. The word "bridle" often appears in the marriage tracts, punning on "bride," obviously, and evoking commonplace analogies between controlling wives and taming horses. Whately compares an obedient wife to a "wel-broken horse, that seemes to have but one soule with the rider, so readily doth she stop or turne or goe with the hand of him that moves the bridle" (*A Bride-Bush*, sig Dd4v). Cleaver continues the analogy: "The breaker of horses, that doth use to ride and to pace them, doth handle the rough and sturdie colt with all craft, rigour, and the fiercnes that may be: but with the colt that is more tractable, he taketh not so great paine. A sharpe and shrewd wife must be pleased and mitigated with love, and ruled with majestie" (*A Godlie Forme*, sig. L7). Not surprisingly, given the horse-taming analogies and metaphors, one marriage tract writer actually condones wife beating. Whately writes, "But for blowes, for strokes with hand or fist, nothing should drive an husband to them, except the utmost extremities of unwifelike carriage." Among those so-called extremes are when the wife curses, swears, gets drunk, or rails. The husband may also beat his wife if she "outface him with bold maintaining, that she will doe as she doth, in despight of him" (sig. R2). Other Puritans, like Smith and Perkins, maintain that spousal abuse is immoral under any circumstances. Reading too literally the Bible's assertion that husband and wife are one flesh, Perkins denounces wife beating because it is a form of self-flagellation: "But he may not chastise her either with stripes or strokes. The reason is plain. Wives are their husbands' mates, and they two be one flesh. And so man will hate, much less beat, his own flesh, but nourish and cherish it" (*Christian Economy*, 172). Even so, when knot metaphors appear in close proximity to horse-taming analogies, it is easy to believe that injunctions against wife beating were ignored. Wife beating was legal in early modern England, though in other contractual relationships it was illegal for a superior to strike his charge; masters were not entitled to beat their apprentices, for example.[20] Only a certain class of people was legally subject to physical abuse. T. E. writes: "if a man beat an out-law, a traitor, a pagan, his villein, or his wife, it is dispunishable, because by the Law Common these persons can have no action. God send the gentlewoman better sport or better company." T. E. thinks the woman can sue in the chancery courts for beatings, but that the "office of husband" entails room for "lawful and reasonable correction."[21] The wife should patiently endure, even if her husband is drunk, profane, or blasphemous. In this situation, the marital bond physically imperils her. As Gouge writes, "Though an husband in regard of evill qualities may carrie the Image of the devill, yet in regard of his place and office he beareth the image of God" (*Of Domesticall Duties*, 273).

The wife has no authority even to rebuke her husband, much less physically punish him, should he be an unfit governor. Even so, the tract writers insist that the marital relationship is mutual. According to Whately, writing in the preface to the third edition of *A Bride-Bush*, for every duty assigned to wives there is a corresponding duty for husbands.[22] But if the wife breaks her part of the covenant, the husband is empowered to discipline her, if not by physical abuse then by other means left unspecified. In contrast, if the husband breaks his part of the covenant, he does so with impunity. Despite the gross inequity, Cleaver claims without irony that "marriage is the supreme and most excellent part of all amitie and friendship: and that it farre differeth from tyrannie" (*A Godlie Forme*, sig. O4v). The imbalance between so-called "mutuals" operates in conjunction with the repetition and indeterminate meaning of marital metaphors, thus further exposing the tracts' subversion of categories of authority and subordination.

The Puritan tract writers did not use their metaphors ingenuously. In fact, many of them are conscious of the instability of metaphor and sometimes draw attention to the potential for double meaning. In *Of Domesticall Duties*, William Gouge exegizes the biblical language of binding and unity and concludes that it conveys both literal and figurative meaning. His willingness to highlight the potential for various interpretations may suggest he is aware of the problems with his own use of metaphor — though he participates in a long tradition of biblical scholars who believe that scripture conveys both literal and figurative meaning.[23] In his interpretation of Genesis 2:24, the critical passage that states that man and wife are one flesh, Gouge declares, "In this place, these words have both a literall and mysticall sense. A literall of man and wife. A mysticall of Christ and the Church. The maine thing which the Apostle aimeth at, is to shew how neerely man and wife are linked together" (*Of Domesticall Duties*, 110). Gouge adds that the literal qualities of the marital union and the emphasis on tying and binding in marital language are modeled on the way Christ and the church are joined.[24] His attention to the double meaning of biblical language concedes the potential for multiple interpretations of his own wordings. Indeed, he exploits the various meanings afforded by the biblical source. Likewise, Thomas Becon and Miles Coverdale, the prefacer and translator of Bullinger's *The Christen State of Matrimonye*, embrace the doubleness of biblical language. They acknowledge that the words they employ to define ideals are open to interpretation, and, like Gouge, they do not repress the possibilities for alternative readings. Becon, like other marriage tract writers, uses metaphors that insist on both bliss and torment in wedlock. Not only does marriage imitate the relationship of Christ to the Church, it also contains sexual excess, one of the three often-stated advantages to marriage. He contrasts the purity of wedlock, achieved through containment, with whoredom by playing with the word "husbands," which he also spells "hausbonds" and "housebonds": "Behold unto what poynte theyse whorysh loose bondes, housebondes, I would have said, are fallen."[25] Like Gouge, Becon manipulates the doubleness of figurative language. But instead of noting the potential for his audience to derive both literal and mystical meaning from his text, Becon creates double meaning by punning, forcing his readers to ponder the etymological drift of the word. Through various rhetorical gestures, Gouge and Becon constantly exaggerate and repeat the importance of union, joining and binding in marriage. The intrinsic instability and duplicity of metaphor, combined with the exaggeration and repetition of the word "bond," overstate the nature of authority. Becon contrasts "house bonds" (husbands) to the "loose bonds" of the single life in order to show the advantages of marriage (as opposed to the celibacy extolled by Catholics). His plays on words also insinuate that if a woman takes a husband, she then becomes necessarily housebound. Often vacillating between praising mutual love and marshaling hierarchical order, Becon and Coverdale freely draw upon a realm of bondage metaphors. Becon calls marriage "holy wedlocke," admonishes "wedlocke breakers," refers to married persons as "yoke fellows," husbands as "husbondes," and claims that people who do not keep within the bounds of marriage should be "banished from the bounds of Christendom" (sigs. A3, A7v, A5, B8). Translating Bullinger, Coverdale discusses the "dewty knot and covenant of married folkes." He calls wedlock a "knot unloseable," and uses words such as "yoke" and "snared" in relation to the unity of man and wife upon marriage (sigs. A6v, B2, B4).

When Gouge insists that there is a literalness to biblical metaphors of marital unity, and when Becon and Coverdale facilitate alternative interpretations of bondage metaphors, they seem to imply that men and women have separate identities until marriage, whereupon the two bodies fuse and the separate identities cease to exist. Articulating this notion of "oneness," the tract writers figure the husband as a kind of mother and the wife as a child. T. E. interprets English law as stating the following: "Every feme covert [married woman] is *quodammodo* [in a certain way] an infant" (*Lawes*, sig. K7). Husband and wife are mutually joined, but the wife, like a child, is inferior, weaker and smaller, and in the Puritans' physiological descriptions of her, she is joined to the husband's midsection rather than to his head or to his feet. Gataker describes her as "a part or a limbe of her husband." The prevalence of allusions to the Adam and Eve story in these tracts allows Gataker to say that the wife, like a child, "had her beginning and her being originally from [the husband]" (*A Wife in Deed*, 8). Because Adam in effect gave birth to Eve, wives are indebted — in addition to being subordinate — to their husbands, thus "bound" to them in yet another sense. Meanwhile, the husband's fantasy of giving birth to the wife, suggested by these constructions, further complicates the metaphors. Belsey argues that the early modern woman has no fixed subject position because as a wife she is subordinate to her husband, but as a mother she is superior to her children. Thus she is only defined in relation to others, unfixed within a system of domestic government. Belsey writes: "In the conventional understanding of the power relations authorized by the fifth commandment, children owe obedience to both parents equally, but at the same time one parent owes obedience to the other. In other words, the wife is aligned with the children, the mother with the father. These subject-positions, offered to the same woman, cannot be held simultaneously without contradiction" (*Subject of Tragedy*, 155). Indeed, an individual woman is duplicated, or split, among her different roles and positions. Marital metaphors of tying and binding attempt to underscore the wife's attachment to the system of domestic governance, but the multiple meanings of such language undermine that attempt; instead of fixing her, she remains unfixed.

Such physiological metaphors conjure an image of the married couple as a set of joined twins or as a monstrously deformed double body — a beast with two backs: Becon writes, "And lyke as the partes of a mans body when they are sundred one from another conceave an exceadig great anguish [and] doloures payne even so ought it to be an exceadig grefe for maried folkes to be separated" (Bullinger, *Christen State*, sig. A6v). This ideal (that husband and wife experience physical pain when they separate) collapses the spiritual realm of "oneness" into the physical and recalls descriptions of the labor of childbirth or the pain of surgical amputation, both of which reinforce the theory that the wife is a "part" of, or appended to, her husband. In other physiological descriptions, the single marital body is imagined as a patchwork of body parts, assembled in a way that personifies the incompatibility between marital mutuality and the domestic hierarchy; the body is figured as a superior male head attached or grafted to an inferior female body. Thus the female is constructed as headless, the male as bodiless — the male supplies the intellect, the eyes, and the ears, while the woman provides the motions, the needs and the feelings. This physical paradigm implies that marriage decapitates women and disembodies men, while suggesting that neither body is at all normative in the state of marriage.

As head of his wife, the husband owns the wife as his possession, though she does not own him. Whately instructs the wife to "remember then that thou art not thine owne, but thine husbands; and a man may doubtless challenge his owne, as his occassions require, and it must be readily granted unto him" (*A Bride-Bush*, sig. D3). Vives narrates the didactic story of a woman who enlists the literal meaning of possession metaphors to reject an adulterous advance:

> And know thou this, woman, that the chastity and honesty which thou hast is not thine, but committed and betaken unto thy keeping by thine husband. Wherefore thou dost the more wrong to give away that thing which is another body's, without the owner's license. And therefore the married woman of Lacedemon, when a young man desired of her that unhonest thing, answered him, I wolde grant thee thine asking, young man, if it were mine own to give that thou askest, but that thing which thou woldest have while I was unmarried was my father's and now is my husband's. (*Office and Duty*, 113)

The "thing" that the woman cannot give away is described euphemistically; whether it be her chastity or her body, the implication that she is a material possession is the same. But Vives's understanding of the single body idea once again inaccurately describes the woman's subject position. Despite Petruchio's assertion in *The Taming of the Shrew* that his wife is "my goods, my chattels, she is my house" (3.2.230), an early modern husband did not really own his wife as if she were an object that could be traded from person to person. For example, a husband could not enjoin his wife to break the law — divine or common. Although the wife was the husband's property, he could not trade, sell or give her away. Physically, women did have some control over their bodies in that they could and did indulge in extramarital affairs.

On the other hand, the woman's identity did dissolve into her husband's upon marriage in that she not only lost her last name but also forfeited control of her assets to her husband. *Legally*, man and wife were considered to be one person in a very literal sense. To wit, T. E. writes, "now because Adam hath so pronounced that man and wife shall be but one flesh, and our law is that if a feofment be made jointly to John at Stile and to Thomas Noke and his wife, of three acres of land, that Thomas and his wife get no more but one acre and a half, *quia una persona* [because they are one person] . . . and by this a married woman perhaps may either doubt whether she be either none or no more than half a person" (*Lawes*, sig. B2v). The legality of the concept that man and woman form only one body upholds a literal interpretation of the tract writer's bondage metaphors: the early modern wife was in fact bound to her husband in more numerous and oppressive ways than he was bound to her. The reason for the inequity stems from fearfulness of Eve's original sin, a story that influences the tract writers' belief that women have power potent enough to invert hierarchy. Plutarch warns: "Such wives had rather bee mistresses and over-rule their doltish husbands, than obey them that be wise and men of understanding."[26]

By insinuating the existence of latent though fearful female power, marital containment language produces a tension between containment and freedom for husbands *and* wives. In Thomas Heywood's *A Woman Killed with Kindness*, Sir Charles portrays this tension when he describes his newly married sister to her husband through conventional marital metaphors: "she's no chain / To tie your neck and curb you to the yoke, / But she's a chain of gold to adorn your neck" (1.1.62–64).[27] Sir Charles's deft rendering of two opposing interpretations of marital metaphors illustrates the tenuousness of the hierarchy in which husbands rule their wives — the hierarchy that such metaphors help to define. Indeed, where the tract writers manipulate bondage metaphors to establish and uphold male authority and female subordination, they can sometimes invert those categories. Without warning, the tract writers modify the purpose of bondage metaphors from reinforcing what they consider to be naturally occuring male authority and female subordination to provoking fear of the opposite — female superiority and male subordination. Becon and the other early tract writers encourage couples to marry when they employ a phrase like "holy wedlock"; they do not want to suggest that wives have the power to bind their husbands to them, which would discourage men from marriage. Nevertheless, such connotations cannot be ignored, particularly at moments when the tract writers caution discretion in choosing a mate. Alexander Niccholes warns both parties that "Marriage lockes faster then the Jaylor, suspition, or the usurer, for he never turnes the key till Doomsday" (*Discource*, 49). Some Puritan writers attempt to ward off hasty marriage by likening wedlock to a kind of halter.[28] In Puritan treatises such as these, the imprisoning connotations of marital language are applicable only when a man marries an unsuitable wife — that is, when he impetuously chooses a wife for her beauty or her money instead of her virtue. Smith explains, for example, "The husband saith, that his wife must obay him because he is her better, therefore if he let her be better than himselfe, he seemes to free her from her obedience, and binde himselfe to obey her" (*Preparative*, 62). Likewise Gataker calls husbands who are ruled by their wives "bond men," implying that their inferiority is tantamount to slavery. Smith's scenario openly posits an inverted hierarchy. Marital bondage metaphors thus help to produce anxieties, or even fantasies, of a world turned upside down, in which women are the authorities and men are their subordinates.[29]

Under the pressure of these anxieties of male subordination, a term like "yokefellows" loses its utopic pastoral associations of oxen laboring equally and begins to suggest containment and punishment of the husband. When a man chooses a wife for her beauty or her dowry, he may find himself less a yokefellow than bound in punishment to a loathsome woman. Smith neatly turns the yokefellow trope and captures the possibilities of inversion: "a Wife is called a *Yokefellowe*, to shewe that she should helpe her Husband to beare his yoke, that is, his griefe must bee her griefe; and whether it bee the yoke of povertie, or the yoke of envie, or the yoke of sickness, or the yoke of imprisonment, she must submit her neck to beare it patiently with him, or els she is not his yoke fellowe, *but his yoke,* as though she were inflicted upon him for a penaltie" (my emphasis) (*Preparative,* 74–75). He adds, "Miserable is that man which is fettered with a woman that liketh not his religion, for she will be nibling at his prayer, and at his studie, and at his meditations, till she have tyred his devotions, and turned the edge of his soule" (53). Note that the pastoral connotation of "yokefellows" dissolves into the prison-evoking language of "fetters" when men are the inferiors. The tract writers thus manipulate bondage metaphors to reinforce the wife's inferiority to her husband in their commendations of marriage. But when they delineate duties and discuss choosing a partner, they reemploy the metaphors to foster anxieties about the husband's grip on his own power. In the dedication to his two marriage sermons, *A Good Wife Gods Gift* and *A Wife Indeed,* Gataker encourages men and women "to knit that sacred knot betweene you" (3). But within the second sermon, *A Wife in Deed,* he notes that a man who chooses a bad wife will "have his table made his snare, his bread his bane, his raising his ruine, his delights his destructions" (51).

Because of the various meanings put into play by bondage metaphors — besides depicting the wife bound in submission to her husband, they identify the potential for the husband to be bound in submission to his wife — the use of these metaphors at once facilitates domestic ideals by encouraging readers to marry and reinforcing the domestic hierarchy, and subverts it by discouraging men from commitment and underscoring the fearfulness of female power. The danger is obvious: discouraging readers from marriage risks throwing people back into the arms of Catholicism. Nevertheless, Puritan marriage tract writers like Gataker, who were still anxious to promote marriage in defiance of the Catholic ideal of celibacy, were also anxious to counsel caution and circumspection in choosing a partner. But the tract writers' excessive containment rhetoric magnifies the tension between promoting marriage and advising caution. In reality, husbands were neither equal yokefellows nor were they helplessly and punitively yoked to loathsome wives. Subsequently, the relative ease with which marriage tract writers duplicate marital bondage metaphors for these opposing purposes undermines their effectiveness in general. In the end, the language the Puritans employ to emphasize their points provided "antimarriage" tract writers with ample opportunity to counter them.

Hercule Tasso and the anonymous author of *A Discourse of the Married and Single Life* typify nonreligious, antimarriage tract writers who exhort men to avoid marriage, drawing liberally from the fount of marital bondage metaphors conventionalized by the Puritans. By focusing only on the negative, punitive connotations of marital containment, Tasso and the others deliberately provoke alternative interpretations. "Tying the knot," for example, takes on a decidedly sinister quality in the phrasing of the antimarriage writers. In the well-known dialogue between Hercule and his cousin Torquato entitled *Of Marriage and Wiving*, Hercule Tasso dissuades men from marriage using a familiar metaphor: "we rather covet libertie then bondage . . . and if we wil seek what is good, and shun what is bad, let us (then) let such alone, with whom being (once) yoaked, we can never be quiet."[30] Tasso quotes Metellus, a Roman who reportedly said, "My fellow citizens . . . if we could be brought into this world without the company of Women, we would all of us studie how to shake off this heavy yoke from our shoulders" (sig. B3). The bondage language in Tasso's translation of Metellus, especially the word "yoke," which originates in Pauline scripture, alludes to the Puritan marriage tracts Tasso opposes. His very lengthy diatribe against marriage, teeming with bondage metaphors, concludes with this pithy quotation: "Wo unto thee and double smart, / If to a wife once yoakt thou art" (sig. F4). Robert Tofte, who translated the Tasso debate in 1599, harps on the equality implied by "yoking," which he finds repulsive, unqualified as it is by a description of the domestic hierarchy that positions husbands over wives, a hierarchy that, as we have seen, is always delineated in the tracts. By eschewing one meaning of marital bondage — that a woman is bound to her husband — the translator furthers Tasso's project of dissuading men from marriage. Moreover, by enlisting alternative meanings implied by conventionalized marital metaphors, these antimarriage tracts expose ambiguities and contradictions inherent in Puritan marital ideals. The price of this exposure is a potential weakening of the culture's patriarchal precepts, which ensure the maintenance of male authority and female subordination.

The absence of a domestic hierarchy in these antimarriage tracts not only convinces men to avoid marriage, but it also, in a backhanded way, empowers women. Though the antimarriage tracts are profoundly misogynist, in terms of their nascent power women come out on top.[31] Tasso disparagingly compares women to "Divels," "the plague" and "murthering Basiliskes" (sigs. B3, C), but his remarks also assume that female power is unimaginably fearful and almost limitless. Further emphasizing female power and control over men, Tasso constantly draws upon women's resemblance to witches by observing their "bewitching company" and their "enchanting whistles" (sigs. B3, C). While it is true that most early modern writers, including Puritan marriage tract writers, believe that all women are innately disorderly and desirous of usurping man's authority, these antimarriage tract writers view women as having the power to do as they please, that is, as having more power than men.[32] In their marital paradigm, women not only come out on top of the social hierarchy, men come out bound and helpless on the bottom. A wife is "an over proude and usurping Tyrant to him that weddeth her" while a husband is represented as a "man that hath both his handes and his feet manacled togither."[33] Tasso explicitly claims that the domestic sphere is analogous to the public one — he writes how women, "that scarce hath bin two daies in her husbands house . . . will straight (as if she were a Princesse) make new laws and orders" (sig. D2v). Improbably the end result of Tasso's invective against women is the image of marriage as a kind of gynecocracy.

In *A Discourse of the Married and Single Life* (1621), an anonymous antimarriage tract writer mimics Tasso's strategy of appropriating metaphors from the Puritans, amplifying their punitive connotations, and upsetting the ideals they are supposed to invigorate. In a polemic that dissuades men from marriage, this author focuses on female power, puts the woman on top, and debases the man. He warns single men, "thou are about to purchase unto thy selfe a wife, and the price that thou must give, is thy liberty; that of a king, thou wilt make thyselfe a Vassall; of a Lord, a servant."[34] Further, he lists famous women who murdered their husbands, and again notes their "bewitching" and devilish qualities: "If [your wife] be foule, thy house will be hell, thy wife the divell, and thy selfe the miserable soule tormented" (sigs. B8v, Cv). Throughout the tract, the author uses marital metaphors common in the Puritan tracts: "The colt is carried unwillingly to the bridle. The bullock is brought by force to the yoke. The thief is drawne by violence to the stocks, and so to the halter. Yet thou runnest violently, and joyfully to thy Inchanter, to thy bridle, to thy yoke, to thy stocks, and to thy halter" (sigs. B3v–B4). In this author's inverted worldview, women rule and men are subject to their choice of horrific bodily punishments.

The author of *A Discourse* forces his readers to see how marital metaphors connote punishment and containment for husbands: "Marriage is called Ligam, because it bindeth a knot, because it knitteth a string, and because it tyeth: and a yoke, because it burdeneth: yet it is farre better to carry a yoke, then to marry a wife, for a yoke is borne in the day, but laid downe at night; but a woman must be endured even to the death" (sigs. H–Hv). For Tasso, marriage is also more burdensome than a yoke. In contrast, the rhetoric of the Puritan marriage tracts falls short of encouraging the literal meaning of marital bondage — at least in reference to the husband's experience. But when the antimarriage tracts are compared to Puritan tracts, we see how the Puritans may also facilitate a slippage from figurative to literal in order to urge the physical containment of women's speech, gadding and vanity. It is easy to see how readers may have derived "uncleane" meaning from, for example, Whately's injunction that the wife avow that her husband is the "tie and tedder, not of mine actions alone, but of my desires and wishes also" (*A Bride-Bush*, sig. Bb3v). Because the slippage from figurative marital containment to literal marital containment would seem to encourage men literally to tie and bind women, the Puritan tract writers apparently did fear that women had the power to invert hierarchy and to wrest control of the social and political spheres from ruling men.

It is true that tying and binding metaphors encourage spouses to maintain their commitment and to procreate. But when applied to each partner's individual marital duties, the bondage metaphors suggest other applications. For example, the husband's duty is to govern and support his family by working outside the house; the woman is enjoined to stay inside the house, and she is often forced to comply with that injunction. In 1591, Henry Smith wrote that a man and wife "must think that they are like two birds, the one is the Cock, and the other is the Dam: the Cocke flieth abroad to bring in, the Dam sitteth upon the nest to keepe al at home. So God hath made the man to travaile abroade, and the woman to keepe home."[35] Similar formulations are found all through the tracts. William Vaughan evokes ancient tradition to explain the practice: "The Grecians accustomed to burne before the doore of the newe married the axletree of the coach, wherein she was brought to her husbands house, letting her to understand, that she was ever after to dwell there."[36] And, as if recognizing and acknowledging that forcing women to stay indoors is oppressive and tyrannical behavior, Vaughan later brags, "Our women here in England, although they be in the power of their husbands, yet they bee not so straightly kept as in mew, and with a guard, as they be in Italy and Spaine, but have almost as much liberty as in France or in Germany" (sig. N7v). Francis Dillingham repeats the dogmatic refrain nine years later: "As the wife must have a care within doore, so must the husband without."[37] And, as a final, but by no means exhaustive example, Whately explains how women should behave when forced into their houses like prisoners: "Wherefore if a woman be so yoked, shee must keepe her place, and shew patience. It is not for a prisoner to breake prison at his pleasure, because he hath met with a rough Jaylor" (*A Bride-Bush*, sig. Ee3). Whately's language concedes that the injunction to keep wives indoors is virtual imprisonment.

To ameliorate the unpleasantness of such containment, some of the tract writers couch injunctions for the wife to stay at home in Aristotelian logic — they say that, as a kind of deputy to the husband, the woman must remain in the house to control and guard it in the husband's absence.[38] Women, of course, had to leave the house in order to take care of basic household needs, and some married women worked outside the house. With these realities in mind, Cleaver lists the times when it is appropriate for women to venture beyond the boundaries of the home. He writes, "There are foure reasons why the woman is to goe abroad. First, to come to holie meetings . . . second, to visit such as stand in neede . . . third, for employment and provision in household affaires committed to her charge. And lastly, with her husband when hee shall require her" (*A Godlie Forme*, sigs. P3–P3v). Robert Burton is infamous for advocating the position that a woman should leave the house but three times: for her baptism, her marriage, and her funeral.[39] But the language in the marriage tracts that admonishes women to stay at home is so strong and prevalent that it is difficult to discern whether readers are meant to interpret it literally or figuratively. Early modern playwrights constantly literalize such injunctions when they lock female characters into their homes or in other kinds of prisons. Shakespeare's Hermione, Marlowe's Abigail, Beaumont and Fletcher's Panthea, Middleton's Bianca and Jonson's Celia all are forced into prisons or enclosures of some kind out of a fear that their freedom will lead to, or has caused, infidelity. Julia in Edmund Tilney's *The Flower of Friendship* recognizes that readers interpret bondage metaphors literally and feels obliged to explain that they are emphatically figurative. She states, "My meaning is not in reciting these examples [of women who never left their houses], to have the married wife continually lockt up, as a cloystred Nonne, or Ancres, but to consider hereby, what respect she must have in going abroade, and what a vertue it is to kepe well hir house" (136–37). Evidently Tilney is aware of the potential for literal interpretation of injunctions to lock wives up. But better to risk husbands jailing their wives than risk the freeing of female will and power.

The anonymous author of the antimarriage tract *A Discourse of the Married and Single Life* incorporates a more strident tone than the Puritans in sanctioning the wife's virtual imprisonment in the house. He quite specifically describes how to contain a woman: "If [the wife] be faire, she can never go abroad . . . [and] all thy business abroad is sure to go to wracke: for her bewitching and attracting beauty will inforce thee to stay within doors . . . If dishonest . . . then would there be putting chains to her hands, making laws for her feet, and restraint for her eies" (sig. C3v). While containing women in various kinds of prisons occurred on the early modern stage, this writer overtly alludes to containment devices like stocks and scold's bridles, which were used to punish women for petty crimes. These punitive devices restrain those parts of the female body that are theoretically prone to excess — the stocks confine the legs, which women might use to stray, and scold's bridles restrict movement of the tongue with which women might gossip and chide.

Because wives are so "bound" to their husbands, the punishment for indecorous marital behavior might be to tighten the ropes — literally. This was indeed the case for early modern wives. The author of *A Discourse of the Married and Single Life* advocates, seemingly figuratively, the making of chains for women's hands and laws for their feet, and he is not alone in using containment words like "chains," "locks," "guards," "bridles," "halters" and "stocks," which connote punishment, even in the context of persuading people to marry. Recall Gataker's formulation that "man and wife are as the stock," the "stock" referring to a tree trunk. Because it was a commonplace for women to submit to punishments, such as the stocks, that really did bind their hands and feet, the language also carries punitive associations. For certain offenses, a woman could be sentenced to the thew, a device much like the pillory to which women were tied by the neck.[40] For speech infractions in the household, husbands, townspeople or magistrates would lock scold's bridles onto women's heads.[41] When Robert Cleaver evokes bondage metaphors like the "bridle of government," when Whately evokes the "bridle of fear," and when the anonymous antimarriage tract writer calls certain women "unbridled and licentious," the literal referent is clear and ominous.[42]

While the tracts often caution that wedlock can be a terrible prison for men if they marry "froward" and peevish wives, they do not register any kind of lamentation over its imprisoning aspects for women. Women, like tamed animals, should be content to abide behind locked doors. Clearly, however, if the man is free to roam the streets and the countryside, he is the partner more at risk of infidelity — he can commit adultery without fear of discovery, and indulge in various sins with impunity; men do not display their sexual transgressions on their very bodies as women do when they become pregnant. Importantly, many people believed that an adulterous wife threatened the inheritance of wealth, a transgression that in turn would threaten the foundations of English power through succession. Gouge concedes the existence of this double standard: "I denie not but that more inconveniences may follow upon the woman's default [adultery] then upon the man's: as, greater infamy before men, worse disturbance to the family, more mistaking of legitimate, or illegitimate children, with the like. The man cannot so well know which be his owne children, as the woman; he may take base children to be his owne, and so cast the inheritance upon them; and suspect his owne to be basely borne, and so deprive them of their patrimony" (*Of Domesticall Duties*, 219). In the early part of the sixteenth century, advocates of marriage, flouting the Catholic glorification of celibacy, based much of their argument on the ways in which children immortalize their fathers and people the commonwealth with strong, able and rich bodies. Through this logic, any qualities in a woman that might predispose her to adultery and encourage her power to bear illegitimate children would have had to be censored immediately.

Given such profound fears of female infidelity, the tract writers' rhetoric specifically discourages sexual transgressions. The physical containment of unruly wives in bridles, stocks, and even in the house lends a coercive aspect to marital metaphors and may also explain the tract writers' emphasis on a woman's individual body parts. To marriage theorists, certain parts of the body seem to have an almost disembodied tendency toward profligacy. Silencing a woman, for example, is accomplished by restraining the tongue; preventing the woman's perceived tendency to wander is accomplished by confining her feet. Anatomizing of the woman's body into synecdochal parts commonly occurs in the marriage tracts, reflecting a tendency to further contain women by depicting them as limbs appended to their husbands instead of as whole and autonomous bodies.[43]

In early modern poetry, the fragmentation of the female body operates as a trope; poets are able to use fragmentation, or blazon, to praise or blame aloof and idealized figures like Petrarch's Laura, Sidney's Stella, Spenser's Elizabeth and Shakespeare's Dark Lady. Nancy Vickers has argued that blazon enables the poet to possess or consume his unrequiting lover despite the woman's detachment from and lack of interest in her male wooer;[44] that is, the poet is able to possess the woman against her will. Blazon and the related device — synecdoche — are, of course, rhetorical strategies; the tract writers employ synecdoche and blazon as they do metaphor — to be eloquent. But the use of rhetorical figures that fragment a woman's body coalesces with the abundance of references to disembodied female body parts in the marriage tracts. The end result is the reinforced image of a woman as a series of limbs and features appended to the male body, which the man, as head, can subsequently "cut off." Thomas Becon advises husbands to "cut [your wife] from thy flesh, that she do not always abuse the[e]."[45] T. E. says that when a woman's husband dies, "her head is cut off" and she has "lost a moiety of herself" (*Lawes*, sig. Q4v).

Some of this strange and violent rhetoric of the body can be explained by the preeminence of the Adam and Eve story in marital ideology. Because Eve was built of Adam's rib, man is never a whole body until he is reunited with the rib upon marriage. Adam then is perceived as a whole body missing one rib; Eve is perceived as the missing rib itself. Tract writers often manipulate the rib allegory to enforce the unity of man and woman in marriage, but that allegory also serves the secondary purpose of substantiating a woman's inferiority to her husband. Smith exemplifies this tendency:

> To honour Mariage more, it is said, that God tooke a rib out of Adam's side, and thereof built the woman. . . . To honour Mariage more yet, or rather to teach the maried how to honour one another, it is saide, that the wife was made of the husband's rib: not of his head, for Paule calleth the husbande the wives head: nor of the foote, for he must not set her at his foote: the servant is appoynted to serve, and the wife to helpe. If she must not match with the head, nor stoope at the foote, where shall he set her then? He must set her at his heart, and therefore she which should lie in his bosome, was made in his bosome, and should be as close to him as his ribb of which she was fashioned. (*Preparative*, 8–11)

Other tract writers tell a similar story.[46] But these anatomical references, like bondage metaphors, encourage alternative interpretations. For example, a statement like "the wife is the husband's rib" is clearly figurative. But a similar statement like "the husband is the head of his wife" carries various meanings — the husband is like the wife's head in that he speaks for her and makes decisions for her, but he is also her head in that he is his wife's leader.

This separation of the female body into parts helps explain the overabundance of tying and binding metaphors throughout the tracts; harping on a woman's fragmented body in the context of bondage metaphors portrays the husband as a unifier who picks up and binds the scattered pieces of an unmarried and thus incomplete woman; alternatively, he becomes a surgeon who cuts away rotten flesh. Gataker theorizes that a bad wife eats away at the marital body, working like a cancer to cause the demise of the marriage. He writes in *A Wife Indeed* that "a bad wife, an indiscreet woman . . . is as a rottennesse in his bones. And she may therefore be compared rather to a wart . . . or a cancer, that consumeth the flesh, wasteth the body parts, and eateth even to the verie heart. For no sorer ulcer than a bad friend, in Sophocles his judgement;

than a bad wife, in Salomon's account" (9–10). Gataker's medical language reinforces the need to imprison the wife by preying on anxieties about disease. Whereas the antimarriage tract writers openly compare women to the plague, Puritans do so by insinuation. If a woman were constructed as part of a man's body, like his rib, and if the two bodies literally become one through sexual intercourse, women can metaphorically contaminate the husband's body through association and literally contaminate the husband's body through sexual contact. As noted earlier, an adulterous wife does more than contaminate her husband with syphilis, she also figuratively contaminates his bloodline by denying his paternity.

Fragmentation of the female body in marriage tracts, whether it be through medical language or a version of blazon, further destabilizes the position of women in both domestic and sociopolitical economies. Just as poets are able to possess a distant woman in a blazon, husbands are theoretically able to contain an unruly woman through their version of blazon. To prevent a wife from committing adultery, William Gouge advocates that she follow these measures:

> For preventing this hainous sinne . . . [be a] diligent keeper of the heart (that lustfull thoughts proceed not from thence) of the eies (that they wander not on the beautie or propernesse of any ones person, or on lascivious pictures, or any other like allurements) of the ears (that they hearken not to inticements of others) of the tongue (that it utter no unchaste and corrupt communication) of the lips (that they delight not in wanton kisses) of the hands (that they use no wanton daliance) of the feet (that they carry thee not too neere to the place where adulterie may be committed) of thy company (that thou be not defiled with others wantonesse and uncleanesse) of thy diet (that it be not immoderate) of thine apparell (that it be not garish and lascivious) of the time (that it be not vainly and idly spent) to omit, I say, these and other like remedies. (*Of Domesticall Duties*, 221)

Gouge's inventory of female body parts in this quotation encourages men to perceive women (and women to perceive themselves) as an assembly of fragmented limbs and features. But when that woman acts subversively, Gataker describes her not as a true limb of the man, but as a prosthesis: "But the Woman that beareth the Name, and standeth in the roome of a wife, but doth not the *office* and *dutie* of a *Wife* is but as an *eye of glasse*, or a *silver nose*, or an *ivorie tooth*, or an *iron hand*, or a *woodden leg* that occupieth the *place* indeed, and beareth the *Name* of a *limbe* or a *member*, but is not truly or properly any part of that *bodie* whereunto it is fastened; it is but equivocally so called" (*A Wife in Deed*, 9). The unwillingness to envision a woman as a series of *contiguous* body parts suggests that marriage theorists such as T. E. saw a woman as "none or no more than half a person" in a literal sense (*Lawes*, sig. B2v). And the grotesque transformation of a real, living person into a *synthetic* fragment shows how easily a man, as head, can "cut off" his wife — cut her from his body, cut her off from social contact, and, in fact, dis-member her from both the marital body and the social body with little or no harm to his own flesh. As Gataker suggests, the wife can easily go from being an organic member of the union to a synthetic one, in which case, while the limb cannot exist without the head, the head can exist without the limb, further weakening promises of marital reciprocity and mutuality.

Such dismemberment language exemplifies the dubious position of the wife in early modern households. When tract writers continually harp on "bonds" and emphasize the contractual obligations of marriage, in addition to comparing a wife to so much excess flesh that can be summarily cut off, their claims about marriage as a partnership or even about wives as deputies in the household lose their persuasiveness. The tracts ultimately leave us with a picture of the wife as bondwoman — a slave to the tempers, idiosyncrasies and desires of her husband. He is the "master in his family" who must "rule like a king," to be "as it were the king in the family" with "royall perogative of being Lord of all," though he has "more authority then a king in his kingdome."[47] Forgetting for a moment the abject situation of wives, that picture of a monarchical husband had potentially serious consequences for the tract writers themselves. In his first speech to Parliament in 1603, James I used common marital bondage metaphors to describe the role of a king — "What God hath conjoyned then, let no man separate. I am the Husband, and the whole Isle is my lawfull Wife; I am the Head, and it is my Body."[48] If there is a relationship among metaphors that evoke bondage in widely disseminated marriage tracts, increased restrictions on women and the increase of power in the English monarchy during the early modern period, then the tract writers, as subjects of the monarch, would find their positions similarly unfixed, unstable and perilous. With, for example, the notion that an unruly woman is not always an essential part of the marital body, the analogy to the sociopolitical realm suggests that unruly subjects under a king can be similarly cut off. Ironically, then, in their rhetoric designed to augment the power of husbands and to further subordinate wives, the tract writers diminish their own positions as subjects of the monarch.

2 • "*Bisket* of *Love,* which crumbles all away"

The Failure of Domestic Metaphor in Margaret Cavendish's Poetic Fancies

Katharine Capshaw Smith

> *Death* is the *Cook* of *Nature*; and we find
> *Meat* drest severall waies to please her *Mind*.
> Some *Meates shee* rosts with *Feavers, burning hot,*
> And some *shee* boiles with *Dropsies* in a *Pot*.
> Some for *Gelly* consuming by degrees
> And some with *Ulcers,* Gravie out to squeese.

In 23 volumes of verse, biography, natural philosophy, essays, plays and epistles, Margaret Lucas Cavendish trumpets her astonishing ideas and impressions, exciting twentieth century literary critics with countless aesthetic, scientific, social, philosophical and moral puzzles to decode.[1] My essay's epigraph, taken from Cavendish's poem, "Nature's Cook," suggests the noblewoman's remarkable imaginative boldness and eagerness to publicize the shocking syncretic aptitude of her poetic mind. However, while scholars of early modern science and protofeminism enthusiastically grapple with Cavendish's mercurial scientific and social treatises, relatively few literary critics comment on Cavendish's first volume of poetry and even fewer examine her verses in any depth.[2]

While critics notice Cavendish's inventive use of household imagery, none explains the reasons for the duchess's unconventional comparisons. In fact, homey metaphors in Margaret Cavendish's first publication, *Poems, and Fancies* (1653), provide a framework through which Cavendish attempts to systematize and explain life experience. Examining her world through the lens of housewifery, Cavendish applies the organization and productive purpose implicit in cooking and in weaving to various confounding issues, such as death, loss of youth and constructions of female beauty. While Cavendish ostensibly hopes to make sense of her world through the domestic, to discover an ordering principle which guides and gives purpose to life issues, the metaphysical tenets undergirding her poetry prevent such a success. In fact, by juxtaposing "huswifery" against the scientific principles inherent in the duchess's depiction of life and death, Cavendish forces the reader to question the significance of the domestic. The poetry's homespun metaphors inevitably buckle under the weight of Cavendish's scientific beliefs, forcing the reader to recognize the domestic framework's inability to annul an atomistic worldview.

Although her poems ultimately depreciate the domestic, in the prefaces to *Poems, and Fancies,* Cavendish craftily employs social constructions of the feminine in order to validate her poetic project. In mapping out an aesthetic and public persona to authorize her efforts, Cavendish implies that her poetic work inevitably results from her gender, as in "To the Reader," when Cavendish explicates the connection between poetry and housework: "for, Housewifery *is a discreet* Management, *and ordering all in* Private. . . . *It is just as in* Poetry: *for good* Husbandry *in* Poetry, *is, when there is great store of* Fancy *well order'd, not only in fine* Language, *but proper* Phrases, *and significant* Words."[3] As a poet expressing ideas in language, Cavendish employs similar strategies of organization and administration as those found in household supervision. Building on this generic similarity, Cavendish envisions the domestic as the conventional arena in which women express their fancies. In "To All Noble, and Worthy Ladies," Cavendish concludes that poetic invention naturally belongs to the creative housewife: "*Poetry*, which is built upon *Fancy, Women* may claime, as a *worke* belonging most properly to themselves: for I have observ'd, that their *Braines* work usually in a *Fantasticall motion,* as in their *severall* and *various dresses,* in their many and singular choices of *Cloaths* . . . [in] all manner of *Meats* to eate: and thus their *Thoughts* are imployed perpetually with *Fancies.*" Women's minds are best suited to poetry, Cavendish asserts, for the evidence of their creativity in clothing and cooking attests to women's artistic nature. Since poetry parallels the products of a creative woman at home, Cavendish frequently likens her verses to clothing and food. In *Poems, and Fancies,* she describes her poems both as a "Garment *of* Memory" ("To Sir Charles Cavendish") for her audience to admire and edibles for her readers to consume: "though they are not of the choicest *Meates* . . . and though I cannot . . . feast you with *Ambrosia,* and *Nectar,* yet perchance my *Rye Loafe,* and new *Butter,* may tast more savoury, than those that are sweet, and delicious" ("To Naturall Philosophers"). In this and other of the collection's prefaces, Cavendish's self-deprecating stance as a poet merges with her assertion of modest success as a cook. As a whole, Cavendish's prefaces employ constructions of women as housewives in order to name wives as artists and to designate household activities and poetic creation as inextricably bound and consummately similar. Cavendish's affinity for domestic imagery continues in the title of her collection *The Worlds Olio* (1655), which reflects the similarity between spicy stew and the text's hodgepodge of short essays on various subjects. An anonymous dedicatory poem to *The Worlds Olio,* "To the Lady of Newcastle," furthers the analogy by entreating the reader to partake of the text: "An *Olio* of Confections, not refrain; / For here's a Sumptuous Banquet for your Brain" (15–16).[4]

By using orthodox expectations for women's work to establish an aesthetic rationale for female poets in *Poems, and Fancies,* Cavendish attempts to deflect criticism of her audacious vocation.[5] In addition to avoiding criticism of female poets, a related reason for Cavendish's emphasis on domestic imagery lies in her position at the historical moment of *Poems, and Fancies'* composition. In 1652, when drafting her verse, the duchess was struggling to reconstruct her identity in relationship to English society and turned to images of the housewife in order to shunt off potential antiroyalist criticism of her text. Although Cavendish had returned to England after an eight-year exile in France to petition the interregnum government for the restoration of her banished husband's estates, the prefaces to *Poems, and Fancies* depoliticize her visit to England and define the author's identity as merely that of a simple homemaker lacking proper occupation. She repeatedly bewails her shortage of employment at the time of the book's composition, saying "I had nothing to do, when I wrot it" ("To Naturall Philosophers"), which suggests a political as well as personal uselessness for the royalist in Commonwealth England. When she mentions her husband's lost wealth and status, Cavendish minimizes the implications of such a ruin, complaining only of a shortage of domestic work: "*I have no* Children *to imploy my* Care, *and* Attendance *on; And my* Lords Estate *being taken away, I had nothing for* Huswifery, *or thrifty* Industry *to imploy my self in*" ("To the Reader"). The duchess's turn to poetry, then, becomes even more explicable, for since she had no occupation as a housewife or as a royalist, and because poetry is next to domestic enterprise, she had no alternative but to write.

Of course, in order to figure Cavendish's relationship to the construction of women as housewives, one might consider the duchess's class and her actual relationship to laboring women. A marchioness at the time of *Poems, and Fancies'* publication, Cavendish almost certainly was not herself involved in menial domestic occupations like cooking and weaving. Also, an enforced distance from the serving class characterizes Cavendish's account of her gentrified youth. A proponent of class division,[6] Cavendish describes in her autobiography her mother's warnings against close interaction with the serving class: "neither were we suffered to have any familiaritie with the vulgar servants, or conversation" (*Memoirs*, 190). Cavendish's personas in *Sociable Letters* (1664) overflow with cautionary advice about servants; one voice asserts that most servants are "Idle, Cousening, Wasteful, Crafty, Bold, Rude, Murmuring, Factious and Treacherous, and what not that is Evil," and another that "I Intrust my Servants as Little as I can, but just what of Necessity I must, for there is an Old Saying, that in Trust lies Treason."[7] Kathleen Jones charts a lifelong distance between the duchess and working women, explaining that in her husband's house Cavendish was never "accepted" by many servants, "a situation which continued to cause problems throughout her married life" (*Glorious*, 55).

In light of this distance, Cavendish's repeated references to herself as a cook and weaver in the prefaces to *Poems, and Fancies* appear exceptionally artificial. However, crafting a housewife persona was for Cavendish a strategic maneuver, for with the increase in popularity of conduct literature, sanctioned conceptions of women's roles became increasingly limited, telescoped, in fact, into the construct of woman as housewife.[8] Conduct book author Edmund Tilney epitomizes this reduction in his *Flower of Friendshippe* (1571), asserting simply that "the office of the woman is, to govern well the household."[9] Peter Stallybrass notes the period's reductionary tendency, asserting that "when the elimination of class boundaries is produced by the collapsing of women into a single undifferentiated group, that elimination is commonly articulated within misogynistic discourse."[10] Unclassifiable as a woman who admittedly preferred more "to write with the pen than to work with a needle" (*Memoirs*, 206), Cavendish in the prefaces to *Poems, and Fancies* cannily exploits the categorical limitations placed on women; she assumes the housewife image in order to justify the writing of poetry and its publication as rustic "*Rye Loafe*, and new *Butter*" for a hungry audience.

A glance at contemporaneous household manuals suggests the similarity between kitchen discourse of the period and the language of Cavendish's poetry. The most popular cookbook in the early seventeenth century, according to Barbara L. Feret, was Gervase Markham's *The English House-wife* (1615), one of the first of these texts to separate categorically cooking from other household occupations, such as weaving, brewing and medicinal cures.[11] While it is uncertain that Cavendish was familiar with Markham, they did share similar backgrounds and values; according to Michael R. Best, Markham "was a younger son from a noble family in decline, and believed in the old, chivalrous virtues, particularly in the ideal of an orderly hierarchical society led by an aristocracy that was noble in action as well as in birth."[12] If not the duchess, than surely William Cavendish, an avid horseman, was familiar with Markham, who published five volumes on the breeding and care of horses.[13] In her poetry, Cavendish wields the language of the kitchen, using phrases that recall cooking manuals like Markham's. Compare excerpts from Markham's recipe for roasted cow udder to Cavendish's poem, "A Heart Drest": "Take a cow's udder, and first boil it well, then stick it thick all over with cloves . . . take vinegar and butter . . . put to it a good store of sugar and cinnamon . . . and so serve it up" (89). Cavendish describes a soured infatuation in similar terms: "*Life* takes a *Heart*, and *Passions* puts therein, / . . .Then take some *Anger*, that like *Pepper* bite, / And *Vinegar* that's sharp, and made of *Spight*. /. . . Some *Salt* of *Slander* put also to that. / Then serves it up with *Sauce* of *Jealousie*" (1–9). Cavendish's use of actual cooking discourse adheres to her poetic self-construction as a "natural" poet, a housewife, one who writes without formal training; she tellingly asserts in "The Claspe," "Give me a *Stile* that *Nature* frames, not *Art*" (5).

However, as Sylvia Bowerbank reminds us, "anyone who has ventured to read ten pages of Cavendish's work knows that her method, or rather her defiance of method, is deliberate" ("Spider's Delight," 395). Cavendish's domestic poetry radically yokes the low discourse of the kitchen to the high discourse of poetry, invoking cooking language within heroic couplets. Her verse speaks both to the experience of the housewife and to the weighty metaphysical themes and approaches of traditional poetry, a discursive fusion that reflects her ingenious formal imagination. Even though her poetry ultimately critiques domesticity, Cavendish reveals her indebtedness to the rhetoric and labor of working-class women, discovering in servant culture a vehicle to assert her epistemological vision. And while Cavendish in life may have never baked, woven or brewed, domestic metaphor enables Cavendish to cross the kitchen threshold imaginatively, freeing her to play the role of middle-class housewife or laboring servant.

Cavendish begins to uncover her opinions on the nature of domestic efforts in her evolving explication of the term "fancy." Cavendish's persona in the prefaces to *Poems, and Fancies* embraces a definition of fancy as capricious imagination, dismissing its products in, for example, "To All Noble, and Worthy Ladies" as "*honest, Innocent*, and *harmlesse Fancies*." But the apparent insignificance of her imagination unravels later in the text when she introduces the "Fancies" section, which contains most of her domestic poetry. Cavendish repeatedly describes her fancy as "Truth" (121) and asks the reader in "To Poets" to take the "Fancies" section most seriously: "*I desire all those which read this part of my* Book, *to consider, that it is thick of* Fancies, *and therefore requires the more* Study" (122). If a reader still cannot grasp the sense expressed by fancy, Cavendish directs her to "*ask a* Poet *where the* Conceit *lies, before they* Censure" (122). And in this section of her book, which contains the poems many critics have dismissed as "ridiculous" and "bizzare,"[14] Cavendish implores the reader "*not to accuse my* Book *for* Non-sense" (122), for with close reading "*the* Truth *will be found out*" (123). Cavendish closes her introduction to the "Fancies" section by again emphasizing the solemn import of her fancies: "*I must intreat my* Noble Reader, *to read this part of my* Book *very slow, and to observe very strictly every word they read; because in most of these* Poems, *every word is a* Fancy" (123).

Cavendish continues her reinterpretation of the term "Fancy" in several of her poems, which emphasize that "*Fancies*, in the *Braine* that *Nature* wrought, / Are *best*; what *Imitation* makes, are naught" ("Of Poets, and their theft," 5–6). Because fancy is close to truth, Cavendish imagines it as the substance, the physical body of poetry: "*Fancy* is the *Form, Flesh, Blood, Bone, Skin; / Words* are but *Shadowes*, have no *Substance* in" ("Of Poets, and their theft," 58–59). As a woman without academic training, Cavendish adopts an aesthetic theory that privileges idea over form, thought over expression, fancy over wit. In the untitled poems that conclude her text, Cavendish again underscores that "*Fancy* is the *Soul* in *Poetrie*" and asks the reader to "Be just, let Fancy have the upper place" (17, 19). While playing the housewife in her book's prefaces, Cavendish is able to deflect criticism of her efforts by constructing her poetry as harmless and innocent, and herself in the nonthreatening position of middle class homemaker; however, the seriousness with which Cavendish treats her fancies indicates that they embody substantive ideas worthy of considerable attention.

In general, the concepts that anchor the domestic poetry in the "Fancies" section of the volume illustrate Cavendish's emerging scientific philosophy. In 1653, Cavendish adhered to an atomistic theory much like that of Descartes and Hobbes, one which asserts that matter is composed of several types of atoms (for Cavendish, long, sharp, round and square) whose movements result from physical forces at work. However, Cavendish's philosophy, according to Lisa T. Sarasohn, diverges from many seventeenth century atomists by virtue of its essential religious skepticism, its "almost complete lack of theological qualifiers necessary to dissociate mechanism from the charge of atheistic materialism" ("Science," 291). In "To the Reader," Cavendish explains that she could not attempt any poetic representation of the Christian god in *Poems, and Fancies*: "*my* Incapacity, Fear, Awe, *and* Reverence *kept me from that* Work. *For it were too great a* Presumption *to venture to* Discourse *of that in my* Fancy, *which is not* describeable." However, this deferential avoidance also might suggest a more deep-seated ambivalence about conventional religion.[15] Additionally, Cavendish believed, like Hobbes, in the materiality rather than incorporeality of the soul, an audacious creed in that age of religious fervor.[16] Critics like John Rogers have examined the overtly scientific sections of poetry in *Poems, and Fancies*, finding in works like "A World Made by Atomes" a perfect example of Cavendish's "atheistic cosmogony" ("Matter," 196), for no governing deity generates the poem's new world; rather, atoms "by their severall *Motions*, and their *Formes*" construct the world "by chance" ("A World," 15, 17). Further, Jay Stevenson argues that *Poems, and Fancies* "repeatedly suggests that there is nothing transcending" Cavendish's atomistic landscape ("Mechanist-Vitalist," 531). For the duchess, materiality becomes the sole reality at the core of life experience. Cavendish's atomistic cosmology also grounds her domestic poetry, investing life and death issues with the brutal weight of religious skepticism and materialism.

The commanding image of domesticity in Cavendish's fancies is the powerful female entity, Nature. The character of Nature, who appears throughout Cavendish's corpus, has often been critically defined as "the conventional view of a feminine nature — Mother Nature or Mother Earth."[17] In *Poems, and Fancies*, however, Cavendish's Nature is no intimate and comforting "Mother." Rather, Cavendish bases her construction of Nature on tenets of atomistic cosmology, for Nature is a character who indifferently destroys, consumes and manipulates material reality, a being concerned solely with matter and never with spirit. To depict Nature's creative and destructive movements, Cavendish imagines Nature as an upper class housewife, a noblewoman who consumes gifts brought by her servants, Death and Life, the cooks in Nature's employ. When Cavendish uses this household framework, ostensibly to make sense out of the human condition, the tension between her atheistic metaphysics and her homey poetic structure forces the reader to question the aptness of domestic metaphor in sustaining existential inquiry. Repeated throughout the "Fancies" section of *Poems, and Fancies*, these poetic failures deliberately and repeatedly point both to Cavendish's seeming desire to invest existence with purpose by using the sanctioned housewife role available to her, and to her final inability to achieve meaning through homespun imagery. Through these repetitions, Cavendish critiques not only the modes of expression available to female poets, but more pointedly the significance of domestic work in the face of blunt metaphysical truth.

Cavendish exposes the essential materiality of human existence in "Nature's Exercise and Pastime," where the duchess expressly calls up Christian associations of sacrificial purpose in death in order to deny such meaning. She describes humankind's relationship to Nature: "Our *Flesh her Meat*, our *Blood* is *her strong Wine*" (6). In this line Cavendish teases the reader with the ultimate Christian compliment, that human death might be as important and significant as that of Jesus. But after holding out that hope for such consequence in death, Cavendish deflates human death's sacramental potential:

> The *Trees*, and *Herbes, Fruits, Roots*, and *Flowers* sweet,
> Are but her *Sallets*, or such cooling *Meat*.
> The *Sea's* her *Bath* to wash, and cleanse her in,
> When *she* is weary, hot, or *Journey* bin.
>
> (7–10)

By equating Nature's devouring of human bodies with her ingestion of "*Herbes, Fruits, Roots,* and *Flowers*" as "*Sallets*," Cavendish collapses the promise that human flesh and blood are anything more than physical, material "*Meat*" and "*Wine*" for Nature's consumption. To continue the poem's disturbing implications, Cavendish buries the literal comparison of flesh to meat among such simplistic and trite homespun comparisons as the night to Nature's bed and the sun to Nature's light and looking glass. Ostensibly, then, the ease with which the poem's speaker positions human death in the natural domestic order should comfort the reader, for it suggests that being consumed as meat is as uncomplicated and fit as is using the sea for a bath. Of course this leveling effect instead astounds by its cold nullification of man's hope for spiritual consequence in death. The title also ironically underscores this effect, for by suggesting that Nature's consumption of human flesh and blood is a mere diversionary entertainment, an "Exercise and Pastime," the poem completely negates any opportunity for death's transcendent meaning.

Cavendish's poems on weaving enact a similar attempt and failure to impose spiritual significance on life events through a domestic framework. In "Nature's Grange," Cavendish uses weaving imagery to imagine that a higher being consciously and deliberately orders and arranges human life. As part of her household duties, Nature deliberately calls human life into existence:

> And *Nature* makes the *Fates* to sit and spin,
> And *Destiny* laies out, and brings *Flax* in.
> For *Nature* in this *Housewifry* doth take
> Great pleasure, the *Cloath* of *Life* to make.
>
> (15–18)

By virtue of its homey conceit, this image offers a comfortable and familiar depiction of life's beginnings, with Nature as a caring housewife who directs her servants at work. However, as Cavendish elaborates on Nature's role as a household manager, the spinning image confounds any discovery of meaning or arrangement in life's creation:

> Thus *Nature* busily doth her selfe imploy
> On every *Creature* small, till they do dye.
> When any dies, that work is done,
> And then a new work is begun.
>
> (23–26)

Cavendish applies the psychology of the housewife to Nature, and thus the homemaker/creator turns unmoved to another task after one of her creations dies. Instead of stressing the joy Nature takes in weaving the "*Cloath* of *Life*," the poem concludes with the dark implication that creating life is "work" Nature easily and nonchalantly abandons. In addition, Cavendish levels the meaning of the "*Cloath* of *Life*" by speaking generally of "*Creature*[s]" rather than specifically of human life as the product of weaving. Human death then, not only inconsequential because it means merely the end of one of Nature's tasks, has the same import as the loss of any negligible life form. Instead of investing human life with significance by demonstrating that life is ordered and premotivated, the weaving metaphor finally trivializes and minimizes the worth of human life, reducing creation to a meaningless chore.

The weaving metaphor in "Soule, and Body" also finally

undercuts Cavendish's attempt to invest human death with significance. Like "Nature's Exercise and Pastime," which evokes and deflates hope of religious meaning in death as Nature's flesh and blood, "Soule, and Body" similarly calls up the promise of spiritual significance in eternal life only to frustrate it. Cavendish uses a clothing metaphor to describe the resurrection, but her emphasis on the earthly activity of weaving divests the resurrection of any religious consequence. The context is entirely secular, for the fates who spin the "*Cloath* of *Life*" in "Nature's Grange" reappear in "Soule, and Body" as those who, under the direction of Nature, create life: "Great *Nature She* doth clothe the *Soule* within, / A *Fleshy Garment* which the *Fates* do spin" (1–2). This comparison of the body to a garment governs the entire poem, ultimately flattening the image's potentially spiritual connotations:

> And when these *Garments* are grown old, and bare,
> With *Sicknesse* torn, *Death* takes them off with care;
> And folds them up in *Peace*, and quiet *Rest*,
> So laies them safe within an *Earthly Chest*;
> Then scours them, and makes them sweet, and cleane,
> Fit for the *Soule* to wear those *Cloaths* agen.
>
> (3–8)

The final lines suggest the Christian resurrection, since the soul will, after death, be reunited with the body. But significantly, Cavendish's resurrection lacks the spiritual associations of sublime union with God and eternal life in heaven which give the Christian resurrection meaning. Instead, Cavendish's weaving metaphor reduces resurrection to the experience of dressing in a clean set of clothes; there is no glorious purpose in donning this refreshed body. By writing from the exclusively secular context of housewifery, Cavendish eliminates the religious significance of the resurrection and exhausts the reader's hope of spiritual meaning in eternal life.

Within the poems that use cooking metaphors, "Nature's Cook" is perhaps the most grotesque and disturbing depiction of Cavendish's cosmology, for it nominally tries to interpret human loss by representing Death as a chef who prepares corpses as various dishes for consumption by Nature. In the surface logic of the poem, as in "Nature's Exercise and Pastime," human death serves the important purpose of sustaining the female deity, Nature. Employing her domestic conceit, Cavendish likens the physical characteristics of particular ailments and tortures to the different modes of food preparation: "Some *Flesh* as *Sage she* stuffs with *Gouts*, and *Paines*, / Others for tender *Meat* hangs up in *Chaines*" (7–8). As Death prepares and transforms human flesh, Cavendish graphically underscores her belief in the essential materiality of the human body; human flesh is simply meat, the elemental material sustaining Nature's existence:

> Some in the *Sea she pickles* up to keep,
> Others, as *Brawne* is sous'd, those in *Wine steep.*
> Some with the *Pox*, chops *Flesh*, and *Bones* so small,
> Of which *She* makes a *French Fricassee* withall.
>
> (9–12)

At this point, Cavendish treats different modes of death with a horrifying playfulness, taunting the reader with those a common person might experience, such as death by drowning, alcohol or venereal disease. As the poem changes tone by moving into even more violent and repulsive descriptions of death, the emphasis shifts from depicting the body as a hunk of meat to describing Death as she graphically excises particular body parts, such as "*Braines*" (19), "*Tongues*" (21) and "*Guts*" (24), in order to create specific dishes. The darkening tone and more brutal images make increasingly concrete the use of human flesh for different culinary creations, emphasizing that no matter what type of death, whether through age, disease or violence, ultimately humanity becomes fodder for Nature's sustenance. Through harsh emotive images, Cavendish forces the reader of "Nature's Cook" to recognize the ultimate meaninglessness of life and death: human remains become fleshy dishes to "please" (2) the ever hungry, aloof Nature. This is the devastating implication of the duchess's materialist cosmology. While Cavendish attempts to use the domestic metaphor ostensibly to offer a purpose for human life, her metaphors fail horribly in bequeathing a satisfying purpose to human life and death; this failure enables Cavendish to convey her metaphysical beliefs with graphic power.

Additionally, the failure of domestic metaphor in "Nature's Cook" highlights the problematic position of the seventeenth century female poet. As the duchess's protective rationale for poetic art and her public image as a "happy wife"[18] emphasize the necessary connection between household tasks and poetry, she must and, in fact, does describe her subject in the most domesticated way possible. And yet, with each example piled upon grotesque example, Cavendish escalates the emphatic inappropriateness of comparing deaths to recipes. Although it is not expressly evident that Cavendish intended to critique the domestic perspective, the sheer number of gruesome comparisons in "Nature's Cook" implies that Cavendish might have been conscious of her conceit's effects. The metaphor's collapse indicates that the insignificant and irrelevant homey framework cannot impose existential meaning on human suffering and death. Additionally, by deprecating the domestic, Cavendish also implicitly criticizes the working class, particularly women whose lives were absorbed in work the duchess may have envisioned as unsatisfying, trivial, and ultimately meaningless.

Cavendish's vivid descriptions of death and possibly her materialistic skepticism may have resulted from her experience with the Civil War.[19] Although Cavendish asserts in "An Epistle to Souldiers" that she "*never saw an* Army *together, nor any* Incounters" (*Poems*, 167), the duchess suffered many personal losses in the conflict; as well as devastating her husband's estate, war took her brother's life, and in June 1648 during a raid on the Lucas estate her mother's and sister's tombs were vandalized, their corpses dismembered and strewn across a churchyard (Jones, *Glorious*, 68). Much of *Poems, and Fancies* takes violent conflict as its subject, as in poems like "A Dialogue between a Bountifull Knight and a Castle Ruined by War," "A Dialogue betwixt Peace and War" and "The Ruine of the Island." Cavendish's poems rarely glorify war; as a materialist, Cavendish could not believe that brave soldiers receive some heavenly reward for their efforts, and as a royalist, Cavendish was on the losing side of the struggle. As in her domestic poetry, in war "*Death* was onely *Conqueror* of all" ("Doubt's Assualt, and Hope's Defense," 22).

Interestingly, several of Cavendish's more graphic verses on war distinctly echo her violent domestic poetry. For example, the explicit "A Description of the Battle in Fight" enumerates the various modes of death on the battlefield in language shared by "Nature's Cook." The structure and phrasing of "Some *burning hot*, as in high *Feavers* were" ("A Battle," 54) tellingly recall "Some *Meates shee* rosts with *Feavers, burning hot*" ("Nature's Cook," 3). Cavendish in "A Battle" even likens body parts to various foods, describing "*Guts* like *Sausages*" (43) and "*blood* as *thick* as *gelly*" (48). While the comparisons of body parts to food render these descriptions particularly ghastly, additionally disturbing is the poem's progression to an equally involved depiction of the soldier's horses in death throes. Again Cavendish underscores her materialist metaphysics; death levels both man and horse, for "All in *death* lay, by *Fortune* they were cast / And *Nature* to new *formes* goes on in hast; / . . . in *death*, all *beasts alike there meet*" (153–56).[20] As the same atomic material in different "*formes*," man and horse both experience a similar insignificance in death. Likewise, in "A Battle between King Oberon, and the Pygmees" Cavendish employs language of the kitchen to detail violence as well as her materialist convictions:

> Here *beasts* and *men*, both in their *bloud* lay *masht*,
> As if that a *French Cook* had them minc'd, *so hasht*,

Or with their *bloud* a *Gelly* boyle,
To make a *Boullion* of the *spoyle,*
For *Nature's table* several *dishes brings,*
By her directions in transforming things.

(209–14)

This passage repeats the domestic strategy and materialist ideology of "Nature's Cook": again Cavendish figures Nature as an indifferent housewife, again both human and bestial bodies are simply different forms of matter, the "several dishes" absorbed into Nature. As the brutal passages from Cavendish's war poems suggest, the Duchess's poetic imagination recurrently associates violent deaths with cooking, a linkage reflected also in the domestic dismemberings of Cavendish's "Fancies," like "Nature's Cook."

In addition to using domestic metaphors to uncover death's lack of spiritual significance, the duchess also employs cooking imagery to investigate constructions of female beauty. Although somewhat less concerned with atomistic cosmology than those poems about life and death, "A Bisk for Nature's Table" and "A Tart" share a similar impulse in their imposition of a domestic framework: these poems presumably attempt to make sense of female beauty by likening women's bodies to edibles. But like the duchess's poems on death, her apparent efforts to understand female physical appeal through comparisons to food ultimately unsettle any certainty about the nature of beauty. As Catherine Gallagher asserts, for Cavendish "there is no privileged perspective of universal knowledge. . . . In Cavendish's poetry, for example, we are invited to see the hunt from the perspective of the hunted animal, the feast from the perspective of the food."[21] Cavendish assumes an overtly satirical approach in these domestic poems. By defining and measuring female attractiveness through the domestic, Cavendish parodies a rhetorical strategy employed by male Renaissance writers, poets who appraise and represent beauty by anatomizing and complimenting women's physiques. Like Renaissance blazon writers, Cavendish examines and assesses distinct physical features of a woman's body, which, in aggregate, should constitute female beauty. However, by imposing a cooking framework on the blazon strategy, Cavendish deliberately sabotages her attempt to discover beauty through her descriptions, for likening women's body parts to foodstuffs destabilizes not only knowledge of beauty, but also conventional masculine attempts to systemize and control women's bodies through language.

Cavendish's satiric voice has only recently been recognized by literary critics; Mihoko Suzuki notices, interestingly, that Cavendish's closet drama "Matrimonial Trouble" (1662) also offers an "energetic critique" of the blazon genre "through an insistence on the materiality of the woman's body."[22] In *Poems, and Fancies*, Cavendish calls up the blazon tradition only to deflate it, providing an example of what Bronwen Price sees as the seventeenth century female poet's public entrance into "conventions and genres in which women are traditionally located as the objects rather than the subjects of speech" ("Feminine Modes," 118). In "A Bisk for Nature's Table," Cavendish initially plays it straight, revealing her aptitude at blazon writing. She delicately describes a female body without explicit reference to food or cooking:

> A *Brow*, that's *Arch'd*, or like a *Bow* that's bent:
> A *Rosie Cheek*, and in the midst a dent:
> Two *Cherry Lips*, whereon the *Dew* lies wet:
> A *Nose* between the *Eyes*, that's *even* set.
>
> (3–6)

Douglas Grant compliments this section of the poem, calling it "charming," most likely because its representations are regular, almost clichés, and tactfully expressed (*Margaret*, 125). But as the poem progresses, the speaker's descriptions increasingly focus on the texture and heft of the woman's body: "A *Body plump, white*, of an *even* growth; / . . . A sound firm *Heart*, a *Liver* good" (11, 13). The evaluative gaze becomes less informed by romantic commonplaces and more concerned with the state of the body as a potential source of nourishment, as meat for a recipe. When the speaker instructs the reader to locate "A *Hand* that's fat, smooth, and very white, / The inside moist, and red, like *Rubies* bright" (15–16), there remain the trappings of romantic compliment in the whiteness and comparison to "Rubies," but the emphasis insistently falls on the body's weight, bloodiness and suitability for consumption. Toward the conclusion of the poem, Cavendish puns on the status of the woman's body as ingredient by requiring "A *Stomack* strong, and easie to digest" (19). When Grant excerpts the poem in his biography as evidence of the "occasionally charming" (125) effect of Cavendish's poetry, he tellingly omits the lines that describe the woman's body as meat. By applying a cooking metaphor to what, if the early passages are any indication, would be a conventional blazon without it, Cavendish arrives at the grotesque image of woman as hearty soup. As in the poems that liken corpses to food, this attempt to demarcate female beauty through food metaphor collapses into the repulsive, suggesting first that, as in her domestic poems on death, women's bodies are merely atomic material that will be absorbed into Nature. But the domestic analogies also lead to an image of horror rather than of beauty, suggesting that neither can a woman's beauty be conceptualized through the domestic nor through the dissecting gaze of the male blazon writer.

"A Tart" employs a similar strategy of anatomizing women in order, ostensibly, to represent and understand the components of feminine beauty. However, this poem does not verge into the grotesque by escalating comparisons of the woman's body parts to meat; instead, it continuously emphasizes the body's status as food material. Life dissects a woman to harvest ingredients for a pie:

> Then did she take some *Cherry Lips* that's red,
> And *Sloe-black Eyes* from a *Faire Virgins Head*.

And *Strawberry Teats* from high *Banks* of white *Breast*,
And *Juice* from *Raspes Fingers ends* did presse.
These put into a *Pye*, which soon did bake.

(5–9)

A brutal and violent image, the mention of the fair virgin from whom the parts are removed stresses the subjected woman's destruction to a greater degree than does "A Bisk for Nature's Table." In "A Tart" the speaker details the process of composing the shell which will contain these parts, "kneads it well: then on a *Board* it laies, / And roules it oft, and so a *Pye* did raise" (3–4), as well as Nature's happy, if cannibalistic, consumption of the woman, "she it much commends" (12). In both "A Tart" and "A Bisk for Nature's Table," the poems' graphic comparisons of a woman's body to food strongly resist a metaphoric reading, and instead compel an image of the monstrous, the opposite of what Cavendish seemingly hoped to achieve in her investigation of beauty.

The duchess's manipulation of the blazon structure reveals her awareness of contemporary masculine poetics, an awareness that challenges her self-presentation as the unlearned housewife poet. In entering the generic conversation, Cavendish assumes the role of the male blazon writer; she is not anatomizing *male* beauty, of course, but takes women as her subject in order to address the treatment of women as objects of the male poetic tradition. Nancy Vickers notes, "The canonical legacy of description in praise of beauty is, after all, a legacy shaped predominantly by the male imagination for the male imagination; it is, in large part, the product of men talking to men about women."[23] Cavendish's voice in the conversation contests male fetishization of women's bodies by materializing the blazon writers' metaphors, making literal the prosecting gaze of the male tradition. The male poet, Cavendish suggests, cannot envision the whole woman, but instead reductively dismembers her. The domestic framework enables Cavendish to uncover the poetic commodification of women's fragmented bodies, for the disjointed women in Cavendish become foodstuffs which can be eaten, enjoyed and forgotten.

In a third category of cooking poems, Cavendish uses a recipe format to grapple with the loss of youth. As in the poems about death and beauty, the domestic framework nominally imposes meaning on an enigmatic dimension of life experience. And as in the other cooking poems, Cavendish exercises the metaphoric failure of the domestic in order to sabotage such an imposition. Recognizing that cookbooks name, measure and arrange ingredients in order to achieve specific results, Cavendish models "A Posset for Nature's Breakfast" on a recipe in order to solidify abstract qualities of youth, to master fleeting youth by permanently fixing its characteristics as foodstuffs. As Elise-Noël McMahon explains, a recipe format is "an obvious, one might say unequivocal, strategy of control . . . of prescribing and documenting detail, and fixing a dish's identity."[24] In "A Posset for Nature's Breakfast," Cavendish attempts to understand the components of an attractive youth by using specific foods to represent and circumscribe his or her characteristics; Life, who in this poem is Nature's cook, arranges and combines these different foods to constitute the young person:

> Life scummes the *Cream* of *Beauty*, with *Times Spoon*,
> And drawes the *Claret Wine* of *Blushes* soon,
> There boils it in a *Skillet* cleane, of *Youth*;
> Then thicks it well with crumbl'd *Bread* of *Truth*:
>
> (1–4)

To make corporeal the youth's intangible qualities, Cavendish selects foods whose sensory qualities resemble the abstractions; blushes are figured as "*Claret Wine*" (2); a lemon represents "*sharpest Wit*" (9). Cavendish then uses the recipe format to attempt to gauge and measure exact amounts of certain qualities needed to comprise the young person: "A handfull of *Chast Thoughts*, double refin'd, / Six *Spoonfuls* of a *Noble*, and *Gentle Mind*" (11–12). On a purely symbolic level, the poem appears to be a clever allegorical exercise, but as the poem's directions become more precise and specific, commanding the exact amounts of ingredients needed, the recipe format begins to undermine Cavendish's attempt to recreate a youth imaginatively through food figures by encouraging the reader to read the recipe literally.

The recipe structure also implies an apprenticeship relationship between the cook and the reader. As McMahon asserts, the recipe reader "is implicated not in watching a demonstration but in taking part in a performance" (193), for by transmitting the directions for the dish's creation, the speaker implies that the reader is producing it as well. This recipe paradigm disables Cavendish's poem, for it forces the reader to consider the creation literally. By contemplating the requirement of "Six *Spoonfuls*" of a noble mind, the reader recognizes that a mind cannot be meted out in spoonfuls, nor can mirth be measured in "A *Graine*" (13). Ironically, then, by adhering to the conventions of the recipe format, the poem forces a literal reading, a reading that ultimately cripples itself because it cannot be enacted; one cannot understand the composition of youth by conceiving of it as a recipe.

"A Dissert" follows a similar pattern. Striving to fix intangible qualities in corporeal form, Cavendish simultaneously recognizes that a youthful state can never be made permanent, especially not through domestic metaphor:

> *Sugar* of *Beauty*, which away melts soon,
> *Marchpane* of *Youth*, and *Childish Macaroon*.
> *Sugar Plumb-words* most sweet on the *Lips*;
> And *wafer Promises*, which waste into *Chips*.
> *Bisket* of *Love*, which crumbles all away;
> *Gelly* of *Feare*, that quaking, quivering lay.
>
> (3–8)

The images of loss and decay in these descriptions work on two levels. First, they point to the fact that bright-eyed promises ultimately expire, as do beauty and new love. But in her attempt to fix these youthful experiences as foodstuffs, as abstractions transmuted into the constant physical form of "Dissert," the food representations disappoint as well, since wafers also finally crumble and sugar eventually must disintegrate.[25] Food representations also cripple her goal of materializing youth's transient attributes since, finally, what the abstractions are transmuted into Nature ultimately consumes. While in "A Posset for Nature's Breakfast" Nature enjoys the "*Meat*" (16) of the young person, in "A Dissert" she similarly incorporates the youthful confectionery: "Then *Nature* rose, when eat, and drink her fill / To rest her selfe in *Ease*, she's pleas'd with still" (15–16). Ultimately the domestic approach, as grafted onto Cavendish's cosmology, necessitates the decay and consumption of the very qualities she attempted to stabilize.

While not all of Cavendish's cookery poems mete out exact amounts of ingredients as does "A Posset for Nature's Breakfast," most of Cavendish's cookery poems do, in fact, read as recipes and construct the reader, just as Cavendish does herself in the prefaces, as a housewife. Several critics have noticed Cavendish's tendency to incorporate and implicate her reader; Elaine Hobby notes that in Cavendish's closet dramas, "the reader is left to spell out to herself the patterns formed in alternatives lived by the characters."[26] Even within *Poems, and Fancies*, Cavendish closes any distance between a female readership and her work by entreating her readers, "strengthen my Side, in defending my *Book*; for I know *Womens Toungs* are as sharp, as two-edged *Swords*, and wound as much, when they are anger'd" ("To All Noble, and Worthy Ladies," iv). This inclusion and implication become an important facet within the domestic poetry, a construct which suggests Cavendish's desire for her readership's involvement in her ideology and in the poems' repeated devaluation of the domestic. As each of Cavendish's domestic poems fails to impose meaning, order or knowledge on life events through homey conceits, Cavendish implicitly forces the reader to embrace an atomistic cosmology. More pointedly, since Cavendish constructs the reader as cook/homemaker, she forces the female reader literally to "follow" the recipes, to recognize the inconsequentiality of the domestic in imposing meaning on life. With the reader as cook, Cavendish asks her to reject the domestic in herself, to discern the triviality of her occupation as a housewife in the face of a materialist cosmology. A devastating critique of women's conventional labors, Cavendish's poetry repeatedly insists on the final insignificance of the domestic.

Additionally, while her prefaces celebrate the domestic's homey productions, other sections of *Poems, and Fancies* insistently challenge the consequence of domestic efforts. In "To All Writing Ladies," Cavendish asks creative women, "let us shew our selves a degree above Beasts; and not eate, and drink, and sleep away our time as they doe." Housewifery serves what Cavendish views as the base business of eating and drinking. For Cavendish, the only individualistic element that can supersede the brutal materialism of life and death is "Fame," for through success in poetry and philosophy, women can avoid becoming "forgotten dust."[27] Cavendish ends this section of her text, which immediately follows the domestic "Fancies" passages, by emphasizing the need for female accomplishment to bolster lasting eminence: "*That though our Bodies dye, / Our Names may live to after memory*" (1–2). Again Cavendish involves the reader in her vision of an achievement that can transcend existence's materialistic essence.

In some of Cavendish's later work she also disparages domestic work, as in *Observations Upon Experimental Philosophy* (1666), where she compares housewifery to the ridiculous processes of experimental scientists.[28] She says of women at home: "they most commonly take pleasure in making of Sweet-meats, Possets, several sorts of Pyes, Puddings, and the like; not so much for their own eating, as to imploy their idle time; and it may be, they would prove good Experimental Philosophers, and inform the world how to make artificial Snow by their Creams or Possets beaten into froth, and Ice by their clear, candied or crusted quiddinies or conserves of fruits, and Frost by their candied herbs and flowers; and Hail by their small comfits" (102). "[I]dle time," that which Cavendish disingenuously uses as an excuse to justify her composition of *Poems, and Fancies*, women waste in pointless domestic creations, much as experimenters squander their energies in nonsensical inquiry. Within the same passage, however, Cavendish returns to her characterization of Nature as a housewife, explaining that "for Nature, being a wise and provident Lady, governs her parts very wisely, methodically and orderly; also she is very industrious, and hates to be idle, which makes her imploy her time as a good Huswife doth, in Brewing, Baking, Churning, Spinning, Sowing, etc." (101). A much later work than *Poems, and Fancies, Observations* describes Cavendish's belief in vitalism and in a hierarchy of matter that positions animate, sensible matter over the insensible. Cavendish's image of a vitalist Nature as housewife does not bear graphic marks of violence and satire; she is entirely metaphoric, bereft of the gripping particulars that undercut the same figure of Nature as housewife in *Poems, and Fancies*.

Of course, one cannot expect consistent feminist statements from Cavendish. As Margaret J. M. Ezell asserts of feminist literary critics working with early modern writers, "there is a tendency to devalue or even to 'reinvent' those [artists] who do not conform to our criteria of 'good feminists.'"[29] No one could argue that Cavendish resembles a twentieth century feminist, for this is the writer who notoriously announces in her preface to *The Worlds Olio* (1655), "there is a great difference betwixt the Masculine Brain and the Feminine. . . . Nature hath made Man's body more able to endure Labour, and Man's brain more clear to understand and contrive than

Womans" (vii). Famously inconsistent on female ability and accomplishment, Cavendish reveals in her treatment of the domestic in *Poems, and Fancies* a willingness to perform the social construction offered her as a woman and wife, but also a strong tendency to undercut the limitations of this role in her verse. Although a modern reader cannot be sure that the collapse of domestic metaphor is deliberate (and not just an incidental byproduct of Cavendish's novel imagination), the sheer number of times Cavendish turns to the domestic lens and the subsequent multiple failures to achieve her ostensible ends suggest that she does in fact recognize the limiting implications of the domestic perspective. Certainly in subsequent publications Cavendish refuses to be bound by the domestic, and treads instead in other masculine arenas, such as natural philosophy, biography, drama, and utopian vision. Even in her first publication, Cavendish suggests that housewifery confines and slights a woman's artistic and human potential.

3 • The "Undividable Incorporate"

Householding in *The Comedy of Errors*

Jessica Slights

The Comedy of Errors is perhaps Shakespeare's most explicit investigation of the competing roles of the household and the marketplace in constructions of self and community. The play traces the misidentifications and misunderstandings that result when a pair of identical twins (both named Antipholus) and their identical slaves (both named Dromio) end up in the same city after years of separation. While the play exploits fully the comic potential inherent in such an implausible state of affairs, at the same time it offers incisive commentary on the relationship between the domestic and the commercial sides of social existence. Antipholus of Ephesus is a well-connected member of the thriving Ephesian business community whose vision of the good life appears to consist in establishing and protecting his reputation as a successful merchant; although he is married, the affective relations of the household seem to exist for him only insofar as they enable his role in public life. Antipholus of Syracuse, on the other hand, is an unemployed bachelor and drifter who dreams of belonging to a loving family, but whose solipsism leads him to fear the loss of independence entailed by participation in community life.

By literalizing the distinction between commercial and domestic identities in the figures of Antipholus of Ephesus and his twin, Antipholus of Syracuse, *The Comedy of Errors* insists not only that selves are shaped in meaningful ways by the network of social relationships in which they participate, but also more particularly that the affective relations of the household play an integral role in sustaining the civic and mercantile bonds of the city. The Antipholus brothers have been formed in different ways by their years of separation. As the action of the play moves to reunite them, the household — whose everyday activities are orchestrated by Adriana, wife of Antipholus of Ephesus, and her sister, Luciana — plays a pivotal role in urging the reconciliation of the competing claims of business and family that have kept the brothers apart. As events in Ephesus lead inexorably to the reunification of the Antipholi, efforts to sever the domestic domain from its public counterpart are exposed as futile, even potentially dangerous, and the household is revealed as both a necessary component of personal happiness and a fundamental constituent of a just and merciful state.

A brief introductory scene introduces the conflict between marketplace and household that propels events throughout *The Comedy of Errors*. The play opens with the arrest of the Syracusan merchant Egeon by Solinus, duke of Ephesus, and his men. As the duke explains to his captive, travel between Syracuse and Ephesus has been declared illegal:

> Merchant of Syracusa, plead no more.
> I am not partial to infringe our laws;
> The enmity and discord which of late

Sprung from the rancorous outrage of your Duke
To merchants, our well-dealing countrymen,
Who, wanting guilders to redeem their lives,
Have seal'd his rigorous statutes with their bloods,
Excludes all pity from our threat'ning looks:
For since the mortal and intestine jars
'Twixt thy seditious countrymen and us,
It hath in solemn synods been decreed,
Both by the Syracusians and ourselves,
To admit no traffic to our adverse towns.[1]

The duke's language here is markedly oppositional. Clearly angered by the memory of Ephesian merchants sacrificed to ratify the Syracusan duke's harsh laws, Solinus uses words and images that are inflammatory, even violent: Egeon's countrymen are "seditious," Syracusan statutes are bloody, the quarrel between the two towns is "mortal." Solinus's speech also consistently places rhetorical and metrical emphasis on the possessive pronouns "our," "your," "their" and "thy." For instance, the line proclaiming the duke's imperviousness to Egeon's pleas for mercy — pleas, incidentally, to which the audience has not been privy — ends with the emphatic spondee "no more." This metrical pattern is then echoed when Solinus makes recourse to Ephesian law to defend his arrest of Egeon. "I am not partial to infringe our laws," he announces, with stresses falling on both the direct object "laws" and the possessive pronoun "our." This pattern is repeated throughout the duke's speech as he emphasizes the phrases "your Duke," "their lives" and "their bloods." Such persistent spondaic punctuation of the regular iambic rhythm of the duke's speech accents both Solinus's insistence on the distinction between all things Syracusan and Ephesian, and the play's larger thematic interest in notions of ownership and belonging.

The penalty for violation of the prohibition on travel between Syracuse and Ephesus, the duke continues, is either death or a substantial ransom:

Nay more, if any born at Ephesus be seen
At any Syracusian marts and fairs;

> Again, if any Syracusian born
> Come to the bay of Ephesus, he dies,
> His goods confiscate to the Duke's dispose,
> Unless a thousand marks be levied
> To quit the penalty and to ransom him.
>
> (1.1.16–22)

While the duke's words underscore the gravity of Egeon's situation, the financial particularities he discusses also highlight the commercial disagreement at the root of hostilities between Ephesus and neighboring Syracuse. According to Solinus, the note of "enmity and discord" upon which the play opens is "sprung from the rancorous outrage" of the Syracusan duke toward a group of Ephesian merchants. Indeed, the duke's speech throughout this opening scene is peppered with specifically economic legalities. The "traffic" in "goods" between the "marts and fairs" of Ephesus and Syracuse is strictly prohibited; political strife has suspended ordinary business and Egeon must "quit the penalty" in order to "ransom" his life.

What begins as a tale of international economic intrigue is quickly domesticated, however. In a substitution that prefigures the influential role of the household later in the play, Egeon offers up not cold, hard currency but domestic narrative in a bid to save himself. Unable to pay his own ransom, Egeon instead recounts to the duke the story of his life and thereby shifts the forum for the play's investigation of such notions as ownership, belonging and the formulation of community values from the political arena to the affective domain of the household. From the start, Egeon's autobiographical tale is a family matter:

> In Syracusa was I born, and wed
> Unto a woman . . .
> With her I liv'd in joy; our wealth increas'd
> By prosperous voyages I often made
> To Epidamium, till my factor's death,
> And [the] great care of goods at randon left,
> Drew me from kind embracements of my spouse.
>
> (1.1.36–43)

The focus of Egeon's tale is as intimate and domestic as Solinus's was public and commercial. The Syracusan merchant speaks fondly of his wife, reminiscing about the early days of their marriage and particularly about his spouse's "kind embracements." Despite its apparent strength, however, the couple's marital bond proves no match for the pull of more public responsibilities. Leaving his wife behind, the young Egeon heads for Epidamium and unwittingly sets in motion events that ultimately lead to the violent rending of his household. Significantly, the marketplace appears as the primary agent of destruction in his dramatic account of a household brutally divided. Egeon insists that business trouble precipitated his fatefully protracted visit to Epidamium, and although he credits the "always-wind-obeying deep" (63) with causing the actual shipwreck that leaves his family "splitted in the midst" (103), he presents the death of his agent, his "factor," as the initial cause of his departure from home. Like Solinus before him then, Egeon posits commercial strife as a direct threat to domestic peace.

The play clearly portrays the affective bonds of the household more sympathetically than the merciless (and potentially violent) commercial ties of the marketplace. Nevertheless, *The Comedy of Errors* insists that in Ephesus the domestic and mercantile realms are inextricably intertwined, locked in a mutual dependency capable of generating both pleasure and terror for residents and visitors alike. While the "joy" experienced by the young Egeon and his bride is clearly due, for instance, at least in part to the "prosperous voyages" undertaken by the Syracusan merchant, these same commercial ventures are just as clearly responsible for destroying that joy not long after. Similarly, while Solinus implies that trade between Syracuse and Ephesus has in the past provided the basis for strong international relations, the souring of these same mercantile ties also leads to bloodshed.

Both Egeon's heartrending domestic drama and Solinus's

politicized account of the immediate threat to the Syracusan merchant's life emphasize the ability of the marketplace to exceed the boundaries of the agora and to influence events in the private realm of the household. Their exchange of stories upon the Ephesian mart also insists on the household's ability to affect life in the public arena. After all, Egeon's tale of a young family first delighted by the arrival of healthy twin boys and then brutally wrenched apart so moves the duke that he allows the old merchant the rest of the day in which to gather his ransom. Egeon disappears from the play after this initial storytelling sequence, but not before his exchange with Solinus has prepared audiences for the continuing battle between the realms of commerce and domesticity that gives the main plot its shape.

Home Sweet Home

I have already suggested that the household is portrayed more sympathetically than the marketplace throughout *The Comedy of Errors*. The primacy of the domestic domain as the source of affective bonds that enable both individual happiness and collective justice is literalized in the play's formal setting. The household assumes pride of place at the physical center of Ephesus. Following classical precedence, Shakespeare's Plautine adaptation is set before three stylized dwell ings. Sandwiched between a brothel and a priory, the house of Antipholus of Ephesus and his family is the focus of most of the play's dramatic action. Bearing the sign of the mythical Phoenix, the household pairs its material centrality with a quasimystical power to draw into its sphere of influence even hardheaded representatives of Ephesus's business community like Balthazar the merchant, Angelo the goldsmith, Pinch the doctor and the Porpentine's nameless courtesan. Like many households in Shakespearean comedy, the Phoenix seems to exert an almost magnetic force even on those only remotely connected to its family matters. In the Padua of *The Taming of the Shrew,* for instance, commercial life is subsumed almost completely into the social, emotional and financial transactions concerning the marriages of Katherina and Bianca; visitors to the city quickly become indistinguishable from its residents as everyone is drawn to converge on the Minola living room to woo Baptista's daughters. In *The Comedy of Errors,* however, the action takes place both literally and figuratively out-of-doors, as the characters gather on the mart before the Phoenix and expose both their domestic and commercial concerns to public view. Rather than being silently elided, the domains of the household and the marketplace are in constant tension, and the pull exerted by the household in Shakespeare's fictionalized Ephesus works to delimit social identity even as it effaces difference in a series of comic confusions.

And there are plenty of comic confusions in Ephesus. By doubling the single set of identical twins he found in Plautus's *Menaechmi,* Shakespeare immediately doubles the potential for comic confusion in his own play.[2] As René Girard has pointed out, however, the mere presence of indistinguishable twins (no matter how many) is insufficient to generate comedy. Instead, he argues, the characters' "stubborn expectation of difference in the face of non-difference" is what produces hilarity in the play.[3] Girard is surely right to insist that many of the play's comedic moments are generated by the characters' persistent refusal to acknowledge the possible existence of human beings "less different from each other than we would like them to be" (69). I want to suggest, however, that the comedy of Shakespeare's play arises more explicitly from the unwillingness of its central male characters to abandon a fantasy of absolute autonomy. Although they are different in temperament and have had varied life experiences, the Antipholus brothers share a persistent belief in their respective abilities to function independent of the affective relations of the household. Antipholus of Ephesus's attention is directed toward the public side of his existence. He expects his wife to entertain his business acquaintances but speaks harshly both of and to her, and exhibits demonstrably little pleasure in fulfilling his domestic responsibilities. Consider, for instance, his words to the goldsmith Angelo as the two men prepare to descend unannounced and late upon Adriana at dinnertime:

> Good Signior Angelo, you must excuse us all,
> My wife is shrewish when I keep not hours:
> Say that I linger'd with you at your shop
> To see the making of her carcanet,
> And that to-morrow you will bring it home.
>
> (3.1.1–5)

Rather than sending word of some unavoidable delay and warning Adriana of his plan to bring guests home to share their midday meal, Antipholus instead slanders her publicly by labeling her "shrewish" and then readies a lie to account for his tardiness. The merchant's lack of respect for his wife and her domestic affairs is again evident when his first words upon hearing her voice are a peevish scolding: "Are you there, wife? You might have come before" (3.1.63). Antipholus has a habit of taking the comforts of his household for granted, when he can be bothered to enjoy them at all. Nevertheless, he is surprised and appalled when his domestic problems begin to affect his work.

Unlike Antipholus of Ephesus who forsakes his domestic relationships for the commercial pleasures of the marketplace in the mistaken belief that the private and public sides of social existence can be isolated one from the other, Antipholus of Syracuse actively seeks out a network of affective relations by searching for his mother and brother. However, he too seems to resent that membership in family and community is necessarily predicated on the acceptance of adult responsibilities that restrict individual freedoms. The more philosophical of the twins, Antipholus of Syracuse is plagued not by the practical expectations generated by marriage, but by the more esoteric fear that finding his family may cause him to lose his sense of himself as a distinct and unfettered agent. Although the specifics of their concerns appear antithetical, the twins share a fundamental refusal to acknowledge that the affective relationships of the household upon which they are ultimately dependent demand by their very nature a degree of self-renunciation. Instead of drawing strength from what Gail Kern Paster calls the "radical connectedness of social experience,"[4] the Antipholus brothers each spend the better part of five acts desperately proclaiming the virtue of self-reliance while trying to shield themselves from the transformative powers of the household.

Despite Egeon and Aemilia's odd decision to use the same name for twin sons who are so alike that they can be "distinguish'd but by names" (1.1.52), we have little trouble telling one Antipholus brother from the other. Antipholus of Ephesus is the consummate insider, an established homeowner and popular businessman connected to Ephesian society through a network of domestic and commercial relationships. Antipholus of Syracuse, on the other hand, is presented as both a civic and an emotional outsider. With neither family nor sovereign to vouch for him in Ephesus, he is rendered both "Hopeless and helpless" (1.1.157) by his homeless state.

Small Cheer and Great Welcome

When the teenage Antipholus of Syracuse leaves home on a quest to find the brother he has lost in infancy, he is also searching for a sense of himself as a participant in a wider community. He is trying, in the vernacular of a later age, to find himself. Both the comedy and the errors of Shakespeare's play result not from the failure of Antipholus's mission, but from its astonishing success. While it appears at first as though the unfortunate Antipholus, like his father before him, will discover not kin but cruelty on the hostile shores of Ephesus, he instead finds himself at the very center of a tumultuous domestic world. An Ephesian merchant has warned him of the danger awaiting Syracusans discovered in Ephesus, and Antipholus knows that one of his countrymen is slated to die for the crime of setting foot on its shores. Instead of facing the executioner, however, Antipholus eventually finds himself dining in the home of a woman who claims to be his wife. The series of misunderstandings that culminates in this strange meal is initiated by a scene in which Antipholus mistakes his brother's slave for his own bondman.

Thinking that he sees his longtime companion Dromio rushing toward him down the mart, Antipholus calls out a friendly query:

> *S. Ant.* . . . How chance thou art return'd so soon?
> *E. Dro.* Return'd so soon! rather approach'd too late:
> The capon burns, the pig falls from the spit;
> The clock hath strucken twelve upon the bell:
> My mistress made it one upon my cheek:
> She is so hot, because the meat is cold:
> The meat is cold, because you come not home:
> You come not home, because you have no stomach:
> You have no stomach, having broke your fast:
> But we that know what 'tis to fast and pray,
> Are penitent for your default to-day.
>
> (1.2.42 52)

Mistaking Antipholus of Syracuse for his Ephesian twin, a breathless Dromio of Ephesus calls the man he believes to be his master home for his midday meal. Dromio's clipped and repetitive speech provides a sharply detailed picture of life at the Phoenix: lunch is served at twelve o'clock, the menu consists of capon and roast pig, meal preparations are being presided over by the mistress of the household, and this mistress is infuriated by her husband's tardiness. Ironically, rather than corroborating Antipholus's marginal identity as a homeless stranger, Dromio — the man he calls the "the almanac of my true date" (1.2.41) — transforms him into the perfect Ephesian family man. Antipholus has suddenly become the master not of one servant and a single bag of gold, but of an entire household, complete with a wife, a sister-in-law, and an obligation to return home in time for meals. Primed to expect aggression in Ephesus, he is wholly unprepared for such a domestic onslaught.

While his unexpected luncheon invitation unsettles Antipholus, it must also seem like an extraordinary instance of wish fulfillment. His appearance in Ephesus has been marked by a profound sense of alienation. Having failed to secure a dinner appointment with the helpful merchant who greets him upon his arrival, Antipholus, "dull with care and melancholy," plans to wallow in his feelings of exclusion by wandering unnoticed amid the hustle and bustle of the mart: "I will go lose myself, / And wander up and down to view the city," he tells Dromio (1.2.20; 30–31). Instead, the young Syracusan wanderer finds himself living out a childhood dream in which the game of "playing house" is instantly made real. A home and a family — those socioeconomic markers of adulthood and civic responsibility — suddenly become his for the taking without his having to work for them.

Early modern audience members would surely have appreciated the attractions of this preadolescent fantasy in which the respectability conferred by marriage and householding seems to appear unbidden out of the mist. In late sixteenth and early seventeenth century England, most young people had to work for a number of years before they had accumulated the financial means that would allow them to inaugurate their own households and thus to participate in society as full-fledged adult members.[5] Indeed, if contemporary conduct books are any indication, there was an almost universal need for young men like Antipholus to leave home in order to earn money and gain work experience before they married and set up house. Like Antipholus, who arrives in Ephesus with only a bag of gold and a head full of stories about a "town . . . full of cozenage" (1.2.97; cf. 1–8), these young men left their childhood towns for the greater economic opportunities afforded by London and regularly arrived in the city with great expectations, some trepidation and few connections.

Fewer than 20 years before *The Comedy of Errors* was written a fictionalized dialogue was published detailing the various kinds of work available to able-bodied men in Elizabethan London and providing practical information for prospective employees on such topics as securing employment, behavior appropriate to an apprentice and safe neighborhoods in which to live in the city.[6] This brief pamphlet purports to reproduce a conversation between an 18-year-old country lad named Puer and a former London servant called Civis. As the text's stock Latin descriptors remind readers, entering into service and establishing an independent household of one's own were more than simply stages in the passage to adulthood; they also marked the transition from the political exclusion of childhood to the public recognition of citizenship. Like Puer, Antipholus of Syracuse is eager to complete the journey from boyhood to citizenship and to establish himself in a wider civic community. But while Puer's success in London will be predicated on his ability to prove himself a responsible and contributing member of society, Antipholus is handed the role of wealthy Ephesian householder on a dinner platter.

Antipholus has doubtless dreamed of playing the part of the prodigal in a benign scene of familial reunion, but the force and speed with which he is absorbed into the chaotic domestic world of Ephesus surely exceeds even his most outrageous imaginings. Indeed, the specter of a demanding household complete with bossy servant and indignant wife plays in unpleasant ways on the young man's fears regarding the search for his mother and brother, and regarding the impact that finding them might have on his sense of individuality. While

Antipholus appears starved for human companionship, he is also wary of reunification with his family. Left alone on the mart upon his arrival in Ephesus, Antipholus reflects on the nature of his pilgrimage. As he soliloquizes on his status as exile, he ponders both the rewards and the potential risks involved in seeking out familial bonds:

> I to the world am like a drop of water,
> That in the ocean seeks another drop,
> Who, falling there to find his fellow forth
> (Unseen, inquisitive), confounds himself.
> So I, to find a mother and a brother,
> In quest of them (unhappy), ah, lose myself.
>
> (1.2.35–40)

Antipholus's rather self-indulgent sentimentality turns on his use of the word "confound." According to the *OED*, to confound is "to defeat utterly"; "to destroy the purity of"; to "put to shame"; "to throw . . . into confusion or disorder"; "to mix up or mingle so that the elements become difficult to distinguish or impossible to separate"; to "erroneously regard or treat as identical."[7] Each of these meanings resonates here as Antipholus experiences the disorientation and uneasiness that come from being a homeless fugitive in a hostile land, and the anxiety that thoughts of being reunited with his family bring. The young Syracusan envisions himself tumbling unchecked, "like a drop of water," through an ocean of undifferentiated humanity. His fears are manifold. Foremost among them is the dread that his attempt to contact "a mother and a brother" will fail and that he will find himself absorbed into the seemingly infinite expanse of humanity that surrounds him, his individuality drowned in a community rendered terrifying by its lack of affective connections.

But of course Antipholus's particular situation puts a new spin on the otherwise rather conventional fear of being lost in the crowd. As an identical twin he has as much to fear from success as he does from failure. As the *OED* reminds us, to be confounded is not simply to be defeated and shamed but also to be "erroneously . . . treat[ed] as identical." As this definition indicates, the search for a brother from whom he is — according to his father — indistinguishable, poses a literal as well as a metaphoric threat to Antipholus. The surfeit of welcome with which Antipholus is greeted in Ephesus is thus comic and horrific at the same time. The audience, primed by Egeon's tale of separated twins, is aware, of course, that the Syracusan's search for his brother is at an end. Antipholus himself, however, is faced with a terrifying literalization of his twinned desires to find and to lose himself in Ephesus. "There's not a man I meet but doth salute me," he reports anxiously,

> As if I were their well-acquainted friend,
> And every one doth call me by my name:
> Some tender money to me, some invite me;
> Some other give me thanks for kindnesses;
> Some offer me commodities to buy.
> Even now a tailor call'd me in his shop,
> And show'd me silks that he had bought for me,
> And therewithal took measure of my body.
> Sure there are but imaginary wiles,
> And Lapland sorcerers inhabit here.
>
> (4.3.1–11)

Rather than taking his measure as a Syracusan, Ephesus greets its visitor with remarkable intimacy, calling him by name, offering him gifts, handling even his body with an easy familiarity. For Antipholus this land of plenty represents not opportunity but evil — it is a place possessed by spirits and sorcerers.

As R. A. Foakes explains in his introduction to the Arden edition of the play, the New Testament associates the city of Ephesus not only with Saint Paul's Epistle to the Ephesians and its familiar admonishments regarding Christian marriage, but also with sorcery (xxix). Acts 19 recounts Paul's visit to Ephesus and identifies the city with "exorcists" and "curious arts,"[8] lending scriptural authority to Antipholus's fears of being set upon by a legion of supernatural predators:

> They say this town is full of cozenage:
> As nimble jugglers that deceive the eye,
> Dark-working sorcerers that change the mind,
> Soul-killing witches that deform the body,
> Disguised cheaters, prating mountebanks,
> And many such-like liberties of sin.
>
> (1.2.97–102)

A single day of wandering about the Ephesian marketplace leaves the visiting Syracusan afraid either that he is about to be attacked by an assortment of mundane rogues (including "jugglers," "cheaters" and "mountebanks") or that he will be driven out of his mind by an array of otherworldly villains ("Lapland sorcerers," "dark-working sorcerers," and "soul-killing witches"). Never suspecting that the apparently magical effects that he encounters are the result of a perfectly ordinary case of mistaken identity, Antipholus experiences his absorption into Ephesian life as a direct challenge to his sanity: "Am I in earth, in heaven, or in hell? / Sleeping or waking, mad or well-advis'd?" he wonders (2.2.212–13). If the young Syracusan's appearance in Ephesus provokes an excess of welcome that is both marvelous and terrifying for him, his arrival has unambiguously unpleasant repercussions for his twin.

Welcome Ever Smiles

Upon returning home to the Phoenix after delaying in the marketplace, Antipholus of Ephesus discovers that he is barred from his own house while an imposter dines inside with his wife. The merchant's astonishment at finding his own door locked against him produces an uncharacteristically plaintive whine: "But soft, my door is lock'd. . . . / Who talks within there? Ho, open the door! . . . / Wherefore? For my dinner: I have not din'd to-day. . . . / What art thou that keep'st me out from the house I owe? . . . / Do you hear, you minion? You'll let us in, I hope?" (3.1.30–54). Antipholus's plaintiveness soon turns to fury, but not before he has revealed a bafflement edged with terror that comes of being denied access to his home. As Antipholus's primal response to his barred door reminds us, the household is a primary source of shelter and sustenance. "I have not din'd to-day," he cries, unable for a moment to believe that his main meal of the day is to be withheld. Dromio's comments also emphasize the importance of the household as source of food and of protection from the elements: "Your cake here is warm within," he tells Antipholus, "you stand here in the cold" (3.1.71).[9]

Dromio's rather impudent intervention is particularly jarring because it constitutes an abrupt shift from the polite patter his master and Balthazar have been engaged in while en route to dinner:

> *E. Ant.* Y' are sad, Signior Balthazar, pray God our cheer
> May answer my good will and your good welcome here.
> *Balth.* I hold your dainties cheap, sir, and your welcome dear.
> *E. Ant.* O, Signior Balthazar, either at flesh or fish,
> At table full of welcome makes scarce one dainty dish.
> *Balth.* Good meat, sir, is common; that every churl affords.
> *E. Ant.* And welcome more common, for that's nothing but words.
> *Balth.* Small cheer and great welcome makes a merry feast.
> *E. Ant.* Ay, to a niggardly host and more sparing guest:
> But though my cates be mean, take them in good part;
> Better cheer may you have, but not with better heart.
> (3.1.19–29)

Harking back to the play's Plautine sources, this scene employs the easy rhythm of rhyming couplets to evoke a mood of relaxed geniality. Antipholus and Balthazar engage in witty banter about social niceties and their dialogue is characterized by a stylish one-upmanship. As Joseph Candido has noted, dinner is presented as "an *exclusively* male concern, an occasion for refined humanist discourse on the relationship of food to friendship."[10] This urbane and masculinized exchange of courtesies is disrupted, however, by the discovery that the gates of the Phoenix have been barred against them and by Dromio's appeal to the various female servants of the household — "Maud, Bridget, Marian, Cic'ly, Gillian, Ginn!" (31) — to open them again. What follows is a comically domesticated echo of the elegant repartee between Antipholus and Balthazar:

> *S. Dro.* Mome, malt-horse, capon, coxcomb, idiot, patch!
> Either get thee from the door, or sit down at the hatch;
> Dost thou conjure for wenches, that thou call'st for such store,
> When one is one too many? Go get thee from the door.
> *E. Dro.* What patch is made our porter? My master stays in the street.
> *S. Dro.* Let him walk from whence he came, lest he catch cold on's feet.
>
> (3.1.32–37)

Instead of refined discourse, Antipholus's friends witness a crude exchange of insults. Rather than being welcomed in "good part" with "better heart" Antipholus and his colleagues are left standing in the "street" catching cold on their "feet." Parodying the highly ritualized badinage of Antipholus and Balthazar, the earthy exchange between the two Dromios as well as later interventions by Adriana and her "confederates" (4.1.17) provide the domestic perspective banished from Antipholus's original account of dinner.

Infuriated by his inability to extend the appropriate hospitality to his business partners, Antipholus decides to exert his dominion over his insolent household through a show of brute force. His plan: to break down the gate and enter his home no matter who tries to stop him. The merchant's indignation has not deafened him to words of reason, however. When Balthazar argues that breaking down doors will do his "yet ungalled estimation" (102) no good, Antipholus is quick to agree and even swifter to propose that they try their luck at the home of the local courtesan instead. Despite Balthazar's aphoristically prescient account of falsity's squatter habits — "Slander lives upon succession, / For ever hous'd where it gets possession" (105–06) — Antipholus seems convinced that this apparent violation of his personal property will be short-lived and that it can pose him no real threat. Falling back on what he assumes is his unassailable reputation as a successful merchant, Antipholus literalizes his defection from the domestic realm by abandoning his attempts to enter his house and leading his guests to the Porpentine. "I know a wench of excellent discourse," he tells his companions, "Pretty and witty; wild, and yet, too, gentle; / There will we dine. This woman that I mean, / My wife . . . hath oftentimes upbraided me withal" (3.1.109–13). Evoking Dromio of Ephesus's earlier suggestion that his master has been known to satisfy his physical appetites elsewhere (1.2.49–52), Antipholus's words remind us that this is only the latest in what is apparently a long list of defections from the domestic realm.

Although he quickly reconciles himself to what he understands as proof of his wife's shrewishness and returns to the mart refusing to have his good time derailed by domestic troubles, Antipholus soon discovers that the household is not so easily divorced from the world of the marketplace. As soon as he emerges from dinner at the Porpentine, he begins to experience the impact that neglect of his household has had upon his business. All of a sudden a merchant who has waited since Pentecost for payment seeks to collect on a debt, the goldsmith from whom he has ordered a chain claims to have remitted it to him already, and Antipholus finds himself arrested for attempted robbery. Antipholus, a merchant "of very reverent reputation, . . . / Of credit infinite, highly belov'd, / Second to none that lives here in the city" (5.1.5–7), has suddenly become a man of "notorious shame" (4.1.84).

As the precipitous downturn in Antipholus's fortunes emphasizes, the household is more than simply a source of subsistence. The *oikos* is also the emotional and moral foundation upon which both agora and polis are built in Ephesus. A man's public participation in Ephesian mercantile and civic life depends upon his role as master of a household. Having abdicated his responsibilities in the domestic realm, Antipholus finds himself alienated from the public realm as well. Social dynamics in Ephesus begin to resemble a game of teeter-totter as the visiting Antipholus slips into the role of master of the household at the Phoenix and the resident Antipholus finds his position as respected merchant mysteriously compromised. When Antipholus of Syracuse arrives in Ephesus he causes (though he cannot see) his brother's sickening fall to earth. Unable to provide the hospitality that is an important part of doing business in his town, and surrounded on all sides by angry creditors, Antipholus of Ephesus discovers that his good name — his most valuable commodity — is not worth enough to ransom a piece of jewelry. Meanwhile, Antipholus of Syracuse has unwittingly assumed both his brother's domestic and commercial identities.

Confounded Properties

Toward the end of the play, just before the climactic moment when the Antipholus twins and their matched pair of servant Dromios finally meet face to face, Egeon is led on stage by Duke Solinus and his officers. And, as it was in the first scene of the play, Egeon's death sentence is temporarily commuted, this time thanks to the clamorous citizens of Ephesus. As he tries to make his way to the site of Egeon's execution, Solinus finds himself surrounded by outraged townsfolk. Adriana appeals to the duke for help in rescuing her husband from the priory, Antipholus appeals for redress against Adriana, various merchants appeal for compensation, and even the town courtesan and the local abbess try to register complaints. Finally the duke loses his temper: "I think you are all mated, or stark mad," he growls at the assembled company (5.1.282). Faced with a series of incompatible — and apparently irreconcilable — accounts of the day's activities, Solinus finds himself unable to make sense of his citizens' stories and hence unable to redress the wrongs with which they have charged one another. The situation is, as Adriana terms it earlier in the same scene, "past thought of human reason" (189).

The action in this scene turns on a play on the word "mated," a synonym in the sixteenth century for both "confounded" and "matched."[11] As the duke's inadvertent pun reminds audiences, the errors and confusions to which the play's resident Ephesians and its visiting Syracusans have fallen victim are interwoven with the various familial and romantic pairings in which they are caught up. Furthermore, this association between being romantically mated — that is, being a couple — and being "past thought of human reason" — that is, being mad — is linked throughout the play with threats to various forms of property. I want to shift now to a discussion of these pairings and to suggest that the affective relations of the household are presented in *The Comedy of Errors* as a positive force that appalls reason and confounds property even as it allows for the reunification of Egeon's family and for a tentative resolution of the conflict between the domestic and the commercial realms in Ephesus.

One of Shakespeare's most focused explorations of the challenge to normative notions of reason and ownership posed by affective relationships appears in the "The Phoenix and Turtle." Published in 1601 as part of a collection of poems appended to Robert Chester's *Love's Martyr, or Rosalin's Complaint, Allegorically Shadowing the Truth of Love, in the Constant Fate of the Phoenix and Turtle,* Shakespeare's elegy recounts the love and death of an unlikely avian couple, the mythic phoenix and an ordinary domestic turtledove. Like *The*

Comedy of Errors, "The Phoenix and Turtle" literalizes the relationship between competing accounts of the self in community.[12] The turtledove is a common bird, a native of England most often associated with constancy in love. The phoenix, on the other hand, is emblematic of the exotic — a symbol for both unique perfection and complete autonomy. According to classical myth, the phoenix survived alone in the Arabian desert. When it had lived for between five and six hundred years, it immolated itself atop a funeral pyre only to rise again from the ashes with renewed youth and vigor. In Shakespeare's poem, however, the phoenix appears to have sacrificed its powers of self-generation. Tamed by its love for the domestic turtledove, the wild phoenix has traded its self-sufficiency and even its immortality for a mortal life enriched by the experience of love.

The poem is written in three sections: in the first, a procession of birds mourn the deaths of the phoenix and the turtledove; in the second, the mourners sing an anthem in which love — represented by the relationship between the phoenix and the turtledove — confounds reason; and in the third, reason speaks a concluding threnody. Whether Shakespeare's poem in fact allegorically shadows the truth of some actual historical love as Chester's title page promises remains a matter for debate. I am less interested, however, in reading the poem as political allegory than I am in using its account of the effects of love on the self to clarify the basis on which *The Comedy of Errors* thematizes the communitarian impulses of the household.[13]

In Shakespeare's poem, the phoenix and the turtledove love as "two distincts."[14] At the same time their relationship is said to admit no "division" (27). This apparently impossible state of being, in which the lovers are both separate yet undivided, in which "either [becomes] the other's mine" (36), destroys the very concept of number and in so doing presents a serious threat to a social order based on normative conceptions of individual identity and on the ownership of private property:

> Property was thus appalled,
> That the self was not the same;
> Single nature's double name
> Neither two nor one was called.
>
> (37–40)

"Property" here refers not simply to the material possessions whose ownership is rendered unclear by love, but also to the uniqueness that ostensibly divides one individual from another. Love, the argument goes, insists on a balance of sameness and difference between lovers. By transforming the self from a singular into a plural, love dismays property. It threatens to render meaningless the notion of a fully differentiated, autonomous self and to collapse the distinctions between "mine" and "thine" upon which notions of ownership are based.

By threatening to destabilize a system of social order that constructs selfhood as the product of outer markers such as possessions, love seems to contravene reason:

> Reason, in itself confounded,
> Saw division grow together,
> To themselves yet either neither,
> Simple were so well compounded:
> That it cried, "How true a twain
> Seemeth this concordant one!
> Love hath reason, Reason none,
> If what parts, can so remain."
>
> (41–48)

Stumped by love's ability to fuse divisions, reason admits that love, despite its clear violation of the rules of logic, has both a purpose and a sense all its own. Like property, reason is confused and defeated by love's insistence that two individuals can exist in a state of inseparable togetherness without ever completely losing their independent properties.

In *The Comedy of Errors* as in "The Phoenix and Turtle" the affective relations of the household destabilize conceptions of the self as a fully autonomous agent and challenge normative notions of reason and ownership. Indeed, romantic love proves itself capable of fantastic transformations throughout the play. In a wonderfully comic moment immediately following the meal he shares with his brother's wife, Antipholus of Syracuse meets up with Dromio before the Phoenix:

> *S. Ant.* Why, how now, Dromio, where
> run'st thou so fast?
> *S. Dro* Do you know me, sir? Am I Dromio? Am
> I your man? Am I myself?
> *S. Ant.* Thou art Dromio, thou art my man,
> thou art thyself.
> *S. Dro.* I am an ass, I am a woman's man, and
> besides myself.
> *S. Ant.* What woman's man, and how
> besides thyself?
> *S. Dro.* Marry, sir, besides myself, I am due to a
> woman: one that claims me, one that haunts me, one that will
> have me.
>
> (3.2.71–83)

Echoing his master's earlier fears about demonic possession, Dromio claims that he has been transformed, made "an ass," "a woman's man," somehow transported out of himself. It soon becomes clear, however, that Dromio is being "haunted" not by a spirit, but by the love of a woman of considerable substance ("she's the kitchen wench and all grease" [96]). Such physicalized images of love's transformative powers occur throughout the play.[15] The most articulate account of how affective relations shape individuals is provided by Adriana.

In the second act, Antipholus of Syracuse and Dromio run afoul of Adriana and her sister on the mart. Believing herself to have been disavowed by a husband she already suspects of adultery, Adriana mistakes Antipholus for his brother and pours out her hurt at being forsaken:

> Ay, ay, Antipholus, look strange and frown,
> Some other mistress hath thy sweet aspects:
> I am not Adriana, nor thy wife.
> The time was once, when thou unurg'd wouldst vow
> That never words were music to thine ear,
> That never object pleasing in thine eye,
> That never touch well welcome to thy hand,
> That never meat sweet-savor'd in thy taste,
> Unless I spake, or look'd, or touch'd or carv'd to thee.
> (2.2.110–18)

Adriana's repeated use of negatives here underscores the irony of Antipholus's bizarre situation. She begins by speaking an odd kind of truth — this woman is not, as she insists, his wife — but her tone is also accusatory. Adriana's intention is to shame with her sarcasm the husband she suspects of philandering, but she also tries to understand his defection and to counter it with an impassioned plea for love and respect. Echoing the water-drop image used by Antipholus of Ephesus in his earlier soliloquy, Adriana offers up a vision of companionate marriage that challenges the rules of reason as clearly as does the love of the phoenix and the turtledove:

> How comes it now, my husband, O, how comes it,
> That thou art then estranged from thyself?
> Thyself I call it, being strange to me,
> That, undividable incorporate,
> Am better than thy dear self's better part.
> Ah, do not tear away thyself from me;
> For know, my love, as easy mayst thou fall
> A drop of water in the breaking gulf,
> And take unmingled thence that drop again,
> Without addition or diminishing,
> As take from me thyself and not me too.
> (2.2.119–29)

Appealing to her husband to recognize her as a valuable and inseparable part of himself, Adriana constructs a picture of marriage in which each spouse has become part of the other so completely that the boundaries between their individual identities have been permanently confounded. Echoing a conventional Protestant trope of marriage as the unification of two bodies, she argues that it has become impossible for one half of this "undividable" union to sever itself from the other without inflicting damage. In a wedding sermon preached in 1607, Robert Abbot, bishop of Salisbury, uses this same image to describe marriage as the spiritual incorporation of husband and wife: "the breach and separation betwixt the husband and the wife, because they are but one flesh, is a thing as unnaturall as is the renting and sundring of one member of the bodie from another. This cannot bee in the bodie without paine and griefe."[16] According to both Adriana and Abbot then, marriage requires the confounding of individual identities. The loss of unconditional autonomy entailed by such a union is not presented as a threat to human happiness, however. On the contrary, Adriana clearly takes comfort in love's ability to compound the self by transforming "me" and "thyself" into "me too," or even, as her homonym insists, *me two*.[17]

Adriana has been accused of rebelliously shrewish behavior, but while her relational conception of selfhood challenges her husband's claims to complete autonomy, I see no evidence that she attempts to undermine his authority.[18] She is certainly infuriated when Antipholus fails to return home for dinner, but, while she lets her frustration show, it would be a mistake to read her comments as an attempt to subvert the patriarchal order upon which her household rests. In the course of a brief disputation with her sister about the respective roles of husbands and wives in marriage, Adriana argues that women should expect respect from their husbands, but she never attacks Antipholus or his role as master of their household. Indeed, it is Luciana's self-righteous tone as much as her husband's behavior that instigates Adriana's remarks. She begins by querying her sister's Pauline assertion that "[a] man is master of his liberty":

Adr. Why should their liberty than ours be more?
Luc. Because their business still lies out a' door.
Adr. Look when I serve him so, he takes it ill.
Luc. O, know he is the bridle of your will.
Adr. There's none but asses will be bridled so.

(2.1.7, 10–14)

Adriana resists the notion that women should allow themselves to be "bridled" by their husbands, but her observation that Antipholus "takes it ill" when she mistreats him hardly constitutes a threat to the stability of domestic life at the Phoenix. Instead, this exchange suggests that the real threat to Adriana and Antipholus's marriage lurks in the marketplace, with "business" that "lies out a' door." Since the precise nature of the business that takes men away from home is not explored here, the presumably legitimate commerce Antipholus undertakes in order to keep his household in roast capon and the illicit trade in which he engages at the Porpentine are neatly conflated.

Adriana's vision of the self as associative and relational constitutes an emotionally charged challenge to the conventional Aristotelian notion that the *oikos* comprises a nonpublic, imperfectly rational sphere dominated by noncitizens (including slaves, children and women) who are unable to access the public, fully rational sphere of the polis and are therefore unable to participate in the formulation of notions of the good.[19] Although she does not seek to participate in Ephesian life as a free citizen herself, Adriana points up the interconnectedness of household and marketplace. On her account of selfhood, business that takes men "out a' door" jeopardizes the stability of the domestic sphere when it is not tempered by a respect for household matters. Similarly, domestic strife is capable of exceeding the bounds of the household and contaminating the public sphere when this balance between the domestic and civic sides of social existence is not achieved. Rather than seeking to challenge Antipholus's household authority, however, Adriana seeks to reinforce the importance of her husband's domestic responsibilities as a means of resisting the intrusion of the commercial world.

She may not be silent, but Adriana's account of marriage suggests that she understands her role as wife as one of chaste obedience. "Come, I will fasten on this sleeve of thine," Adriana promises Antipholus, "Thou art an elm, my husband, I a vine, / Whose weakness, married to thy stronger state, / Makes me with thy strength to communicate" (2.2.173–76). As her use of this highly conventional emblem for relations of dominance and deference to describe the relationship between husband and wife suggests, Adriana's view of marriage is hardly subversive. Her picture of a vegetable love that allows a woman to draw strength from her husband does have a darker side, however. While strength can be passed between a couple, so can weakness. Using the image of a cannibalistic natural world, Adriana offers a logical proof for the importance of faithfulness in marriage:

> I am possess'd with an adulterate blot;
> My blood is mingled with the crime of lust:
> For if we two be one, and thou play false,
> I do digest the poison of thy flesh,
> Being strumpeted by thy contagion.
> Keep then fair league and truce with thy true bed,
> I live dis-stain'd, thou undishonored.
>
> (2.2.140–46)

According to Adriana, a husband's adultery poses a threat to his wife because marriage has transformed both partners into two inseparable halves of a romantic union. As Camille Wells Slights has pointed out, Adriana's eloquent plea for fidelity in marriage is hardly the "tirade of a comic virago bent on mastery."[20] Nevertheless, the logic of Adriana's depiction of the corrosive effects of adultery does imply that both husband and wife are vulnerable to contagion through each other.

It is perhaps tempting to understand the fact that Adriana

addresses her heartfelt entreaties to a stranger rather than to her husband as a mitigation of her views on adultery and as an ironic challenge to her conception of relational selfhood. I would argue, however, that her misidentification of Antipholus of Ephesus is best read as a literalization of the transformative powers ascribed throughout the play to the affective relations of the household. Just as Dromio of Syracuse becomes an ass in the course of his encounter with Adriana's kitchen wench, so Antipholus of Syracuse becomes an Ephesian family man in the course of his meeting with Adriana. The play offers proof that Antipholus's metamorphosis is more than a superficial error when the young Syracusan courts Luciana. Speaking to his beloved, Antipholus declares:

> It is thyself, mine own self's better part:
> Mine eye's clear eye, my dear heart's dearer heart,
> My food, my fortune, and my sweet hope's aim,
> My sole earth's heaven, and my heaven's claim.
>
> (3.2.61–64)

Antipholus's account of love bears a striking resemblance to Adriana's commentary on the nature of matedness. Echoing Adriana's paradoxical language — Luciana is both herself and his "own self's better part" — Antipholus declares himself ready to trade his solitary life for the joys and responsibilities of a household of his own. Describing his autonomous existence as "feeble, shallow, weak" (3.2.35), identifying as vine rather than elm, Antipholus seeks strength in a loving relationship with Luciana: "Are you a god?" he asks her, "Would you create me new? / Transform me then, and to your pow'r I'll yield" (39–40). As Antipholus's vision of romantic partnership insists, dependency in love is not gendered. It is, rather, the inevitable product of the affective relationships that give household life in Ephesus its shape.

Antipholus's desire for love appalls property by its willingness to breach the autonomy of the self in favor of a romantic union. It also appalls Luciana, however, for whom Antipholus's proposal is the talk of a two-timing husband intent on bedding his sister-in-law. She associates such a trespass of propriety with madness: "What, are you mad, that you do reason so?" she asks the ardent Antipholus. To which Antipholus, foreshadowing Solinus's exasperation at the end of play, replies, "Not mad, but mated" (53–54).

At the beginning of *The Comedy of Errors* the Antipholus brothers are intent on defining the properties of a fully individuated self — that is, they are preoccupied with ascertaining the constitutive features of a self construed as completely autonomous agent. By the end of the play, however, both men have discovered that unqualified autonomy is possible only outside the bonds of community. As events in Ephesus demonstrate, commitment to the affective relations of the household entails sacrificing a degree of personal freedom — just the kind of willing alienation of self associated with madness. A conception of reason predicated on the existence of a self dissociable from the social relations that surround it must be confounded before the errors of the play can be resolved. Adriana's notion of the "undividable incorporate" insists that selves are constituted by the affective relationships in which they participate, and that division of self from community, of commercial identity from domestic identity, of family member from family member is not simply destructive but ultimately impossible. *The Comedy of Errors* thus emphasizes the importance of understanding the household as a constitutive feature of civic life. The good life, the play suggests, may be defined in the public spaces of the marketplace and the forum, but these spaces are in turn sustained and affected by the lived experience of the household.

4 • "That dead commodity, a wife"

Sexual and Domestic Economy in Aphra Behn's Comedies

Pilar Cuder-Domínguez

As the first woman professional writer, Aphra Behn has deserved special attention in modern times. Many are the critical appraisals that have tried to come to terms with her elusive figure and with the contradictions that run through her writing. In her recent examination of Behn's life and work, S. J. Wiseman declines to find a unified line of thought. It is her argument that Behn's work "is constantly marked by generic and commercial contingencies, and the nature of the work she produced makes it hard to locate a 'real' Aphra Behn." Despite such undeniable difficulty, at least two major fields of work can be said to have emerged in these last decades of Behn scholarship. First and very importantly, feminist scholars have looked at topics concerning the actual or metaphoric display of women on the stage, either as actresses or as playwrights. As Ros Ballaster suggests, "[j]ust as the prostitute simulates sexual pleasure for material gain, the actress and the playwright display their bodies/work simultaneously to conceal and reveal their other agenda, to demonstrate their capacity to be agents in their culture, whether politically (the playwright) or financially (the actress)." The period's slippage between the prostitute and the actress affected the female playwright in that, as Elin Diamond well observes, "the status of the professional writer indicated immodesty: the author, like her texts, became a commodity." Related in some measure to this central issue are those studies which center on voyeurism, eroticism and gendered violence.[1]

A second field of work concerns the politics of state in Behn's plays. Although Behn's royalist positioning was never a secret, and has long been addressed as one more of those aspects that contributed to the shaping of her work, for most critics sexual politics have tended to take precedence over state politics, and only recently have close readings of such issues in her plays been undertaken. Not long ago, Ballaster pointed out the need for such a task, claiming that for the female playwright of the Restoration, "loyalty in state or party politics does not by any means come second to their loyalty to their sex." Susan J. Owen agrees with this interpenetration of party and gender politics, arguing as well that a separate focus on women writers sometimes means that "they are *not* considered in the context of 'high' politics, and this impoverishes our understanding."[2]

Bridging the gap between gender and state issues lies a third ground of scholarly debate, which focuses on the politics of marriage. Lawrence Stone's key historical study opened up a whole field of inquiry when he maintained that: "Between 1660 and 1800 . . . there took place the far more radical shift from [the arranged marriage to the love marriage], with the children now normally making their own choices, and the parents being left with no more than the right of veto over socially or economically unsuitable candidates. At the same time there was inevitably a marked shift of emphasis on motives away from family interest and towards well-tried personal affection."[3] Most of Behn's dramatic work is located precisely at such a historical junction and thematizes the clash between the marriage of convenience and the love marriage.[4] Critical assessments of this conflict have identified its class and state reverberations as well, inasmuch as Tory and Whig allegiances often crystallized around it.

A further aspect of the marriage subject is the role that women's portion, or dowry, played, important because, according to Stone, it increased dramatically in this period: "The seventeenth century saw a sharp rise in the size of marriage portions paid by the bride's parents to the groom's parents. This rise meant an increase in the economic stakes of marriage, and so enhanced the position of the wife. By her marriage portion she was now making a major economic contribution to her husband's finances."[5]. These two major phenomena explain both the high recurrence of the topic of marriage in Restoration drama in general and in Aphra Behn in particular, and the usual emphasis on money matters in its treatment. Moreover, one might even contemplate the notion that relationships, motivations and actions in Restoration comedy come down to a money problem more often than not. It is an inescapable fact that the Restoration hero-rake is characterized as much by his extravagant use of money as by his libertine mores: he is perpetually in debt, he pawns all his properties, he gambles away all he has, and so on.[5] Women too, are bound up in an economic system that defines them as commodities to be exchanged between families. Either as maids, wives or widows, women's worth is shaped by their exchange value. Indeed, the Restoration saw the emergence of mercantilist codes that ruptured the social order: "As the violence of civil commotion subsided, the importance of economic factors pressed more and more on people's consciousness. . . . Large commercial institutions like the Bank of England and the Stock Exchange were started, and shortly came to seem as much part of the establishment as royalty or the Church of England. London swelled in size and importance. Although the hegemony of aristocracy and gentry was still assured, capitalist values associated with the middle classes were spreading upwards."[6]

All things considered, the scant attention that the interpenetration of economic values and love liaisons in Behn has merited among critics is rather surprising. Only Charles H. Hinnant seems to have pursued this line of work, in the understanding that "mercantilism and its values began to permeate the more established idioms of Restoration comedy. One finds these values enshrined . . . in language — the witty metaphors and similitudes employed by its major characters."[7] I wish, therefore, to explore the economic issues at stake in the love plots of Behn's comedies, with added emphasis on the way that money and property affect her female characters at whichever stage of the exchange process they may find themselves: before, during or after marriage.

Virgo and/or Meretrix:
The Rover *(1677) and* The Feigned Courtesans *(1679)*

The Rover (1677), considered Behn's most successful play, and by far the one most often discussed by critics, shows young women as exchange tokens meant to be circulated among men. The much celebrated opening scene focuses on the plight of its two young protagonists, the sisters Florinda and Hellena — the one to be married to old Don Vincentio, the other reserved for the nunnery — as they vigorously counterargue their brother Don Pedro's reasoning:

> *Flo.* I hate Vincentio, sir, and I would not have a man so dear to me as my brother follow the ill customs of our country, and make a slave of his sister; and, sir, my father's will I'm sure you may divert.

. . . .

Ped. [But] you must consider Don Vincentio's fortune, and the jointure he'll make you.
Flo. Let him consider my youth, beauty and fortune, which ought not to be thrown away on his age and jointure.
Ped. 'Tis true, he's not so young and fine a gentleman as that Belvile; but what jewels will that cavalier present you with? Those of his eyes and heart?
Hel. And are not those better than any Don Vincentio has brought from the Indies?
Ped. Why how now! Has your nunnery breeding taught you to understand the value of hearts and eyes?
Hel. Better than to believe Don Vincentio's deserve value from any woman: he may perhaps increase her bags, but not her family.
Ped. This is fine! Go, up to your devotion: you are not designed for the conversation of lovers.
Hel. [aside] Nor saints, yet awhile, I hope. — Is't not enough you make a nun of me, but you must cast my sister away too, exposing her to a worse confinement than a religious life?
(1.1.62–92)[8]

From its very onset, the play brings to the foreground the clash between the male will to power and economic calculation on the one hand and the resisting female will to freedom and affection.[9] In the course of the action, Florinda and Hellena will have to find their own ways to marry the men of their choice, the cavaliers Belvile and Willmore respectively. This subversion will take place in that most subversive of milieux, the carnival.[10] Florinda will elope with the more conventional Belvile, while Hellena will first have to defeat a rival before she can tame the "gay" Willmore.

This "other" woman is the famous courtesan Angellica Bianca, a woman who has decided that, as "inconstancy's the sin of all mankind, therefore [she's] resolved that nothing but gold shall charm [her] heart" (2.1.34–35). As Joseph Musser suggests, Angellica represents a threat to Hellena's success by offering not only an alternative to Willmore, but also an alternative to Hellena's way of love. As much a commodity as the virtuous sisters, Angellica has nevertheless decided that she will both market the "goods" and reap the benefits without any man's intervention. A portrait at her door advertises her price, a thousand crowns a month, an outrageous sum which, to the astounded Frederick, is "a portion for the Infanta" (2.1.110), a *dictum* which emphasizes once more the commonalities of all women's place in this trafficking. As John Franceschina aptly points out, even the faultless Florinda is caught up in this bind: "Out of doors, 'undress'd,' Florinda is taken for a whore by Willmore, who responds to her protests with an offer of money. Willmore's attempt to purchase Florinda is significant, as it reinforces the mercenary-erotic praxis of the play in which money not only purchases (and maintains) the image of the female but supports the male image of self-worth."[11]

Behn's strategy seems to be to highlight the sameness in women's plights while correspondingly deemphasizing their differences. A case in point is Angellica's often-quoted denunciation of men's mercenary attitudes concerning marriage, which we might expect from Florinda rather than from a courtesan: "When a lady is proposed to you for a wife, you never ask how fair, discreet, or virtuous she is; but what's her fortune; which if but small, you cry 'she shall not do my business,' and basely leave her, though she languish for you" (2.2.90–93). Moreover, in the bartering segment that precedes their lovemaking, Angellica's rhetoric of courtesan love in addressing Willmore ("And will you pay me then the price I ask?") progressively gives way to the rhetoric of "free" love: "The pay I mean, is but thy love for me" (2.2.146, 152). This is no more and no less than what Hellena herself demanded from the hero.[12]

However, despite all these ambivalent signs, a woman cannot be simultaneously honest and a prostitute. Their culture endows each woman with an economic value whose signifier is either the honest woman's dowry or the prostitute's fees and whose signified is, respectively, the possession or the lack of maidenhead. *Virgo* and *meretrix* thus belong to different economic modes, two different "traffics" of women. These identities are mutually exclusive; they are built on their mutual difference, and so they remain as fixed, opposite poles throughout *The Rover*, in spite of the momentary blurrings of identity. This fact is hinted at in the rivalry that separates Hellena and Angellica Bianca: Willmore *must*, in the end, choose one or the other.

Behn further explores this analogy between the prostitute and the honest woman two years later in *The Feigned Courtesans*.[13] What in the earlier comedy remained safely at a distance, only occasionally and transitorily close to the point of mistaking one identity for another, is shown in this later play as too close for comfort: all the female characters are simultaneously honest women and prostitutes. In this comedy as well we find two sisters in a similar plight: Marcella is engaged to the deformed Count Octavio while Cornelia is meant to spend her life in a convent. Having run away from home, they hide in Rome under the false identity of prostitutes while they figure out what their next step may be. Allegedly the vizard mask that the sisters temporarily adopt is meant to hide them from their guardian. As such, it is simply one more disguise, which offers them "a relative freedom of speech and action that the modest woman, who proves her virtue by silence and seclusion, cannot easily claim in her own person."[14] However, the line between honesty and whoredom is, from the beginning of the play, rather blurred. When Marcella and Cornelia first enter the stage, they complain about their lack of money; since they cannot possibly live off thin air, this period of independence must soon draw to an end:

> *Cor.* [O]ur money's all gone, and without a miracle can hold out no longer honestly.
> *Mar.* Then we must sell our jewels!

> *Cor.* When they are gone, what jewel will you part with next?
> *Mar.* Then we must —
> *Cor.* What, go home to Viterbo, ask the old gentleman pardon, and be received to grace again; you to the embraces of the amiable Octavio, and I to St. Teresa's, to whistle through a grate like a bird in a cage? For I shall have little heart to sing.
> (2.1.107–15)

Faced with the choice of either confinement or marginality, these women will attempt to renegotiate the terms of their situation. The negotiation, as their conversation makes clear, can only be based on their one asset: their "jewel" or maidenhead. Needless to say, this is not without risk, for they must walk a very narrow and slippery path between seeming and being. Actually, on their entering the stage, they have passed by the very men they are trying to avoid, their uncle Morosini and Marcella's fiancé Octavio, neither man having recognized them:

> *Mor.* Stay, stay, what women are these?
> *Oct.* Whores, sir, and so 'tis ten to one are all the kind; only these differ from the rest in this, they generously own their trade of sin, which others deal by stealth in: they are courtesans.
> (2.1.25–28)

Octavio's misogynist remark is nevertheless extremely enlightening, since with it Behn strikes home the truth she had also attempted to put forward in *The Rover*: patriarchy makes of all women, one way or the other, commodities for sale. The difference between honest women and prostitutes is the result of the different methods patriarchy deploys in marketing the goods — that is, the women. This is why this play, much more so than the earlier comedy, recurrently engages the notions of marriage and prostitution in terms of economic modes.

Two such modes are contrasted in the love dialogues between the women posing as courtesans and their gallants. One is a residual mode, a pseudofeudal, aristocratic notion that bestows the highest value on landownership. As applied to the issues of love and women, this is the language of possession and exclusivity, whose mouthpiece is Fillamour, Marcella's gallant. He defends from the beginning that "the lawful enjoyment of [a pretty, witty and young] woman, and honest too, would be a blessing" (1.1.55–56). In the alternative economic mode, possessing land is not the basis of wealth; rather, wealth results from the circulation and distribution of goods. This mercantilist mode clearly identifies Galliard (the rake hero Cornelia desires), who believes in using and consuming, not in possessing or reserving, as Fillamour does:

> Pox on't, my knight's [Fillamour's] bound for Viterbo, and there's no persuading him into safe harbour again. He has given me but two hours to dispatch matters here; and then I'm to embark with him upon this new discovery of honourable love, as he calls it, whose adventurers are fools, and the returning cargo, that dead commodity called a wife!
>
> (4.2.311–16)

To Galliard, men in love are like trading vessels, but the risks Fillamour takes do not bring him profit; instead, his only reward in seeking "honourable love" will be a "dead commodity," a wife, dead because it does not circulate, and in failing to bring in more gain, loses all value altogether.

These two approaches are dialogically contrasted in the play, not only in the conversations between the promiscuous Galliard and the more conventional Fillamour, but even more pointedly in Fillamour's dealings with Marcella posing as the prostitute Euphemia:

> *Fil.* Oh, I could talk eternity away,
> In nothing else but love, couldst thou be honest.
> *Mar.* Honest! Was it for that you sent two thousand crowns,
> Or did believe that trifling sum sufficient
> To buy me to the slavery of honesty?
>
> . . . .
>
> *Fil.* No, I would sacrifice a nobler fortune
> To buy thy virtue home.
> *Mar.* What should it idling there?

> *Fil.* Why, make thee constant to some happy man,
> That would adore thee for't.
> *Mar.* Unconscionable! Constant at my years?
> Oh, 'twere to cheat a thousand,
> Who, between this and my dull age of constancy,
> Expect the distribution of my beauty.
> *Gal.* [*aside*] 'Tis a brave wench.
>
> . . . .
>
> *Fil.* This wealth together would enrich one man,
> Which dealt to all would scarce be charity.
> *Mar.* Together? 'Tis a mass would ransom kings!
> Was all this beauty given for one poor petty conquest?
> I might have made a hundred hearts my slaves,
> In this lost time of bringing one to reason.
> Farewell, thou dull philosopher in love;
> When age has made me wise, I'll send for you again.
> (4.1.78–112)

Although both codes commodify women, the more conventional discourse voiced by Fillamour dangerously borders on the misogynist speech of confinement and imprisonment whose most extreme representations in the play are Morosini and Octavio. On the contrary, Galliard's libertine ethics can empower women, as shown in his repartée with Cornelia in 2.1 above. Although the bartering sequence draws from Willmore's with Angellica in *The Rover*, here Behn goes further in that both speakers commodify themselves and try to strike a bargain, each of them being at the same time the buyer and the seller of "goods," that is, simultaneously subject and object of the transaction. In *The Rover*, however, Willmore was the only prospective buyer and Angellica the commodity for sale:

> *Gal.* And have you no kind message to send to my heart? Cannot this [Euphemia's] good example instruct you how to make me happy?
> *Cor.* Faith, stranger, I must consider first; she's skilful in the merchandise of hearts, and has dealt in love with so good success hitherto, she may lose one venture, and never miss it in

> her stock, but this is my first, and should it prove to be a bad bargain, I were undone for ever.
> *Gal.* I dare secure the goods sound —
> *Cor.* And I believe will not lie long upon my hands.
> *Gal.* Faith, that's according as you'll dispose on't, madam: for let me tell you, gad, a good handsome proper fellow is as staple a commodity as any's in the nation; but I would be reserved for your own use! Faith, take a sample tonight, and as you like it, the whole piece, and that's fair and honest dealing I think, or the devil's in't.
> *Cor.* Ah, stranger, you have been so over-liberal of those same samples of yours, that I doubt they have spoiled the sale of the rest. Could you not afford, think ye, to throw in a little love and constancy, to inch out that want of honesty of yours?
> (3.1.183–201)

Even though with such discourse Behn opens up a space of equality, the fact still remains that the libertine code that underlies this mercantilist rhetoric is male-gendered. The empowerment that it can bring about for women is denied by a patriarchy which accords them only one asset, virginity or "honor." Once it is traded, women are "undone for ever," as Cornelia remarks above. That is why, once cornered, Cornelia will have to retreat and protect her virginity from Galliard by confessing that she is no prostitute, but "a maid of quality" (4.2.155).

Such is not the case of Laura Lucretia, the third young woman in *The Feigned Courtesans* who poses as a prostitute. Contracted to but having never met the young and attractive Julio, brother to Marcella and Cornelia, she enjoys in Rome a brief period of freedom before her impending marriage. Very much like Hellena in *The Rover*, she goes out in disguise, meets Galliard by chance, and falls in love with him. Laura Lucretia too is determined to have her way, but unlike Hellena, she displays a dangerous carelessness regarding her honor:

> *Sil.* But with permission, madam, how does this change of petticoat for breeches, and shifting houses too, advance that love?
> *Lau.* This habit, besides many opportunities 'twill give me of

> getting into his acquaintance, secures me too from being known by any of my relations in Rome; then I have changed my house for one so near to that of Silvianetta's, and so like it too, that even you and I have oft mistook the entrance; by which means love, fortune, or chance, may with industry contrive some kind mistake that may make me happier than the rest of womankind.
> *Sil.* But what shall be reserved then for Count Julio, whose last letters promise his arrival within a day or two, and whom you're then to marry?
> *Lau.* Reserved for him? A wife! A wife, my Silvio,
> That unconcerned domestic necessary,
> Who rarely brings a heart, or takes it soon away.
> *Sil.* But then your brother, Count Octavio, do you not fear his jealousy?
> *Lau.* Octavio! Oh, nature has set his sort and mine at odds,
> And I can know no fear, but where I love.
> *Sil.* And then that thing that ladies call their honour —
> *Lau.* Honour, that hated idol, even by those
> That set it up to worship? No,
> I have a soul, my boy, and that's all love;
> And I'll the talent which heaven lent improve.
> (2.1.158–81)

Here Laura Lucretia shows an alarming forgetfulness of the consequences of her passion, which Hellena in *The Rover*, summarily described as "a cradle full of noise and mischief, with a pack of repentance at [her] back" (5.1.456–57). Her willingness to part with her virginity (signaled by the shift from prose to verse which underlines the seriousness of her intent), though eventually unfulfilled, is a crime which, in the mercantilist terms of this rhetoric, would amount to robbing her husband-to-be of a valuable commodity reserved for his use and consumption. Furthermore, this constitutes a threat to patriarchy which cannot go unpunished, and thus, unlike the more careful Marcella and Cornelia, Laura Lucretia is not allowed to marry the man she loves, and must instead accept Julio as originally arranged. Though not literally, at least metaphorically she had lost the very item that allowed the other two women to renegotiate and improve the terms of their bondage. As Diamond points out: "In Restoration comedy no witty unmarried woman was really witty unless she had property *and* a maidenhead. Behn's virgins may re-'design' their cast of characters but they cannot change their plot. Ultimately their masquerade is dissimulation in the classic representational sense: a veil that hides a truth. Hellena's mask merely replicates the membrane behind which lies the 'true nature' of woman: the equipment to make the requisite patrilineal heir."[15] Even while denouncing the double standard applying to men and women, Behn must perforce accept it. In the end, her characters must return to the safe but confined sphere of marriage. Nevertheless, those who understand the rules of the game, who have insights into the workings of what Sedgwick termed the bonds of "male homosocial desire" can enjoy the relative advantage of husbands they are congenial to. That is the best deal they can get.

Merry Wives and Widows: The Lucky Chance *(1686) and* The Widow Ranter *(1689)*

Jacqueline Pearson has pointed out that there is a darkening vision in Behn's later plays that distinguishes them from her earlier work: "Many of the later plays emphasize women's emotional, economic and sexual vulnerability and devise extreme images for this and for the contradictory demands made on them by society. In most of the early plays forced marriage is a danger which the heroines successfully escape: in the later plays it is often a trap into which they have already fallen."[16] It is certainly true that Aphra Behn's later comedies, like *The Lucky Chance* and the posthumously performed *The Widow Ranter*, display a larger scope and, together with the ubiquitous maid, they scrutinize the situation of other women in the marriage market. Of the three female protagonists in *The Lucky Chance*, only one is the archetypal maid in distress.

Diana, like her predecessors Florinda in *The Rover* and Marcella in *The Feigned Courtesans*, is being forced to marry the fop Bearjest though she loves Bredwell:

> *Sir Feeble.* Enough, enough, Sir Cautious, we apprehend one another. — Mr. Bearjest, your uncle here and I have struck the bargain: the wench is yours with three hundred pound present and something more after death, which your uncle likes well.
> *Bea.* Does he so, sir? I'm beholding to him; then, 'tis not a pin matter whether I like or not, sir.
> *Sir.* How, sir, not like my daughter Di?
> *Bea.* Oh Lord, sir, die or live, 'tis all one for that, sir. I'll stand to the bargain my uncle makes.
>
> (1.3.125–33)

Though Behn does not save us the grossness of this mercenary arrangement, Diana's troubles deserve only minor attention in the comedy and are predictably solved once more with an elopement.

A variation in the pattern is introduced with the position of Leticia, who has just married the old alderman Sir Feeble Fainwould (Diana's father) after he deceived her into believing that her lover Belmour, to whom she was contracted, is dead. "Poor and helpless,/And much reduced, and much imposed upon" (2.2.50–51), as she herself explains, Leticia has to trade her "jewel" or maidenhead for Sir Feeble's wealth and the security it affords her. This central image shapes the various encounters between the new husband and wife, with the old Sir Feeble offering Leticia jewels for a smile, or a kiss: "Alas, poor pupsey, was it sick? Look here, here's a fine thing to make it well again. [*Shows a jewel*] Come, buss, and it shall have it. [*Kisses Leticia and gives her the jewel*] Oh, how I long for night" (2.2.99–102). The consummation the old lecher so much desires is, however, delayed by Belmour, who tricks him out of Leticia's bed. The first time he uses the pretext that London is up in arms due to some plot, but Sir Feeble returns home before Belmour and Leticia manage to escape, she bearing a casket with the jewels in yet another metaphoric displacement of her depriving him of his right to deflower her.[17] Finally, Belmour comes up with the idea of terrorizing Sir Feeble's guilty conscience with his own "ghost." Out of his wits, Sir Feeble finally gives his blessing to the union of Belmour and Leticia, whose contract takes precedence over his own marriage.

But by far the most frequent use of this rhetoric of sex and money devolves on the third woman in the play, Lady Fulbank, another young woman married to an old man but in love with the young rake Gayman, whose advances she has been virtuously resisting for some time. The rivalry between husband and lover for Lady Fulbank's love and favors will be played out in terms of hard cash and property. At the opening of the play the husband, Sir Cautious, has the upper hand: Gayman has spent all his money on presents and gifts for Lady Fulbank in vain, and is indebted to Sir Cautious as well, so that he is reduced to the most extreme poverty and, under the name Wasteall, has gone into hiding at an inn of ill repute. As elsewhere in Behn's comedies, however, women do not remain passive onlookers. Informed that Gayman is about to lose his land to Sir Cautious, Lady Fulbank takes things in her own hands and steals the money he needs from her husband, sending it to Gayman under the pretense that it is from a secret admirer. Like the old men in the play, Lady Fulbank now has the power to buy the object of her desire. When Gayman receives the money, he decides that its source is no other than:

> Some female devil, old, and damned to ugliness,
> And past all hopes of courtship and address,
> Full of another devil called desire,
> Has seen this face, this shape, this youth,
> And thinks it worth her hire. It must be so.
>
> (2.1.186–90)

Lady Fulbank's agenda goes even further. In this instance as everywhere else in this comedy, money matters thinly veil the granting of sexual favors. Lady Fulbank's empowerment in stealing her husband's money is the prologue to an assignation with Gayman under the disguise of a secret admirer. Thus, a woman is shown to possess the power to redistribute wealth as much as to "pollute" the line of inheritance, two faculties that are in fact intimately related, even though in the dramatic action it may seem otherwise.[18]

As the action bears on, the balance between the old husband and the young lover is being redressed, thanks to Lady Fulbank's agency. The turning point will be the famous gambling scene (4.1), which again decides sexual privileges under the guise of material gain. Sir Cautious, suspecting Gayman of having stolen his money, designs to play dice with him in order to see his gold: "I shall go near to know my own gold, by some remarkable pieces amongst it; and if he have it, I'll hang him, and then all his six hundred a year will be my own, which I have in mortgage" (4.1.231–34). However, not only does Sir Cautious not get the proof he wants, but he loses to Gayman all the money he is carrying besides. Playing on his avarice, Gayman then convinces Sir Cautious to wager a night with Lady Fulbank against the whole sum:

> *Gay.* You have moveables, sir, goods; commodities —
> *Sir.* That's all one, sir; that's money's worth, sir; but if I had anything that were worth nothing —
> *Gay.* — You would venture it; I thank you, sir. I would your lady were worth nothing.
> *Sir.* How so, sir?
> *Gay.* Then I would set all against that nothing.
> *Sir.* What, set it against my wife?
> *Gay.* Wife, sir; aye, your wife.
> *Sir.* Hum, my wife against three hundred pounds? . . . *[aside]* What a lavish whore-master's this: we take money to marry our wives, but seldom part with 'em, and by the bargain get money.
>
> (4.1.379–404)

The contest between Gayman and Sir Cautious is based on the implicit notion of wife as a commodity, and such a one that, in mercantile parlance, it fails to get money because it does not circulate anymore. Its exchange value is "nothing," with a sexual innuendo that becomes even more evident when Gayman wins the wager. Asked then by Lady Fulbank what the wager was, Sir Cautious dejectedly replies it was "only a small parcel of ware that lay dead upon my hands," to which Gayman rejoins: "But I shall improve 'em, madam, I'll warrant you" (4.1.457–59).

Thus the husband is forced to facilitate his own cuckolding, in what, as Warren Chernaik has remarked, is a recurrent theme in Restoration comedy.[19] The double entendres continue as Sir Cautious smuggles Gayman into his wife's rooms inside a chest that carries "prohibited goods," out of which he promises Lady Fulbank "some fine knick-knack will fall to thy share" (5.4.63–70). And while he waits in the antechamber he feels "as restless as a merchant in stormy weather, that has ventured all his wealth in one bottom" (5.7.1–2). Sir Cautious's fortunes have now sunk, just as Gayman's reach their highest with the news, at the close of the play, that he has inherited two thousand pounds a year from an uncle. Once more, wealth goes hand in hand with sexual prowess, whereas Sir Cautious is not only comparatively less rich than at the beginning but has also lost his wife.

Nevertheless, the changes in the fates of the male characters leave Lady Fulbank's untouched: though the commodification she suffers from her husband as from her lover in the gambling scene might disempower her, the dignity she displays, as she solemnly vows that she will never again go to bed with a husband who has so prostituted her, sets her above such reification. She chastises Gayman and Sir Cautious, the latter for his lack of morals and the former for his impulsiveness, and both for having used her in some measure. Such behavior, which denies women's agency, is clearly presented as difficult to forgive or forget. Though the conventions of the comedy press for a reconciliation between the parties concerned, the playwright resists them in order to provide an open space for female autonomy. Sir Cautious, ashamed of himself, promises Gayman that he will bequeath him fortune and wife, and even though Gayman accepts, he then turns to ask for Lady Fulbank's consent. Her reply is ambiguous, thus signaling that she is very much her own mistress: the men's handlings need not determine her fate. Therefore, Behn seems to defend the possibility of women's autonomy even inside marriage, though this autonomy, as in the case of the maids of earlier comedies, can be understood only in very relative terms. As Peggy Thompson explains, Behn always "acknowledges the social and economic forces that allow no alternatives."[20]

Yet another autonomous woman was Behn's last creation. *The Widow Ranter, or the History of Bacon in Virginia* is, properly speaking, a tragicomedy, which combines the heroic plot of the subtitle with the comic action surrounding the figure of the Widow. Rich widows were, needless to say, much sought after: a re-circulating commodity for fortune-hunters. Antonia Fraser records several examples of seventeenth-century wealthy widows courted to the point of harassment:

> In 1653 . . . Dorothy Osborne went to dinner with a rich widow, middle-aged and "never handsome," who had "broke loose from an old miserable husband" with the avowed intention of spending all his money before she died. . . . [T]he widow's palpable state of siege thoroughly amused her. For all the widow's frank words concerning the use to which she intended to put her late husband's money, and despite her lack of physical attraction, she was, wrote Dorothy, "courted a thousand times more than the greatest beauty in the world that had not a fortune." They could hardly get through dinner for the disturbance caused by letters and presents pouring through the door in order to persuade the widow to change her mind.[22]

Indeed, in *The Widow Ranter,* Behn equates the wealth of the widows in the colony of Jamestown to the wealth the New

World has to offer enterprising subjects. The play opens with the arrival of Hazard, a younger brother who has gambled away all he had and has bought passage to Virginia in search of fortune. There he meets with his old friend Friendly, who has lived in Jamestown since he inherited a plantation and who immediately directs Hazard towards two likely sources of income: a widow and a widow-to-be. Friendly suggests that Hazard should take up residence at Madame Surelove's (the wife of a rich old merchant who is in ill health and currently away in England and in ill health) on the pretense that Hazard is the husband's kinsman. Thus he can patiently await the husband's demise while he courts the wife. If this plan does not suit Hazard's fancy, Friendly has an alternative, the Widow Ranter, whom he describes as:

> [A] woman bought from the ship by old Colonel Ranter; she served him half a year, and then he marry'd her, and dying in a year more, left her worth fifty thousand pounds sterling, besides plate and jewels: she's a great gallant, but assuming the humour of the country gentry, her extravagancy is very pleasant, she retains something of her primitive quality still, but is good-natur'd and generous.[23]

Both women will then be under siege for the wealth they may bring the conqueror, just as the town itself suffers the double threat of the Indians and General Bacon. In fact, the connection is later made explicit as Bacon takes the principal ladies of the town hostage in his tug-of-war with the town council. Ranter, however, is not among them, which sets her apart for her extraordinary character. Friendly's description above is pointedly understated, for unlike the more conventional Madam Surelove and Friendly's own beloved, the virginal Chrisante, Ranter is outspoken, direct, and even fairly vulgar. Her unladylike behavior also involves drinking and smoking.[24] Above all, she is practical and clear-minded, and exhibits an evident understanding of her situation as a valuable commodity, as in this exchange in first meeting Hazard:

> *Ran.* What, are you like all the young fellows, the first that they do when they come to a strange place, is to inquire what fortunes there are.
> *Haz.* Madam, I had no such ambition.
> *Ran.* Gad, then you're a fool, sir; but come, my service to you; we rich widows are the best commodity this country affords, I'll tell you that. (227)

Placed in an independent position substantiated by wealth, this woman will have her way, and to that purpose she is not willing to abide with the niceties (or the hypocrisy) which restrict women's actions. In her love chase of Daring, one of Bacon's officers who in turn prefers Chrisante, Ranter will prove that she can take what she wants. Wearing breeches, she goes to Bacon's camp in order to rescue Chrisante and so prevent marriage to her lover. Impressed by the widow's "daring," the young officer acknowledges that her unladylike manner and her courage suit him best of all: "Prithee [marry me and] take me in the humour, while thy breeches are on–for I never lik'd thee half so well in petticoats."[25]

Though in Restoration drama women in breeches were erotic objects, in the character of the Widow Ranter Behn seems to be feeling her way towards the figure of an androgyn that may transcend the conventional images of women displayed in the period:

> [T]he Widow Ranter is indeed a highly novel figure, blending masculine self-confidence and independence with erotic attractiveness, and despite her unfeminine behaviour and her gleeful debunking of male presumption she retains the full sympathies of the audience and is not forced to recant or metamorphose into a chaste and modest belle in the end.[26]

Chernaik too perceives that Ranter, like the central character of the Duchess of Newcastle's *Bell in Campo* (1662), Shadwell's *The Woman-Captain* (1680), and Southerne's *Sir Anthony Love* (1691), is "a genuinely androgynous figure, a woman whose male dress is not a temporary disguise but expresses her inward nature, with all its contradictions, freeing capacities and feelings which in other circumstances would have remained hidden."[27]

The playwright's late work seems to become more complex, and comes to problematize and go beyond the flat characterization of women to be found elsewhere in Restoration drama. As this analysis of the rhetoric of sexual and domestic economy in her comedies has attempted to show, Behn was at this stage in the process of shifting from the intense focus on the conflicts of arranged marriages that pervade her early work to a wider understanding of women's positioning in the marriage market. The diminishing attention she bestows on the stereotypical young virgin (though still ever present) is fairly noticeable, and she tentatively includes other scenarios, like the adulterous affair in *The False Count*. However, Behn remains always sensitive to issues of wealth and correspondingly, power, as much as to the changing features of her society's economic system. It is by means of such rhetoric and its multifaceted nuances, and most particularly in the bartering exchanges that pepper her comedies, that she manages to both expose and subvert female reification even as she explores new venues for female intervention. Above all, here as in her fiction, she is concerned with resisting women's commodification, and with the creation of spaces that allowed for women's autonomy.

5 • Bloody Relations
Murderous Wives in the Street Literature of Seventeenth Century England

Susan C. Staub

> For thus doth St. Peter preach to them: *Ye wives, be ye in subjection to obey your own husband.* To obey is another thing then to control or command, which yet they may do to their children and to their family, but as for their husbands, them must they obey and cease from commanding and perform subjection.
>
> — from "Homily on the State of Matrimony"

It has become a commonplace that early modern women had no legal existence apart from marriage. Maids, wives or widows, they were governed by their relationship and subordination to husbands or future husbands. When T. E., the first commentator on laws relating specifically to women, defined women's legal status, his definition was clear and uncontested: "Women have no voyse in Parliament, they make no lawes, they consent to none. All of them are understood either married or to be married and their desires are subject to their husband." The author continued with only measured sympathy, "I know no remedy, though some women can shift it well enough."[1] Thus in theory, marriage represented a kind of civil death for women, granting them no recourse under the law for crimes they suffered nor accountability for those they committed.[2]

But women's legal position in early modern England was less clearcut than T. E.'s general assessment indicates. In fact, the very existence of T. E.'s text calls into question the idea that women had no legal existence in the period. With the heading "The Women's Lawier" running throughout the five books, the work appears to be a guide for lawyers preparing legal defenses of women. Why would there be a need for such a manual if women had no voice, no consent, no desire — no legal existence? As Frances Dolan has explained, even T. E.'s phrase "shift it well enough" "constitutes wives as subjects of desire . . . maneuvering *within* a subjection presented as repressive, by bending, if not breaking the rules." The definition of wives as "*femes coverts,*" as women legally covered or subsumed by their husbands, seems a kind of legal fiction that is everywhere confounded in the period. And if we consider Dolan's gloss of "covert" as sly and stealthy maneuvering, by her very definition the *feme covert* undermines the system meant to contain her. Nonetheless legal authorities often go to great extremes to maintain this definition of the wife, even to the point of creating the category of the "married spinster." The fiction of the married spinster allowed judges to separate the wife from her husband and hold her accountable for her actions, while at the same time maintaining her status as subordinate to her husband. These ambiguities run throughout the period. As several recent scholars have shown, this was a time of unusual marital ferment in which women's place in the social and legal scheme was ambiguous at best. Marriage was in crisis in the late sixteenth and early seventeenth centuries, "the site of a paradoxical struggle to create a private realm and to take control of it in the interests of the public good," as Catherine Belsey explains it.[3]

Conduct books and marriage manuals offer absolute statements on the need for wifely submission, arguing, "If she be not subject to her husband, things will goe backward and the house will come to ruine."[4] Yet even the *Homily on the State of Matrimony*, with which I began this essay, opens a potential gap in the definition of the wife as subsumed in her husband. The *Homily* instructs wives to obey their husbands, pointing out, "to obey is another thing then to control or command, *which yet they may do to their children and to their family*" (my emphasis). To "command" is to possess identity and agency. But this agency is limited to the household, and even there it is restricted to children, servants and other domestic matters. The husband remains the ultimate authority. Although the woman's position of wifely subjection is clearly delineated in text after text, the period displays considerable anxiety about that position. The popular press also participated in this cultural exploration of female agency, and given the ambiguities evident in domestic and legal texts, it is no wonder that the pamphlet literature focuses on the household as the potential site of female power. But in its depiction of wifely power, the popular press almost always constructs female agency as violent.[5] Murdering wives must certainly be among those "who can shift it well enough" in the seventeenth century. Representations of wives who murder their husbands occupy an important place in the writings of early modern England — in legal tracts, dramas, ballads and pamphlets. Popular pamphlets, sometimes also called newsbooks, were occasional, brief publications, ranging from two to 60 pages in length. They were usually published in response to a sensational or phenomenal event, something as simple as an earthquake, the appearance of a "blazing star" (a comet) or other natural "act of God," or something as strange as the birth of a two-headed baby or the miraculous return to life of an executed criminal. But by far, the most popular subject was murder, particularly murder by women.

The history of the crime pamphlet is shadowy. Many of these writings were posted or sold in public places, and since they were inexpensive, costing a penny or twopence, a wider range of consumers could afford them than could afford more elaborate literary texts. As Tessa Watt points out, however, it is difficult to ascertain the exact audience for these kinds of publications: "the idea that the broadsides and chapbooks were aimed at and consumed by a definable social group may be a myth. The audience presupposed within the cheap print itself appears to be inclusive rather than exclusive." Literacy during this period is equally difficult to access, and these texts further muddy the waters. While scholars conjecture literacy rates as high as 78 percent for London men (with literacy judged by the ability to sign one's name), most agree that the literacy rate for women was much lower.[6] Yet many pamphlets specifically address a female readership. Still others offer evidence of women's writing ability. In *A True Discourse of the Practices of Elizabeth Caldwell*, for instance, Caldwell purportedly writes a long letter to her husband before her execution; another pamphlet, *A Fairwarning to Murderers of Infants*, on the other hand, depicts the woman dictating a letter to her children because she cannot write. This text does offer evidence that she can read, however, referring to specific religious writings that she read while in prison to help her repent her actions.

Most of the authors of these texts are also lost to history. Although a few of these pamphlets have been attributed to literary figures such as Thomas Kyd, John Taylor and Anthony Munday, most of the writers remain anonymous or obscure. Many crime pamphlets seem to have been written by preachers or other clergymen who sought to warn and edify their readers. Yet there can be no denying that, morality aside, even the religious figures wrote because these stories were so titillating and sensational. And money must have played at least some role. For example, Henry Goodcole, one of the most prolific crime writers from the period, seems to have written to supplement his salary as ordinary of Newgate Prison. Apparently, the publication of one or two crime accounts could more than double his meager annual stipend.[7] That these pamphlets proved so lucrative suggests a public interest in violent crime.

Clearly, the public was fascinated with criminal women. A cursory survey of ballad entries in the Stationers' Register for the years 1569–1640 reveals no fewer than 25 titles depicting female murderers.[8] These ballads, coupled with the many pamphlets and plays based on "true-life" crimes committed by women, suggest the level of popular anxiety about female criminality during the period. But the public's appetite for these writings suggests more than a taste for blood and gore. It evinces a cultural preoccupation with women's behavior, and because the violence depicted is predominantly domestic, points toward growing instability within the institution of marriage. But more importantly for my analysis, this literature suggests that the conflict within the marital realm brought with it a concomitant change in the status of women, however dubious. That women were shown committing and being executed for their crimes marks a new consciousness of them as individuals.

At first glance, the popular accounts of women who murder their husbands seem to represent women as possessing unequivocal autonomy and subjectivity. In theory, the married woman was subject to her husband; as T. E. styles it, a husband and wife "are but one person, and by this a married Woman perhaps may either doubt whether shee bee either none or no more than halfe a person." Legally, the husband was held accountable for his wife's actions, her identity contained within his. It has been argued, however, that in instances of serious crime, women gained a separate legal existence.

T. E. explains, "In matters criminall and capitall causes, a feme covert shall answere without her husband." Or, in the words of Margaret Doody, "Women as felons were legal beings."[9] In instances of capital offense women could be tried and executed just as men might be.[10] Further, in the pamphlets and ballads retelling these crimes, women are often given a voice as they confess and explain the motivations for their actions. Catherine Belsey points out the double effect of the required confession in this literature: "The supreme opportunity to speak was the moment of execution. The requirement for confessions from the scaffold, so that the people could see how church and state combined to protect them from the enemies of God and society, paradoxically also offered women a place from which to speak with a hitherto unimagined authority which was not diminished by the fact that it was demonic." The popular crime literature of early modern England, then, further uncovers the ambiguities inherent in the definition of the wife as *feme covert*. As a wife, the woman has no identity apart from her husband yet she is the center of the family, itself a microcosm of society at large. She is granted authority in matters of the household and over her children and servants. Likewise, she has no autonomy, yet in some instances she can be held accountable for her crimes. By exposing such contradictions these works provide a locus for female agency and voice, at least tacitly. While many of the laws seem constructed particularly to contain women, to prevent them from transgressing the accepted social and sexual order, this literature seems to show them doing just that.[11]

Husband murder — far more than infanticide or child murder — posed the greatest threat to the social order and received the most attention in the popular press. So severe a breach of the marital hierarchy was this offense that it was given its own legal category, that of petty treason. Petty treason "was an aggravated form of murder, as consisting in one of the following three acts: Homicide of a master by a servant; of a husband by his wife; and of an ecclesiastical superior by his inferior." Husband murder was analogous to high treason in that both abused "the obligations of duty, subjection, and allegiance" that an inferior owed a superior. Just as the treasonous subordinate violated the "confidence which the king presuppose[d] in his subject" so the insubordinate wife disrupted the "natural, civil, and even spiritual relations" she held with her husband.[12] Unlike infanticide and child murder, which stem largely from the perpetrator's desire to adhere to social formulations of appropriate behavior (the virtuous maid or good mother), husband murder overturns the domestic hierarchy. Because this crime is such a blatant and brutal disruption of the ordered household, the popular press exhibits an almost obsessive concern with it. At least until the middle of the seventeenth century, accounts of husband murder greatly outnumber accounts of wife murder. Yet as several scholars have shown, women were not excessively violent during this period; in one survey of assize records from 1559 to 1625, wives, not husbands, were the victims in three-quarters of the cases of spousal homicide.[13] We can assume that these numbers remained constant throughout the seventeenth century. Perhaps this literature focuses on murderous wives precisely because their crime was more unusual and hence more horrendous, but it seems more likely that husband murder received attention because it represented a fundamental subversion of the domestic hierarchy. There was, after all, some support for male violence as a kind of household discipline; the wife's assault on her husband, on the other hand, was virtually never justified.

Clearly, these accounts mean to provide examples of the household gone awry, and by negation they offer a definition of the properly ordered family. Yet some of these narratives seem merely sensational and exaggerated accounts of wifely villainy and offer little explanation for the wife's actions. Because they offer no real motivation, they skirt the issue of wifely agency. The case of Anne Hamton, whose story is told in *Murther, Murther. Or, A Bloody Relation how Anne Hamton dweling in Westminster nigh London, by pouson murthered her dear husband* offers a good example of popular depictions of marital breakdown. In this case, the husband is the picture of appropriate husbandly behavior. A "very laborious man," he delights "in nothing more but to see his wife pleasant."[14] The wife, on the other hand, gossips and spends all the money the husband earns. In the early modern period, the wife's duties in the household were rigidly defined and were meant to complement the duties of the husband. The husband's responsibility was to "get goods"; the wife's was to "gather them and save them." The husband should "get money and provisions"; the wife was ordained not to spend vainly. The husband was instructed to be skillful in talk; the wife should boast of silence.[15] Before the crime is committed, the husband in this narrative offers a textbook example of good husbandry. He exerts authority over his wife but does not abuse that authority: "hee always spoke in a very loving manner unto her, except she overmuch provoked him" (4). In contrast, the wife is a "light housewife," with all its connotations of moral laxity, who, while the husband is working, spends her time gossiping with one young fellow or another and wastes all the family's resources. The wife, then, disrupts the proper houschold that the husband attempts to uphold. This disruption is characterized as a contest for speech and money, two of the more common signifiers of power within the domestic sphere as presented in this literature.[16]

Once the murder's inception is recounted, the crime seems almost laughable because it is so excessive given the text's description of the wife's circumstances. Complaining that her husband "was an enemy to good fellowship," Anne is swiftly moved to murder when her landlady advises, "hang him, cut his throat, or poyson him, for he is not fit to live upon the earth amongst good fellowes" (4). Anne then proceeds to poison him with double the necessary dosage. Poison is the most frequent method used by wives to murder their husbands in popular accounts and represents a perversion of the prescribed wifely duty of providing nourishment for their families. This crime, then, constructs the wife as a kind of "anti-housewife."[17] The murder here occurs abruptly and quickly; the pamphleteer provides no real motivation for the wife's actions, thus denying Anne any real agency. She is goaded into action by her female companion. Nonetheless, the text expresses incredible anxiety about female companionship and its potential intrusion into the ideally secure space of the household.

The pamphleteer insists that this story should serve as a warning to women of the dangers of insubordination. Speaking directly to his potential female readership, he admonishes, "Harken to me you that be wives, and give attendance you which as yet are unmarried, regard the words of St. Paul which commands that every wife should love her own husband as Christ the church" (1). The title page offers the same admonition. Nonetheless, one suspects that the sensationalism of the case prompted its telling more than morality. The author revels in the details of the death, describing the corrupted body in graphic terms: the body literally bursts with poison, the fingernails peel, the hands swell into great boils, the belly "seemed as if hot irons had beene thrust into it" (5). In its depiction of the explosion of the husband's body, the narrative literalizes the explosion of the household that the prescriptive literature sought to prevent.

Although most crime pamphlets include a confession as a way to reincorporate the criminal back into the social order, the confession here is deferred. Perhaps recognizing that his readers would expect to hear the criminal's repentance, the author calls the reader's attention to the omission and promises a more perfect relation later. Whether intentional or not, however, the omission of the customary confession serves to silence the vocal, gossipy woman of the narration. The goal of containing the unruly woman is achieved in this text just as effectively as if a confession had been delivered.

Yet in many ways, as frightening and horrific as their crimes are, many of these women do not really seem dangerous. Their actions are so extreme and so unmotivated that they become caricatures. In the story of Anne Hamton, in fact, the author seems to recognize the ludicrousness of his narrative and opens the pamphlet with a disclaimer: "Gentle Reader, It is not my purpose to make thee now laugh" (1). Far more compelling are the accounts that try to explain the reasons for the murders, thereby at least recognizing the potential for wifely agency. Interestingly, although they do not dwell on the fact, most of these accounts illustrate the wholesale breakdown of the marriage; both husband *and* wife are shown violating the household order. Henry Goodcole's *The Adultresses Funeral Day* vividly illustrates this more complex examination of marital disorder. Goodcole, chaplain at Newgate Prison and a master of the crime confession genre, depicts husband murder as a fundamental breakdown not just of domestic order, but of the natural order as well. He links it with other unnatural activities — "Catamatisme, Sodometry, Paracity, many headed murders and the like."[18] All are symptomatic of a world out of joint: "Now what the reason may be conjectured in these our latest, but worst days: that so many nefarious acts, equaling, if not far surpassing those perpetrated in former ages, should be new committed. . . . I can give no other reason then this, the contempt of the feare of God, and the neglect of the Sabbath." Although his explanation for the instability within the household is simplistic — heedless disregard of God's commandments, most specifically of the Sabbath — his narrative actually presents a much more detailed picture of marital discord. In *The Adultresses Funeral Day* he focuses on the most dangerous of the "grand Malefactors" plaguing the social order, the "poor wretched creature" Alice

Clark. Although this pamphlet relates the story of the murder of Alice's husband (a man ironically named Fortune), the title, *The Adultresses Funeral Day*, suggests that Goodcole's interest is as much in Alice's sexual transgression as in the murder. The title foregrounds the initial transgression that almost inevitably leads to the greater crime of murder in these narratives. Almost all female misconduct derives from a sexual lapse. As the popular literature presents it, the consequences of female unchastity are devastating.

As Goodcole's narrative illustrates, while criminal writers view murderous wives as fearful, commonly they also seek to explain their crimes away by offering sometimes elaborate motivations for them. Alice's story is a study in victimhood, from her early seduction and impregnation by her employer to a forced, loveless marriage, and finally to the abuse she suffers at the hands of her husband. Goodcole's stance seems strangely sympathetic, making allowances for the woman's actions in light of the circumstances she finds herself in. He admits, "Her injuries, and harsh and unmanly usage spurred on by the instigations of the divill, *almost* compeld her to what she did . . . so they were *almost* beyond the strength of Nature for her to suffer" (sig. B2v; my emphasis). In the course of the narrative Alice is betrayed by four men. The pamphlet offers most of the typical motivations for murder: spousal abuse and neglect, forced marriage, and seduction by another man. The difference is that it includes them all in one case.

Believing in the power of confession to purge the sinner of guilt — "If a sinner be at any time silent, he is but the Devil's Secretary"[19] — Goodcole devotes the greater part of his story to Alice's confession rather than to the actual crime. The confession serves two purposes: first, it provides a public display of the unruly woman surrendering to God, the ultimate patriarch. And second, though perhaps unintentionally, it grants that woman at least limited authority and subjectivity: "to speak is to possess meaning, to have access to the language which defines, delimits and locates power. To speak is to become a subject."[20] Occupying center stage for the moment, the woman tells her life story, ordering it and offering justifications for it as she speaks.

The first explanation the wife offers for her crime is that she is in a forced, loveless marriage. Enforced marriage frequently provides motivation for husband murder. In Thomas Deloney's ballad on the murder of Page of Plymouth, for example, the wife laments,

> In blooming yeares my Father's greedy mind,
> Against my will, a match for me did find;
> Great wealth there was, yea, gold and mony store,
> But yet my heart had chosen long before [. . . .]
>
> My chosen eies could not his sight abide;
> My tender youth did scorne his aged side:
> Scant could I taste the meate whereon he fed;
> My legges did loath to lodge within his bed.[21]

While most murder accounts serve as a warning about what happens when women overstep their place as submissive wives, frequently they admonish the husbands and fathers as well. In the *Murder of M. Page of Plymouth*, for example, the father is held at least partially responsible for Page's murder. He abuses parental authority by forcing his daughter to marry against her will. At a time when companionate marriages were becoming more common, a forced marriage was often considered no marriage at all.[22]

Alice Clark also complains of physical abuse by her husband. The legitimacy of a husband beating his wife was heatedly debated in the prescriptive literature of the period. Although violence within the household was sometimes considered justifiable as necessary discipline, most theorists prohibited excessive physical correction. In his *Apologie for Women*, William Heale, for instance, rejects this form of discipline outright, arguing that wife beating is "not only unlawful, but an odious, unmanly, and unseemelie thing." In fact,

Heale's discussion of wife beating uncovers another disjunction in the theory that the husband and wife are one flesh: "No man did ever willingly hurt himselfe; or if any man hath, certainly he maie iustly of all men bee helde a madde man: and therefore what mutual blowes can lawfully passe between man and wife; who are one and the selfesame?"[23] Since most marriage theorists decry excessive beating as a means of wife control, the wife's attack on her husband in this situation, if not justifiable, is at least understandable. (In at least one other instance in the popular literature, "Anne Wallen's Lamentation for the Murthering of her Husband," the wife murders her husband after repeated beatings and her action is considered justified.) Goodcole supports the wife in this claim, noting the marks on her body that prove the abuse she suffered.[24]

Rather than meeting blow with blow, Alice chooses the more passive but more effective action of poisoning him. Yet she claims at one point that she did not poison her husband at all, but that he grabbed the poison out of her pocket before she could stop him. She implies that the husband was actually suicidal, pointing out that he had earlier attempted to drown himself but was prevented from doing so at her urging. Despite other places where he expresses sympathy for Alice, here Goodcole views her insistence that her husband actually killed himself as little more than a rationalization. Nonetheless, he includes her rationalizations in his narrative, seemingly to undermine her credibility and negate the pity the reader may feel for her because she was abused. To pity her is to acknowledge her as a complete human being with her own needs and desires.

Finally, the wife argues that the murder was instigated by her lover, Henry White. White, she claims, convinced her to kill her husband and gave her the money to buy poison. "That it were better for one to be hanged, then to endure so discontented a life," he glozes, and promises to marry her upon her husband's death (sig. B3v). The instigation to murder by a lover is a fairly common element in these stories and serves to caution women to beware flattery and smooth words, whether of the devil or of their lovers. Furthermore, this explanation for the crime affords the woman little agency and thus, it would seem, little culpability — but such is not the case. Once the murder has been committed, White rejects Clark, ostensibly in fear that having betrayed her husband she might betray him as well. At this point Goodcole intercedes to censure men who seduce women: "A great clog unto such a mans conscience, if it be true, to seduce a woman unto his will, and so leave her" (sig. B3). Nonetheless, his sympathy is qualified by the phrase, "if it be true."

Goodcole's attitude toward his subject is equivocal throughout. Sometimes he casts doubt on the confession by questioning Alice's veracity and by labeling her defense "a lame excuse, or strange delusion" (sig. B3). In other places he seems to verify the truth of her claims as he does when he notes the marks of abuse present on her body. He seems to exonerate her of total blame by placing at least partial responsibility on the men in her life — her employer, her husband and her lover. He even berates her neighbors for their failure to provide "good counsell" (sig. B2v), suggesting a kind of social control and responsibility beyond that of church and court. Crime writers frequently advocate neighborly responsibility.[25] Goodcole implicates the neighbors in *Natures Cruell Step-dames* as well, likening the mother's temptation to kill her child to a house on fire: If her house had been set on fire she would have raised such an outcry that her neighbors would immediately have helped her, but "her heart was here set on fire by hell," and they ignored her need. Rarely, however, does Goodcole allow Alice's confession to stand completely on its own. Although he concedes some voice to the woman, this voice is never left unchecked by the male voice of the pamphleteer.

Kyd's *The Murder of John Brewen* provides another example of an adulterous affair that leads to husband murder. Here Anne

Welles's lover, John Parker, convinces her to poison her husband and marry him. Two years and two children later, Parker still refuses to marry Welles: "The varlet, hearing the great mone shee made unto him, was nothing moved therewith, but chorlishly answered, shee should not appoint him when to marrie: but if I were so minded (quoth he), I would be twise advised how I did wed with such a strumpet as thyselfe: and then reviled her most shamefully."[26] Like Clark's lover, he argues that she who would poison her husband might poison him as well. In this tale, too, the treatment of the woman is ambivalent. We learn that Brewen forces Anne to marry him under threat of imprisonment and that she is mistreated and abused by Parker. Although the sympathy toward Welles is measured, early in the narrative she is called a "proper young woman" and a "nice maiden." Parker, on the other hand, is "accursed," "chorlish" and a "varlet." Nonetheless, Anne suffers the greater punishment when the murder is discovered — she is burned at the stake; Parker is hanged.

Sympathetic treatment alongside vile invective is fairly common in these accounts. More unusual is the almost entirely benevolent depiction of the female criminal in Gilbert Dugdale's *A True Discourse of the Practises of Elizabeth Caldwell*, the story of a botched husband murder.[27] Elizabeth's complicity in the crime is minimal — she stands by while another woman puts ratsbane in her husband's oat cakes. Though she immediately regrets her compliance, before she can stop them, the husband and several neighbor children eat the cakes. As luck would have it, the poison only sickens her husband, who "by way of vomit [was] saved." Nonetheless, a neighbor's child, two dogs, and a cat do eventually die.

Like other accounts, the bulk of this narrative is devoted to Caldwell's confession, but there is little of Goodcole's characteristic ambivalence here. From the moment of her imprisonment, Caldwell is depicted as a godly woman more concerned with the conversion of her fellow prisoners than with her own fate: "from her first entrance into prison, till the time of her death, there was never heard by any, so much as an idle word to proceede out of her mouth, neither did shee omit any time, during her imprisonment, in serving of God, and seeking pardon for her sinnes, with great zeale and industrie, continually meditating on the Bible, excluding her selfe from all company, saving such as might yeeld her spirituall comforts, as learned Divines, and such, the faithful servaunts of God" (sig. B2). Ironically, though an adulteress and an attempted murderer, Caldwell becomes the epitome of piety and rectitude. She takes an active part in the reformation of her fellow prisoners and in the 300 or so people who visit her daily. Although unusual for this kind of literature, the transformation of the criminal here is similar to that which occurs in yet another pamphlet, Richard Watkin's *Newes from the Dead*.[28] This account relates the strange case of Anne Greene who was hanged for infanticide in 1651 but miraculously came back to life after her execution. In order to explain her survival and God's apparent beneficence toward her, Watkins remakes Anne into the epitome of proper womanhood. This pamphlet also includes a series of poems written by Oxford students, some of whom even compare Anne's resurrection to Christ's. In both these cases the criminal becomes perversely sanctified through her crime.

As I have suggested, women in these criminal accounts are typically given some authority in their confessions. Here, however, not only is the woman allowed to speak but to write as well. Dugdale includes a letter purportedly in Caldwell's own hand. In the letter, Caldwell reconstructs herself as a kind of Christian martyr, sacrificing herself for the salvation of her wayward husband: "if the losse of my blood, or life, or to endure any torments that the world can inflict upon me, might procure your true conversion, I should esteeme it purchased at an easie rate" (sig. Cv). As often happens in these accounts, the recasting of the criminal as saint reconciles the criminal with the state in a final act of atonement. Yet the situation seems even more complex in this instance because Caldwell posits herself as the wronged party. She places the blame for her actions at least partially on her husband, who in his neglect of his wife left her at the mercy of seductive and sinful personages: "[Remember] how poore you have many times left me, how long you have beene absent from mee, all which advantage the devill took to subvert me . . . wrought upon my weaknes, my povertie, and your absence, untill they made me yeeld to conspire with them the destruction of your bodie," Caldwell chides him (sig. 2v). While the text is overtly concerned with wifely submission, it seems equally aware of husbandly duty. In a twisted reversal of criminal culpability, Caldwell piously intimates that her husband is actually the one in need of heavenly forgiveness. Piety — not poison — inverts "the hierarchy of marital authority" in this pamphlet.[29]

The autonomy granted the woman seems especially unusual here. Caldwell even dictates the terms upon which she dies, exhorting her companions to pray, calling for her Bible, reading and praying to God and finally requesting that a hymn be sung as she meets her death. There is power here and Caldwell is given the privilege of speech, but except for her mild criticism of her husband, she speaks only in religious platitudes. Whereas her crime implies a resistance, her confession actually defers to patriarchy. Further, the narrative does not end with Caldwell's death. As a counterpoint to the saintly and devout Caldwell, Dugdale returns to one of her conspirators in the crime, "that uncharitable creature, Isabel Hall, widdow," before ending his narrative. Like other female criminals, Hall is defined by her marital status and, as a widow, ultimately seems more dangerous than the married Caldwell because she exists outside of direct male control. As the narrative concludes, Dugdale shifts total blame onto Hall, calling her "the onely instrument of this timeless action" (sig. D3). Apparently, class plays as big a part as gender here. Caldwell is obviously a gentlewoman; Hall comes from the lower classes. Unlike Caldwell, who is contrite and repentant, Hall denies everything. Paradoxically, by rejecting speech, Hall retains her subjectivity and power. She is the unruly woman who refuses to be tamed by confession. When seen as a foil to Elizabeth Caldwell, Isabel Hall offers the real threat to the dominant social order. Although Dugdale seems, then, to express total sympathy for his subject, the shift in focus to Hall at the end of the narrative suggests a refusal to admit any goodness in a more average woman and allows him to complete the saint/sinner dichotomy. Caldwell, with all her contrition and devotion, is an anomaly.

Even in the more notorious cases, the authors usually provide at least minimal explanations for the wives' actions, though such details are often not developed. In the story of Thomas Arden's murder, for example, Arden's land grabbing and greed at least partly mitigate his wife's guilt and suggest that she was not the only one who wished him dead. Holinshed's account even intimates that Arden facilitates Alice's affair with the servant Mosby because of this greed: he "was yet so greatly gyven to seek his advauntage, and caryd so litle how he came by it that in hope of atteynynge some benefits of the lord northe by meanes of this mosby who could do muche with hym, he winked at hir filthie disorder, and both permitted, and also invited Mosbie verie often to lodge in his house."[30] Arden's actions represent an abuse of male authority as he becomes the most reviled of early modern stereotypes — the wittold, or willing cuckold. This is hardly a sympathetic endorsement of Alice's behavior but does at least suggest the complexity of her actions.

Perhaps the most extreme depiction of the collapse of the household, and surely one of the most sensational accounts, is the story of Mary Hobry (or Aubrey), the French midwife, who murdered her husband and disposed of his body by chopping it into parts and leaving the pieces in various places along the Strand. There are at least four versions of Hobry's crime: two pamphlets (one with an attached ballad, sung to the tune of "The Pious Chieftans's Exhortation") and two broadside ballads.[31] It is not hard to imagine why the story of Mary Hobry would have caught the early modern public's fancy. She is transgressive in every way: she is French, she is a midwife and she is Catholic. And she is preternaturally strong, acting alone and accomplishing a feat of incredible physical strength. She does not choose poison, the typical female murder weapon, but brutally and physically kills her husband by strangling him with his own cravat. Although two of the accounts express doubt that she could have carried out the crime of strangling and disposing of her husband's body by herself, the court decides otherwise.

The most developed of these narratives is told in *A Hellish Murder Committed by a French Midwife.* This pamphlet differs from the more typical crime pamphlet because it purports to be the actual legal deposition of the witnesses and of Mary Hobry herself. Its tone is legalistic and precise, and because it records the examinations of 18 witnesses, including Hobry's son, it renders the full horror of the crime in vivid detail. But it also provides a more complete picture of the trouble within the household than other accounts do. In some ways the emphasis on Hobry's nationality — she is almost always referred to as "the *French* midwife" — serves to construct her as cultural "other" and thus makes her less threatening. The pamphlet's record of her speech, frequently in French with an English translation provided by the author, further creates her as foreign — alien, incomprehensible, perhaps even base. (Interestingly, the French phrases are only presented in the witnesses' depositions; Hobry's testimony is recounted in English, except for her signature at the end verifying its accuracy.) By emphasizing her foreignness, the text can offer consolation to the Englishman (or woman) reading it by linking the barbarity of the crime to nationality. No Englishwoman would perpetrate such a crime. The hints at Hobry's Catholicism may serve a similar purpose, at once demonizing her and the hated papist religion that she practices.[32]

Most of the witnesses are neighbors who recount the constant battles within the Hobry house. Given the amount of neighborly surveillance here, it seems particularly curious that no one did anything before the anger erupted into violence. As the neighbors relate it, the emphasis is almost completely on Hobry's angry speeches against her husband, what one deponent describes as "dangerous words." Although everyone agrees that Denis Hobry, the husband, is a drunk, a "Libertine and Debauchee to the Highest Degree" (39), they focus instead on Mary Hobry's abusive language. One witness testifies that he heard her curse her husband more than 40 times, calling him "Dog, Drunken Villain, and other the Fowlest Words of Reproche" and "C'est un Chien; C'est un Yvrogne" (2). Repeatedly, the witnesses tell of Hobry's threats to murder her husband. The emphasis here is consistent with the early modern construct of gender, which places speech at the center of patriarchal authority. To have speech is to have agency, as I have argued earlier. The woman who speaks neither in acquiescence nor in answer to her husband reveals an independence that threatens the patriarchal order. Since she ignores the social tenet requiring female silence, she may very well ignore other rules of marriage as well and end up with a man other than her husband in her bed. Verbal assertiveness in women is associated with sexual assertiveness: "Love thy wife / As thy life, / Let her not go thou know'st not whither; / For you will alwayes live in strife / If she keep not her lips together," as one seventeenth century balladeer phrased it.[33] In this account, however, adultery is never an issue; nonetheless, the authority of the patriarch, the husband, is undermined by Hobry's independence. Strangely enough, in a text that so foregrounds unchecked female speech, Hobry's voice is obscured. Amid the voices of the many witnesses, hers is drowned out, as it must have been before she committed the crime. Though many of the witnesses chastise her for her transgressive speech, no one seems to have really heard her because no one helped her.

As a midwife, Hobry is self-sufficient. With her own profession, she earns money and respect and has an identity outside the household. In fact, as the narrative depicts it, she is the breadwinner, not the husband. The wife is described as "industrious," the husband as profligate. At least part of the conflict derives from the husband squandering all her hard-earned money on drink. By allowing the wife to earn the family's income, he abandons one of the important responsibilities that his authority is hinged upon. In particular, as a midwife, Hobry seems the very embodiment of female power. In her role as midwife, she presides over childbirth, itself a site of female empowerment. Further, the position of midwife, according to Adrian Wilson, overturned the normal distinctions of class and rank, giving her authority over both men and women of a higher social class. And the midwife possessed a unique authority in early modern courts, offering expert testimony in infanticide, child murder and rape cases. As Percival Willughby depicts them, "midwives will follow their own ways, and will have their own wills."[34]

Nonetheless, despite the narrative's focus on her autonomy, we learn from her testimony that she, too, is a victim. The most telling detail, and the one that the text glosses quickly over, is the fact that Hobry had endured years of sexual abuse, and on the night of the murder, her husband had raped her. The wife's description of the abuse she endured that night is graphic and brutal: first, the husband begins beating her in the stomach and breasts; then he grabs and squeezes her so hard that blood starts coming out of her mouth. Then, forcing upon her "the most Unnatural of Villanies," he "acted such a Violence upon her Body in despite of all Opposition that she could make, as forc'd from her a great deal of Blood, this

Examinate crying out to her Landlady, who was (as she believes) out of distance of hearing her. This Examinate told him, *I will immediately Rise and Complain to the Neighbors*: Whereupon he took her Forcibly by the Arm, and threw her down on the Bed, being before sitting up to rise; and after this, Bit her like a Dog &c" (33–34). Despite the author's discrete "&c," the magnitude of the crime is clear. As Frances Dolan points out, Hobry raises the "hue and cry" that the law says she must to prove that she did not consent. According to Bracton, the medieval legal writer, the raped woman "must go at once and while the deed is newly done, with hue and cry, to the neighboring townships and there show the injury done to her to men of good repute, the blood and her clothing stained with blood, and her torn garments."[35] But the situation for Hobry seems even more dire than that of other victimized women because the rapist is her husband; the symbol of law enforcement within the household is here the lawbreaker. Further, since rape had been constructed as a property crime at least since the Middle Ages, consent does not seem to be at issue here at all. As the wife is her husband's property, any assault against her is a crime against the husband. But what happens when the perpetrator is the husband himself? If T. E.'s discussion of rape is any indication, no crime has occurred: "if any virgin, widdow, or single woman be ravished, shee her selfe may sue an Appeale of rape, prosecute the felon to death, and the kings pardon (as it seemeth) cannot helpe him. If a feme covert be ravished, shee cannot have an Appeale without her husband."[36] And yet the text, seemingly aware of the wife's dilemma, shows a remarkable amount of self-consciousness on the part of the wife. Her self-questioning — "What will become of me? What am I to do! Here am I Threatend to be Murder'd, and I have no way in the World to Deliver myself, but by Beginning with him" (34) — depicts her despair so sympathetically that her separateness as a human being is unequivocal. Such a strategy almost demands that the reader examine the boundaries of a husband's control over his wife's body.[37] It seems that the wife in this narrative has no choice: to save herself, she must kill her husband. The contradictory position of the wife that we have noticed throughout this literature is most acute here. Hobry is her husband's possession, legally without autonomy, yet she is accountable for her reaction to his brutalizing of her. The law only recognizes the death of the husband; Hobry's suffering seems of little consequence.

On the surface, the crime literature of early modern England presents women felons (and by extension all women) as threatening and monstrous — "matchlesse monsters of the female sex," as Goodcole would have it. But if these women are monsters they seem distinctly impotent — monsters with talons blunted and claws clipped. Their actions are almost always explained with reference to men (or the devil), and we soon realize that it is not the woman's story that's being told here but the man's. If these women are subversive, they are so only momentarily and are quickly incorporated back into patriarchy as victims. As reprehensible as these women's actions may be, the narratives invariably show that men are ultimately in power. Containment is affected by glossing over blame. Although men are revealed to be culpable, that culpability is minimal. Similarly, women are held accountable for their actions, but they are rarely shown acting on their own. Although their crimes suggest that these women act in defiance of male control, the narratives persistently depict them acquiescing to men, whether in confession or murder. The pamphlets, then, give power to the women only to deny it. This contradiction seems central to the genre and to the period.

6 • "The infant of your care"

Guardianship in Shakespeare's *Richard III* and Early Modern England

Heather Dubrow

Although revisionist studies of *A Midsummer Night's Dream* have posited the suppression and violation of its female characters, a related but significantly different form of resentment splinters the surface of the play in its opening lines. "She lingers my desires," Theseus observes of the moon, "like to a stepdame or a dowager, / Long withering out a young man's revenue" (1.1.5–7).[1] A dowager, introduced into this passage through the linguistic surrogacy of a simile, by definition assumed the rights and privileges of her dead husband; the reference to such women and to stepmothers hence crystallizes fraught issues of guardianship and substitution, linking material and familial losses as it does so.

The preoccupation in this passage with that putative guardian the stepparent recurs throughout the texts of early modern England. Sidney, too, mentions a stepmother, a deflected version of maternal origins, in the originary, opening sonnet of *Astrophil and Stella*. The plot of *The Faerie Queene*, like that of many romances, often pivots on substitute parents. Other, nonliterary cultural texts are equally concerned with stepparents and their implications; thus in his influential marriage manual *Of Domesticall Duties* (1622) William Gouge alerts his readers to the "fearefull tragedies" and "lamentable mischiefes" that can issue from the machinations of these conniving guardians.[2]

Surrogate parents of many types also recur throughout Shakespeare's own canon, where, as in *A Midsummer Night's Dream*, stepmothers and stepfathers often figure other types of proxy. *All's Well That Ends Well*, a play in which both the king and the Countess of Rossillion replace dead parents, achieves its comedic closure through other forms of substitution. In *Hamlet*, Claudius is stepfather as well as uncle, a role of which contemporaries would have been more aware than most recent critics have been. Claudius's position as a substitute tropes the broader preoccupation with displacement and with replacement in the divergent senses of substituting and of returning something to its proper position that structures the play: the villain who has taken the place of a king insists that the king's son resume his own place at court; Hamlet survives because one letter is substituted for another; Laertes dies because swords are exchanged, and so on. The queen in *Cymbeline* is the prototypical evil stepmother; Dionyza assumes a comparable role in *Pericles* after the eponymous hero entrusts his daughter, "the infant of your care" (3.3.15), to her; not coincidentally, the play opens on that most abhorrent form of proxy, incest.

Shakespeare's representation of stepparents is echoed and expanded in his preoccupation with many other types of guardianship as well. The frequency with which characters take — and on occasion travesty — that role is telling. Orlando and Adam, for example, symbiotically assume it toward each other in a play where Oliver deforms it and where even Duke Senior proves a problematical guardian for the four-legged citizens in his sylvan kingdom. One sign of Lear's lack of power is his inability to protect those who also protect him, the retainers; in this and other instances throughout the play, the loss of that material version of shelter, the physical abode, both creates and tropes the characters' loss of the ability to guard others and be guarded. The speaker in the sonnets identifies his unfriendly Friend as a faulty guardian of treasure. And not the least reason for Shakespeare's preoccupation with romance is its tense exploration of the interactions between good and bad guardians; the genre whose signature episode is the return of a lost child by a beneficent protector is populated, as we just recalled, by that prototypically bad guardian, the stepmother. Shakespeare's romances, not surprisingly, sometimes blur the distinction between good and bad protectors. Witness the relationship between Marina and Lysimachus and Prospero's gloss on his storm: "No harm: / I have done nothing but in care of thee" (1.1.15–16).

Why and how, then, do Shakespeare's plays, like so many early modern texts, represent the phenomenon of stepparenting and cognate types of guardianship, and why do they engage with the problems adumbrated by Theseus? These questions are as broad as they are significant, encompassing as they do not only the material issues that interest so many critics today but also the workings of gender, of representation and of literary tropes.

I

Generalizations about the prevalence of surrogate parents and the larger questions about guardians they pose must be bracketed with cautions, thus providing an exemplary instance of the potentialities and dangers of practicing cultural history. Mortality statistics vary from one region to another, yet again demonstrating the perils of basing generalizations on London and the court. Social and economic historians disagree among themselves about rates of death and remarriage and therefore about the precise likelihood of what would today be called blended families.[3] Nonetheless, the early death of parents was indisputably frequent: scholars have estimated that about one-third to one-half of the population had witnessed the death of at least one parent by the time they themselves married.[4] Because of the mortality crisis of 1557–1559, a period when death rates rose sharply in a number of regions, many members of Shakespeare's audience were especially likely to have endured the loss of a mother or father early in their own lives. And remarriages occurred often enough for bereaved children to experience the anxiety expressed by the third plebian in *Julius Caesar*: "I fear there will a worse come in his place" (3.2.111).

Many texts of Tudor and Stuart England emphasize the threats created by such guardians. A Renaissance translation of Petrarch, the *Phisicke against Fortune*, conflates such dangers with the devastation of fire: "Who so having children by his first marriage, bringeth a Stepmother among them, he setteth his house afire with is *[sic]* owne handes." More immediate to the early modern period are Gouge's warnings in *Of Domesticall Duties*. He insistently emphasizes the responsibilities of stepparents, flagging the danger that they might instead prove irresponsible and exploitative. Tales of such exploitation also appear in the account of the eponymous hero's problems with his stepfamily in Lucy Hutchinson's *Memoirs of the Life of Colonel Hutchinson*. Ilana Krausman Ben-Amos's *Adolescence and Youth in Early Modern England* issues a shrewd warning about the accuracy of biographical narratives written long after the event even as it acknowledges the pervasive traumas occasioned by parental loss. But however one evaluates the reliability of a given record like the Hutchinson memoir, it is clear that in the early modern period as today, stepmothers and stepfathers were widely regarded as very threatening.[5]

A culture whose history included lord protectors like Richard, Duke of Gloucester, men rightly perceived as primarily protecting their own interests, is likely to have been particularly conscious of analogous perversions of guardianship in the domestic sphere. And antagonism originally and guiltily directed toward the dead parent might readily be deflected onto stepparents and other caretakers, especially if they provided some rationale for doing so. But the anxieties expressed by writers like Gouge and Hutchinson also stem more immediately from the institution of stepparenthood itself. To begin with, Gouge's linguistic usage when he stresses that stepparents serve in the stead of mothers and fathers draws attention to semiotic and epistemological threats. Stepparenthood signals the complexities of representation in general and substitution in particular and in so doing carries with it implications for arenas ranging from the workings of rhetorical tropes to the problematics of gender. Surrogate parents both are and are not the parents they represent; if the dead are absent presences, so too in this sense are the living stepparents. Thus on one level they draw attention to the vulnerability of the individual family members they replace while on the other hand they testify to the longevity of family roles. The mother is dead, long live the mother — an emotionally charged statement whether maternity is perceived as beneficent, as suffocating, or as both at once. And such assertions are further destabilized in that the death of one mother reminds one of the vulnerability of her substitutes as well. These types of instability may help to explain the tendency, noted above and traced acutely by Marianne Novy, of splitting parents into good and evil versions.[6] Similarly, self-serving stepparents and guardians at once signified protection and ironically redefined that concept in ways that suggested that protection and signification itself were as vulnerable as the life of a parent.

From yet another perspective the introduction of a stepparent could complicate mourning in several ways. Clearly the processes of substitution might help a child redefine a relationship with the dead parent.[7] On the other hand, it is not hard to imagine scenarios in which new parents too quickly or too insensitively attempt to impose themselves as substitutes, thus interrupting the trajectories of mourning. Whereas parental substitutes could complicate the workings of grief, arguably the changes in religious and social modes of mourning that resulted from the Reformation in turn complicated familial surrogacy. These shifts in customs and rituals threatened patterns of grieving and recovering in that certain highly significant ways of expressing grief, and in so doing maintaining a reassuring relationship with the dead, were curtailed in the course of the sixteenth century. In particular, the Reformation eschewed practices connected with purgatory — a concept that redefines guardianship in terms of intercession. Anthony Low finds in *Hamlet's* repression of references to purgatory an enactment of that radical change. "The emotional and psychological consequences of the abolition of the doctrine of purgatory and curtailment of prayers for the dead," the social historian Ralph Houlbrooke observed, "constituted one of the great unchartable revolutions of English history."[8]

Houlbrooke goes on to speculate, persuasively enough, that this rejection of Catholic mourning rituals might decrease fear of suffering in the next world; but Joshua Scodel's suggestion that the same change emphasized the barrier between the dead and living is equally persuasive and more significant to an analysis of early parental loss. In particular, at the beginning of the sixteenth century the culture that built the ritual of parental blessing into quotidian domestic practices offered a continuation of that ritual in the belief that a dead parent could intercede for the living. In denying the possibility of that sort of intercession, Protestantism again displaced the dead parent. Not the least reason *A Midsummer Night's Dream* and other texts are so concerned with substitution, then, is that truncating the relationship with the dead parent put more pressure on its alternative, the several forms of surrogacy we have explored.[9]

Bereaved children were liable not only to, as it were, wicked stepmothers and stepfathers but also to many other apparently well-meaning guardians. The records of the Court of Orphans testify to the machinations of unscrupulous stepfathers as well as other male relatives.[10] Uncles clearly had many opportunities for such exploitation, and it is telling that the villain in the popular ballad "The Children in the Wood" is one, as are his analogues in *Hamlet* and *Richard III.* Given the emphasis on threatening male relatives in these and other renditions of parental loss, the focus on stepmothers rather than stepfathers in so many literary texts, notably *Pericles* and *Cymbeline*, provides a particularly telling instance of the gendering of anxieties.

In addition, many abuses resulted from the workings of wardship, an institution that deserves more attention than it has yet garnered from students of early modern literature.[11] Developed by the Tudors as a source of revenue, the system exemplifies the pragmatic efficiency of those monarchs. Wardship, which was based on medieval conceptions of financial obligation and of marriage practices, again demonstrates the need to nuance generalizations about protocapitalism with the recognition that feudal practices survived — and were skillfully deployed — in the laws regulating wardship no less than in land law. And most germane to this study is its profound effect on the material as well as the affective consequences of parental loss. Fathers sometimes attempted to avert those sorry effects through such devices as passing on property while they were still alive, but nonetheless the potentially abusive system continued to flourish.[12]

Whereas the monarch might benefit financially by retaining a wardship, it was through their sales that most benefit accrued to the crown. And it was through such sales that a number of abuses indisputably arose. Ascertaining just how corrupt the national administrators of the system were remains problematical. Lord Burghley, master of wards between 1561 and 1598, took gifts, but so too did many other Tudor officials; weighing the evidence against him, the historian Joel Hurstfield does not wholly exonerate him but persuasively asserts that he was generally fair and judicious.[13] Whether or not one seconds that verdict, however, it could not be pronounced on many of the guardians created by the wardship system. Anticipating the antics of twentieth century ambulance chasers, they were known to file petitions in anticipation of the death that would turn a child into a ward. Many of these so-called guardians were more concerned with the financial profit they could gain from their ward than the child's education or spiritual well-being; witness among a host of other examples the marriages into which wards were often forced.

Moreover, both the policies of the wardship system and the practices of individual guardians intensified the displacement associated with parental death. The surviving mother received little if any preference in the assignment of wardships, but the temptation merely to read this as yet another instance of the disempowerment of women needs to be qualified by the recognition that when male relatives sought to become guardians, their relationship to the child did not necessarily ensure that they would succeed. In the reign of Edward VI, only one-fifth of wardships were sold to the mother, a relative, or trustees chosen by the father or were granted to the ward him- or herself; during Mary's reign the figure came close to one in three, but in the opening years of Elizabeth's reign, it declined again to one in four. In 1587–1590 one-third of all grants went to such parties, an improvement but hardly a reversal of a disturbing pattern.[14] Because of it, a child who had suffered the loss of a parent might well be forced to move far from home and in effect lose the other parent as well, thus suffering another loss of control. The unscrupulous guardians provided by the wardship system not only displaced parents but in another sense often effected the geographical displacement of their charges, demonstrating how often spatial control both creates and figures other types of power, a pattern we will encounter as well in *Richard III*.

Yet one needs to remember that although the primary effects of wardship or other types of guardianship were more likely to be traumatic than liberating, bereaved families, like unhappy ones, are not all alike. It is not hard to imagine comedic scenarios culminating in relief, emancipation and the formulation of a new society, as it were, around a beneficent stepparent. In his autobiography the Renaissance minister Richard Baxter explains that shortly after his mother's death his father married a woman "whose Holiness, Mortification, Contempt of the World, and fervent Prayer" were "Exemplary"; this paragon was, he announces, a "Special Blessing to our Family."[15] Though, as we have seen, autobiographies famously distort what they claim to report, the passage reminds us that stepparents might be very positively perceived or represented or both. As Quintilian observes in 8.6 (*Quintilian's Institutes of Oratory*), the term a trope substitutes for the original one may be better than that original.

Nor were the social institutions of early modern England inevitably exploitative of bereaved children. The dog that doesn't bite the man stands less chance of headlines; the social institutions that oppose exploitation and the individuals who disdain it are likely to be neglected in an academic culture that prizes conflictual paradigms for social interactions. In fact, preventing the abuse of children was one agenda of another cultural institution, the Court of Orphans. Nonetheless, the fact remains that on the whole the material and emotional consequences of parental surrogacy were indeed threatening. Moreover, though the contrast between cultural myths about unscrupulous surrogate parents and the more positive behavior of some of them was no doubt sometimes a source of relief, it could again erode categories, spinning judgments and perceptions until they whirled as dizzyingly as a Van Gogh cypress.

Stepparents, other relatives and the guardians appointed by the wardship system had a profound impact on not only the affective but also the material consequences of the early loss of a parent. Those who live in a society of life insurance, pension plans and so on may too easily forget the financial devastation that the death of a breadwinner could bring. In the discussion in *Of Domesticall Duties* cited above, Gouge devotes considerable attention to the economic results of parental death. Warning of the disasters that can result from the machinations of unscrupulous stepparents or other guardians, he sedulously urges parents to prepare a will and ensure that reliable surrogates will be responsible for their children (esp. 569–74, 580–83, 585–86). He proceeds to assert that the majority of guardians, rather than protecting the child, are all too likely to pursue their own financial interests.

Studying early parental death invites us to rewrite one of the most common new historicist generalizations about early modern England. It has become common, indeed commonplace, in studies of that period to trace crises of representation to the theater. Though much of the criticism in question is incisive, yet again we need to acknowledge that the domestic realm anticipates, glosses and nuances events often associated largely or entirely with the court and theater of London. Critics have noted the theatricality of deathbed scenes, but the remarriages that succeeded them were in certain senses no less theatrical.[16] A generation that had grown up seeing mothers and sons assuming the roles of a deceased paterfamilias and stepparents representing and misrepresenting the progenitors they replaced learned a great deal about theatricality, performance and cross-dressing without going to the Globe.

II

Loss and his "imperial jointress" (*Hamlet*, 1.2.9), recovery, are the reigning monarchs in Shakespeare's conception of history; they quarrel, struggle with each other for supremacy, flirt with other partners, yet repeatedly seize each other in the embrace that generates the narrative of these plays. The history plays enact the relationship between deprivation and recuperation generically through the interplay between tragedy and history, though merely to associate the former with loss and the latter with recovery is to oversimplify their dynamic since each genre typically traces the interaction of both states. Recurring frequently throughout this group of plays, the myth of Eden offers a model for such patterns.[17] As the prologue to *Henry V* insists, the monarchs in question also stage the relationship of loss and recovery metatheatrically. And much as *Henry VI* opens with the body of a monarch on the stage, so throughout the history plays the death of a parent, whether it be the father of a small child or a nation, is both harbinger and figure of other types of loss, many of them related to surrogacy.

The connection between deprivation and recuperation is as fraught and unstable in the histories as it is elsewhere in the canon. At many junctures in Shakespeare's texts in this genre, orderly succession apparently models many other forms of recuperation, yet Henry IV's desperate hope that it will legitimate the rule of his son, as well as the problems associated with child kings, demonstrate the tensions in this pattern. In a host of other ways as well the history plays render the relationship between loss and recovery problematical even while they endorse the possibility of some forms of the latter; thus their author reminds us that the writers of history and their audiences may have many motives, including dubious ones, for finding, or imposing, a segue to regeneration. The epilogue to *Henry V* implicitly warns of this very danger. Shakespeare, I maintain, does not write the Tudor myth of history, but he repeatedly writes about it. And in the histories, as in *The Rape of Lucrece*, he writes about cognate attempts to reshape disaster into forms that serve the ends of the teller.

In none of Shakespeare's history plays, however, is the interplay between loss and recovery more central or intriguing than it is in *Richard III.* That dynamic subsumes and unites many other issues that have interested readers of the drama, such as the viability of providential interpretations and the extent to which characters other than Richard himself, notably Richmond, are untrustworthy or even evil.[18] The extraordinary encounter between the grieving Anne and Richard, though usually analyzed in characterological terms, is in fact a paradigm of how the relationship between loss and recuperation works throughout this drama. For in a sense this play, like *Macbeth,* is all about whether one can securely bury one's dead — that is, whether one can negotiate the consequences of loss in ways that discourage the repetition of it, notably in the form of ghostly visitations, and thus protect the living from those who attempt to take the place of the dead. When Richard interrupts the funeral procession, he demonstrates his predilection for interruption of all types; the man whose untimely birth obstructed the normal gestation period breaks into Margaret's curse in 1.3.233, breaks into patterns of succession. His late arrival cuts short plans to crown his nephew. By obstructing linearity as realized in the spatial movement of the funeral procession, he stages the ways he will obstruct narrative movements from loss to recuperation.

The interaction of loss and recuperation that structures the whole play is at its most intriguing and its most relevant to this study in its relation to the loss of parents and the patterns of surrogacy that result. In a text that stages the demise of not one but two kings and famously pivots on that of innocent children, several incidents also draw attention to the immediate fears and long-term consequences of the death of parents, implicitly but insistently relating the public and private spheres. Act 2, scene 2, the episode in which Clarence's children learn of his death, does not serve any significant narratological or characterological functions; instead, it not only anticipates the fate of their cousins, who have also lost a father, but also gestures toward the larger issues intertwined with the death of parents in the play. The dialogue here insists on the danger that event creates for the young: "Why do you look on us, and shake your head, / And call us orphans, wretches, castaways" (2.2.5–6). The answer to that question is not that such children are alone, but that they may be surrounded by too many unscrupulous relatives, notably uncles, a point with obvious relevance not only to members of the royal family but also, as we have seen, to the many members of Shakespeare's audience who had lost a parent early in their lives. Similarly, the wailing of the royal women in this scene hints at their recognition that they are powerless to protect these children, a situation that echoes the plight of many widows whose offspring entered the wardship system. Elsewhere in the play, language — notably Richard's pyrotechnics — controls loss, but here the elegiac laments express their speakers' lack of control. The scene also establishes indeterminacy and the anxieties it breeds as another consequence of the children's bereavement. Thus the presence of these children's male relatives creates uncertainties reminiscent of those caused by burglary, another version of loss. The children are confused about which of their uncles they can trust and whether or not their father is dead (in one of the many versions of failed or distorted protection in the play, their grandmother is attempting to shield them from that knowledge).

Yet most suggestive, and most predictive of the ways the play will subsequently analyze the loss of parents, is Clarence's son's description in this scene of how his "good uncle Gloucester" (20) behaved: "Bade me rely on him as on my father, / And he would love me dearly as a child" (25–26). For these lines, in which the connective "as" echoes the syntax of a simile, represent the first of many times this play acknowledges the link between the substitutions effected by parental death and those created by metaphoric language. Familial substitution, as it were, tropes the act of troping: in both cases the replacements are unalike and alike, a dual role signaled by the connective "as"; in both cases the process of linkage destabilizes and complicates. In both, the use of "as" at once exposes an absence and promises, however reliably, to fill it. Both parental and linguistic substitutes recall the twinnings, themselves not coincidentally associated with absence and loss, in *The Comedy of Errors* and *Twelfth Night*. On one level, Richard's assertions are just heavily ironic, while on another their uncle indeed desires that Clarence's offspring will be like children to him, who will turn to him for guidance and whom he hopes to manipulate even more easily than adults. The lines also remind us yet again that if Richard, like other Vices, creates unnatural separations and divisions, he also delights in generating unnatural familial bonds.[19]

Many issues raised by Clarence's children recur when their cousins the princes arrive in London in act 3, scene 1. In drawing attention to the surprising absences of his other uncles, his mother, brother and Hastings, Prince Edward reminds the audience that literal, material absences represent the absence of protection and a stable political and personal family. To paraphrase Queen Elizabeth, given that those uncles are absent, what will betide on the young prince? These gaps in stage appearances also gesture toward the role of ghostly presences throughout the play: the dead and dying kings who represent lost hopes for reconciliation and stable leadership and the dead personages enumerated in the hypnotic wailing of the women. It is not surprising that a coffin figures early in the play, and ghosts make their cameo appearances toward its end, for the drama, like *A Midsummer Night's Dream, Pericles* and *Cymbeline,* is concerned with the presence of those who are not present and the absence of those who should be.

As the scene progresses, it engenders another type of gap. Its emphasis on seizing the Duke of York from sanctuary signals the literal permeability of the religious house in which he resides, a material manifestation of the corruptibility of religious leaders in this scene and elsewhere in the play, men whose principles can readily be permeated with specious arguments, whose perceptions are as soft and easily spoiled as a strawberry. The decision to take away the young duke also represents the unreliability and the frailty of metaphoric sanctuaries, whether they be the Tower in its ambivalent role, the tellingly named Lord Protector, or the armor of wit this ill-fated young man attempts to wear.

Above all, the episode demonstrates the limitations on the maternal body in its role as sanctuary for a child denied a father and other more powerful guardians. Notice the wording of Buckingham's command: "And from her jealous arms *pluck* him perforce" (36; my emphasis). Later, in a line that does not refer specifically to the mother's arms, the reference to "seizing" (47) suggests the necessity of a more violent act. But the fact that the Duke of York can be plucked, a verb that might be used for, say, those strawberries (or the godly gardener who arranges for their delivery), suggests that maternal arms offer little protection indeed. Many studies of the play have emphasized the limited agency of its women, and others have reactively drawn attention to the power of their curses, but this passage, like the experience of many widows and their young children, provides a new and chilling perspective on one crucial type of impotence.

Female powerlessness and the power and powers of several different males are at play when the scene presents the effects of parental loss, especially the likelihood of surrogacy. The episode stages a stately minuet of expressed deference toward the princes, against whose notes we hear the cacophonous noises of Richard's assertions of his will. The badinage about whether the Duke of York may — and can — have his uncle's weapons literally and materially enacts other issues of power. The opening scene of act 3 implicitly compares several versions of power: the potency of Prince Edward's status, the efficacy of language as used both by the princes and their evil uncle, references to the military might that the heir to the throne hopes to achieve and the force of premeditated cunning.

In the most telling power play of the scene, and the most intense reminder of the dangers facing those who have a Lord Protector — or a guardian from the wardship system — rather than a reliable father, Richard arranges his charges' accommodation. As acute about the significance of space as any contemporary Marxist critic, this uncle, who earlier directed the body of one of his victims away from Chertsey and to White-Friars, here pretends to give his nephew the choice of where to stay:

> Where it seems best unto your royal self.
> If I may counsel you, some day or two
> Your Highness shall repose you at the Tower;
> Then where you please, and shall be thought most fit
> For your best health and recreation.
>
> (63–67)

On one level the speech simply endows the prince with the major decision about long-term accommodations while offering a firm recommendation about temporary plans. But observe too the deference of the first line and the tentativeness of the conditional segue into "shall" (65), whose insistence is immediately blurred by the emphasis on choice in the final lines. And then the Machiavel who delights in manipulating others to do his bidding revealingly qualifies the ascription of choice to the prince in a line that could refer to himself but elides subject and agency: "shall be thought most fit" (66). In the Olivier film, this speech reduces the prince to a quivering child, an impression intensified by the high angle shot. The Tower, an ostensible guardian that is instead the site of betrayal, is the inanimate analogue to the Lord Protector Richard.

The concern for threatened inheritances that I have been tracing in act 3, scene 1 preoccupies Shakespeare no less than William Gouge. Shakespeare's "whole tragic period can be seen as a reckoning with the problem of inheritance from one generation to the next," C. L. Barber and Richard P. Wheeler observe, though they proceed to explore the point largely in relation to inheriting masculine authority.[20] Similarly, the plots of Shakespeare's histories may justly be described as variations on the theme of inheritance, whether it be of Gaunt's lands or Bolingbroke's dubious behavior or England itself. These and many other texts, like the passage from *A Midsummer Night's Dream* on which I opened, demonstrate the imbrication of the material and the affective consequences of inheritances. Threats to a legacy may imperil both sustenance and status, as Orlando insists at the opening of *As You Like It.* At the same time, an inheritance represents the continuing presence of a parent, whether for good or ill, with caskets or admonitions or little changeling boys gesturing toward the power of a revenant. Shakespeare's preoccupation with guardianship in its many senses is manifest in the frequency with which it is a guardian of some type, whether Olivier or the queen in *Cymbeline* or, in a very different sense, Falstaff, who threatens the inheritance in question. Richard, like many guardians in the wardship system, is plotting to appropriate the legacy of the princes; but Richard, unlike those guardians, is after nothing less than a kingdom, with all the material and political perquisites associated with it.

Tyrrel's description of the princes' murder intensifies several issues raised by this scene. Their prayer book reminds us of the church and churchmen who failed to offer them sanctuary; their sleeping in each other's arms recalls the maternal arms from which the younger prince was plucked. They are embracing each other in a world that has failed to embrace and protect them, a failure facilitated by their loss of a father and realized in the figures of false or weak would-be protectors. In particular, if we accept the argument that the embrace recalls the popular ballad to which I referred earlier, "Children in the Wood," one of the most telling links between the two plots is that both cast an uncle as the principal villain, reflecting the cultural suspicions about that role.[21] Thus Tyrrel's description demonstrates the broader implications of parental loss and guardianship in *Richard III*: the child deprived of a parent loses one form of protection and acquires what may variously be reliable substitutes and simulacra.

Indeed, as this passage reminds us, *Richard III* engages thoughout with both familial and national resonances of protection and protectors. Through both dramatized action and wordplay, the *Henry VI* plays similarly draw attention to the irony of so-called protectors who instead threaten or destroy. "He will be found a dangerous Protector" (*2HVI* 1.1.164), Carlisle acutely prophesies, while in the next play in the series, the king's declaration to Warwick and Clarence, "I make you both Protectors of this land" (4.6.41) draws attention to the danger that the title Protector will not oblige its bearer to protect anything but his own interests. Similarly, the word "protect" and its cognates resonate throughout *Richard III*, appearing no fewer than eight times, with half those instances referring specifically to the title of the Lord Protector and the other half deploying the term more broadly.[22] In usages that anticipate Richard's perversion of his status as Lord Protector, the concept often acquires pejorative or ironic undertones, as when Clarence asserts that the king is sending him to the Tower to protect him — "His Majesty, / Tend'ring my person's safety" (1.1.43–44) — or when Hastings is accused of being "protector of this damned strumpet" (3.4.74). Whether manifest as political memory, ideological imperative or linguistic play, the question of protection is central in this text, as it will be in so many later Shakespearean plays.

As these references suggest, Shakespeare's allusions to guardianship are rooted in cultural history and cultural memories. *Richard III* draws on remembrances of England's recent history under a Lord Protector, playing them against the role of such figures when Henry VI and Prince Edward were in their minority. Perhaps such debates also reflect remembered anxieties of what would ensue if Elizabeth produced a child late in life, hence opening the possibility of a protectorship, maybe even one with a foreign husband in that role. In any event, it is revealing that in a play with as many choric interludes as a Bach passion, the citizens comment chorically on only one issue other than their immediate decision about the kingship of the cunningly devout, devoutly cunning Richard. In act 2, scene 3 they discuss in some detail the situation of a country with a child ruler, debating whether his uncles would be a source of wise counsel or dangerous "emulation" (25), thus signaling the significance of such problems to Shakespeare and his audience.

In a text that so repeatedly relates the familial to the national, the ambiguous status of a Lord Protector mimes the instabilities of familial roles; the civil war engulfing England is staged through uncivil behavior, and worse, among the family members in the play. Those familial roles are repeatedly travestied, as when Richard insistently declares that Queen Elizabeth is his mother. In particular, family members who might be expected to guard and nurture do the opposite; to signal the importance of that issue, of all the incidents on which he might have opened his story, Shakespeare begins it when the king, far from caring for Clarence, imperils him, and when Richard, ostensibly caring for Clarence, betrays him. It is telling, too, that Clarence's dream suggests that he harms himself when hoping to protect Richard: "Strook me (that thought to stay him) overboard" (1.4.19). This is but one of many times in the text when a family member who thinks to stay a fall in fact cannot or will not do so. In short, if the lust for power distorts sexual encounters in the play, so too does it twist the *caritas* that should characterize familial relationships. The situation of a child who, after losing a parent, is surrounded by dubious surrogate caretakers is a synecdoche for the situation of families as a whole and for that family the state.

All these connections between the surrogate parents of a child and the Lord Protector of a state draw attention to the complex workings of patriarchal paradigms. On one level, of course, Richard's behavior toward his unfortunate nephews merely mimes and glosses his relationship to England. Yet the princes are in no sense responsible for their fate, whereas in the national arena a series of fools and knaves colludes, wittingly and unwittingly, with Richard's machinations, a contrast that gestures towards contemporaneous debates about the responsibilities of the subjects of a tyrant. Here, as is so often the case, patriarchalism functions not by simply equating king, father and husband but rather by establishing a dynamic of both comparisons and contrasts.

Richard III also explores political questions in the national and domestic arenas in relationship to broader questions about representation and surrogacy. The bereft children who must rely on surrogates crystallize not only analogous political issues but also the relationship between surrogacy and representation. Richard's pious claim that he will love the late Clarence's son "as a child" (2.2.26) gestures toward the instabilities of figurative language and their connections to a range of different forms of substitution. As Marjorie B. Garber points out, in Clarence's dream metaphor masks the lineaments of his subconscious; similarly, other dreams and prophecies rely on the surrogacy of figuration. That form of substitution has mixed results in the play, but they are generally negative or at least dubious. If, as Garber elsewhere suggests, Richard's deformity is catachresis, the play invites us to speculate on whether metaphor itself can in fact be distinguished from catachresis. How often is it too deformed? In any event, metaphor indubitably conceals truths from those who cannot read it properly, as in Clarence's and Hastings's misinterpretation of dreams. And so *Richard III* demonstrates the necessity — and the difficulty — of reading both substitute words and substitute guardians accurately.[23]

Other types of surrogacy in *Richard III* extend and further complicate the play's valuation of it. The text's preoccupation with substitution is manifest in its repeated appearance even in more neutral contexts, such as Stanley's statement, "I, by attorney, bless thee from thy mother" (5.3.83). But more often surrogacy involves danger and recalls what is missing, what has been displaced and replaced. The ghosts not only represent absent people but also recall the absence to which I referred above, the loss of the concept of purgatory and of the potentialities for intercession connected with it: these figures are surrogates who gesture toward missing and possibly deeply missed forms of surrogacy. When Queen Margaret uses the verb "usurp" (4.4.109) in reference to Queen Elizabeth's putative stealing of her place as queen, she reminds us of the political ramifications behind certain types of substitution, and in fact that verb is repeatedly used for Richard's behavior (see, for example, 5.3.112). Richard, as we have already seen, famously promises to replace the husband and father he has murdered. And throughout the play we witness characters suborning others to do evil in their stead; Tyrrel is like his employer in this as in many other ways.[24] And yet *Richard III* qualifies its emphasis on how proxies may threaten and deform. It is no accident, I think, that the dying King Edward not just once but twice uses terminology that draws attention to Christ's role as substitute for sinful man, in the first instance even deploying polyptoton to reinforce the point and in the second referring to a cognate form of replacement — representation: "I every day expect an embassage / From my *Redeemer* to *redeem* me hence" (2.1.3–4; my emphasis), and "The precious *image* of our dear *Redeemer*" (2.1.124; my emphasis).

III

If the evocation of guardianship within *Richard III* engages with the social and cultural history of Shakespeare's England, it also gestures toward problems and challenges in late twentieth century America. So many roles in the academy and in our culture at large involve versions of guardianship; witness the university that still uneasily maintains some version of *in loco parentis*, the mentee to a junior faculty member, the foster parent, the stepparent, the board overseeing a nonprofit organization, the legislator concerned about children reading pornography, and so on. Radically different though all these instances are, they do involve certain similar problems, issues that are as intriguing to debate as they are difficult to resolve. How is the guardian's obligation to protect weighed against conflicting values, such as the privacy and the agency of the person being protected? And when and how does otherwise beneficent guardianship become an excuse for irresponsible assertions of power, with the obligation to shield disguising the darker motives behind it? An amendment to the Southern Baptist statement of beliefs was announced shortly before I began this essay: the revised document includes the statement that a woman should "submit herself graciously" to the leadership of her husband, who should in turn "provide for, protect and lead his family."[25] As *Richard III* demonstrates, it is as irresponsible to ignore the dark implications of that statement as it is to gloss guardianship only in such negative terms.

7 • "She is herself a dowry"

King Lear and the Problem of Female Entitlement in Early Modern England

Stephanie Chamberlain

> An ancient estate should always go to a male. It is mighty foolish to let a stranger have it because he married your daughter
>
> — Samuel Johnson, from *Boswell's Life of Johnson*

In 1605, George Clifford, third Earl of Cumberland, died, leaving his 15-year-old daughter Anne sole surviving heir. Although the Cumberland estate was legally entailed to the "heirs of his body lawfully begotten" — in other words, heirs general, not male — George Clifford nonetheless willed the lands and offices to his brother Francis, designating that Anne receive a £15,000 cash settlement in lieu of a landed inheritance.[1] Only in the event of a failure in the collateral male line would the lands and offices of the Cumberland estate revert back to Anne, an inheritance already legally hers by virtue of the ancient entail. At the age of 19, this displaced heiress married an ambitious 19-year-old earl (who did not support her claims as heiress, but was greedy for a lesser, quicker settlement), initiating a bitter, protracted struggle over who was legally entitled to the estate. Anne's uncle, her husband (who was prone to overspending) and eventually James I attempted unsuccessfully to coerce her into accepting a cash settlement that would terminate her prior claim as heiress to the lands and offices of her late father. When the Clifford collateral male line ultimately failed, Anne finally came into her legally protected rights as "daughter and sole heire of ye right honoble George Earl of Cumberland."[2]

Anne Clifford's tumultuous inheritance struggles provide a fitting introduction to a study of the problem female entitlement presented to an early modern English society. That George Clifford preferred a brother over a daughter — in other words, a collateral male over an heir general — betrays, I would argue, an anxiety about the efficacy of female inheritance within a society strongly protective of patrilineal descent. Heiresses took landed estates into marriages where other men and other families assumed control of the patrimony, enjoyed its profits and obscured the land-based patrilineage. Moreover, descent thereafter was traced through matrilineal lines, challenging notions of early modern patriarchal identity and calling into question constructed gender and social hierarchies. George Clifford's response seems less that of an indifferent father surreptitiously undercutting his daughter's rights than that of an expedient legal maneuver designed to avert the threats produced when the male line failed.

The conflict that began with the death of Clifford over the issue of female entitlement finds poignant expression on the Jacobean stage in Shakespeare's *King Lear*. In the opening scene, an aging Lear, lacking a male heir, ritually divides his kingdom into dowry and inheritance for his three daughters.

In what constitutes a scripted cultural performance, Lear portions out sections of his kingdom as estate according to provisions within the common law. Dowry, at once the mechanism through which marriages are contracted to protect social hierarchies as well as to secure marital and political alliances, also becomes a means by which to endow daughters with lands, property and cash within a social system favoring primogeniture. However, Lear's increasing irrationality in the opening scene of the play, during the division of his kingdom between conniving daughters who will quickly abuse their patrimony, raises the knotty issue of female entitlement within a patriarchal society. For although Cordelia never directly participates in her sisters' villainy, her status both as legitimate daughter to the king of England as well as queen to England's rival, France, ultimately implicates her in her siblings' actions, as well. Indeed, a marriage to France carries with it dangerous overtones, for under the restrictive laws of coverture, this alliance would give her husband a governing interest in English lands. In the terms of anthropologist Victor Turner's theoretical model, the scene can be understood as constituting a social drama, a disruptive communal event which must be consensually resolved before the public peace can be restored.[3] Cordelia's swift disinheritance, followed by the stylized vilification and deaths of all three heiresses, becomes one solution to a world badly disrupted by female entitlement.

Female entitlement took many forms in early modern England, with far-reaching consequences for fathers, husbands, and even brothers. At her marriage, a woman brought a dowry or marriage portion, which was normally given by the bride's father to the groom's father, ostensibly to pay for the couple's maintenance as well as to guarantee payment of the bride's jointure upon the death of her husband. The marriage portion was then used by the groom's family to provide for its daughters, to pay debts and to purchase land. The will of

Thomas Stoner (1431), for example, specified that the proceeds of his son's marriage be used to marry his five daughters. The making of a marriage became an even more lucrative business by the mid-sixteenth century, when the release of previously held monastic lands at the dissolution allowed families to use the cash proceeds of marriage to engage in the practice of estate building. John Isham, for instance, used proceeds of his marriage to the widow of a London mercer to purchase lands that would eventually lead to his status as a great landowner.[4]

Female entitlement also impacted the male-privileged system of inheritance in early modern England. The practice of primogeniture, whereby the eldest male child inherited all of his father's lands, had been increasingly preferred in England since the eleventh century as a means by which both to build and to keep large landed estates intact, to guard against what John Day has termed the "extreme pulverization" of land.[5] Primogeniture, in concert with the device of the entail, kept landed estates large. Female inheritance, whether single or partible, inevitably divided family lands, an occurrence the practice of primogeniture had been designed to protect against. Such a system would seem to have prevented daughters from inheriting anything other than cash and moveable goods from their fathers' estates. In practice, many landowners were left without male heirs, and in such cases daughters inherited, in part because, though a nearly equal number of males and females were born, the higher early male mortality rate meant that more daughters survived than sons. Eileen Spring has calculated that, in fact, as many as 42 percent of early modern English women could be made heiresses as a direct result of common law provisions. Under the common law, the daughter's right to inherit came at the exclusion of any surviving collateral males — nephews, uncles or brothers. As the early modern commentator of *The Lawes Resolutions of Womens Rights* (1632) notes, "land descended must alwaies goe to heires of the blood of the first purchaser, and the case may bee such that a female shall cary away inheritance from a male." Such a possibility must have proven frightening to an early modern English society protective of patriarchal privilege. Yet, as James Holt has observed, "in the absence of male heirs in the same generation, [the daughter] was the only means of continuing the lineage, the only legitimate route whereby her father's blood could be transmitted." To preserve lineage, daughters were thus allowed to participate in an otherwise male-privileged system of inheritance. And therein lay the problem.[6]

Despite a prevailing legal and moral imperative to provide for daughters, female entitlement proved increasingly problematic, generating escalating economic and psychological burdens that strained the limited resources of a changing early modern English society. As Lawrence Stone has pointed out, "daughters were a serious economic drain on the family finances." Whereas younger sons were usually only marginally endowed (and in some cases, not at all), daughters required significant dowries, usually given in the form of cash, if they were to secure the kind of marital alliances which would bring prestige to the family.[7] At her marriage in 1601, for instance, Elizabeth Isham required a portion of about £1,000. When Elizabeth Spencer married John Craven in 1634, her father funded an even larger portion of £6,000: a noteworthy 600 percent rate of increase in just 33 years. Granted, the size of the portion was affected by many factors, including the status as well as the financial resources of the family. The case of the well-endowed Judith Lewyn is illustrative. Her marriage to John Isham in 1607, brother of the above-mentioned Elizabeth, took place only after some fairly competitive dowry negotiations. Mary Finch has found evidence of "no less than nine prospective brides" for the groom, including Alderman Swinnerton's daughter, "who would have a 'great portion' of city money, the widow of Sir William Skeffington with a jointure of £300, and Sir Anthony Tyringham's daughter, who would have a £1,500 if not £2,000 portion." Conversely, Katherine Hyde's father was able to negotiate a reasonable dowry figure of just £1,400 in 1603 because of the groom's recognizably inferior social ranking.[8]

Regardless of the landowner's status, funding dowries was often a difficult enterprise, requiring innovative solutions to remain competitive in a market favoring ever-increasing cash reserves. Simply put, early modern English estates were often land rich, but cash poor. Landownership, which provided a means for long-term wealth and continued social status, also became a curse to those sorely in need of large cash reserves. Because estate lands were frequently entailed upon future heirs, owners were unwilling or, in some cases, unable to sell even portions of them to raise cash. Before long-term mortgages became available early in the seventeenth century, some estate owners were, in fact, forced to lease sections of their lands in an attempt to raise funds for the payment of, among other debts, marriage portions. To help fund marriage portions of just 2,000 marks each for his six daughters, the financially strapped Sir Thomas Tresham leased some of his pastures.[9] That marriage portions were often paid in installments provides further insight into the challenge of funding dowries in early modern England. Anne Clifford's hotly contested inheritance/marriage portion of £17,000, for instance, was paid over a period of ten and one-half years.[10] Katherine Fitzwilliam's father took an even more innovative approach to the challenge of dowry funding. When his daughter married Sir John Lee in 1633, her father, the second Baron Fitzwilliam, promised a portion of £2,200. At the time of the marriage, however, he could only pay £1,000; Sir John was subsequently given a mortgage on lands held by the baron for the remaining £1,200.

Final payment of promised portions frequently did not take place until after the death of the landowner, creating considerable debt for his heir who was required to satisfy estate obligations on his newly acquired lands. John Isham II's 1605 inheritance, for instance, was encumbered both by the only partially funded marriage portions of his sisters as well as his mother's jointure claims. To satisfy his sisters' claims, he assigned them a term in his manor at Lamport "towards theire better satisfaccion" of their unpaid portions. John's mother eventually agreed to relinquish her jointure claims of an annuity of 20 marks and legacies within her husband's will in exchange for £154 5s. 4d., a lease of Pale House for 60 years and an annuity of £60 for her life. It was not until she died in 1621 that John Isham was finally released from the debt his father incurred through female entitlement.[11] As Margaret Spufford has concluded, required provisions for daughters, younger sons, and widows frequently created a heavy burden on the inheriting son, making "the distinction between primogeniture and unigeniture, on the one hand, and partible inheritance on the other . . . a very blurred one."[12]

From a psychological perspective, female entitlement was an equally great burden to bear, especially where the transmission of land was involved. Simply, female inheritance was viewed as patrilineal decline. Indeed, one of the greatest fears associated with the succession of heiresses was a corresponding loss of patrilineal identity. Eileen Spring has argued that "the succession of a female came to be held not the natural means of continuing the family, but the end of the family, its very dying out." Male heirs perpetuated paternal names, preserving lineages and thus family heritage. Female inheritance threatened a loss of patrilineal identity as daughters moved into marriages where entitlement lands virtually disappeared during the term of coverture. At best, ownership of patrilineal lands was subsequently traced back through a matrilineal line; at worst, patrilineal lands settled upon a female heir became identified with another patronym. The case of Agnes Bussy, only child and heir of the wealthy John Bussy, is illustrative. In 1539, she married Edward Brudenell, son of Sir Thomas

Brudenell. For her portion, her father settled all of his lands and manors first to himself for life, then to Edward and Agnes and their heirs. Although Agnes was heiress to her father's estate, the Bussy lands would subsequently be traced back through the Brudenell patronym, first through Edward and then through heirs of his body.[13] It is this threat of patrilineal loss, I would argue, which haunts the text of *King Lear.*

From its opening lines, an air of decline pervades Lear's world. Sensing his approaching demise, this aging king draws his court together to assign dowry and name heirs to his estate. As he declares: "We have this hour a constant will to publish / Our daughters' several dowers, that future strife / May be prevented now" (1.1.41–43).[14] Despite the fact that the assignment of dowry and inheritance constitutes a standard cultural practice, there exists, nonetheless, an unmistakable sense of anxiety over the impending division. Because Lear has no sons, he at least initially plans to divide his estate in a way surprisingly consistent with common law provisions, which stipulated equal division among female heirs. However, Kent and Gloucester's whispered concerns, which open the play, provide strong evidence of an uneasy feeling of disruption occasioned by the impending division:

> *Kent.* I thought the King had more affected the Duke of Albany than Cornwall.
> *Glou.* It did always seem so to us, but now in the division of the kingdom[15] it appears not which of the Dukes he values most; for equalities[16] are so weighed that curiosity in neither can make choice of either's moiety.
>
> (1.1.1–6)

That the planned division is not viewed as equal is immediately evident, indicating perhaps an awareness of a possible favoritism at odds with communal expectations of the common law. Samuel Johnson, puzzled by the planned division, suggests that "there is something of obscurity or inaccuracy in this preparatory scene. The King has already divided his kingdom, and yet when he enters he examines his daughters, to discover in what proportions he should divide it."[17] As interesting is the fact that the two express concern not simply over a division of land between daughters, but between the sons-in-law who will subsequently control it. This concern has especially important implications in the case of Cordelia and her as yet unnamed French husband-to-be.

Lear's odd "love test" during the course of this ritual event, moreover, openly violates provisions of the common law, which, as noted, stipulated an equal division of the estate among female heirs. His unexpected and, for Cordelia, unnerving, "which of you shall we say doth love us most?" (1.1.49), rewrites the terms of female entitlement as conditional rather than obligatory — dependent upon the whim of a decidedly anxious paternal authority. The love test can itself be read as a perversion of the espousal or "trothplighting," a ritual routinely performed in early modern England to cement marital agreements. During this formal ritual, the engaged couple publicly professed their love for one another, with the recitation of prayers and the exchange of promises, all to ensure that the engaged couple could legally enter into such an agreement, that no impediments existed which would invalidate such an alliance.[18]

Lear's "espousal," performed in the presence of court witnesses, recasts this father/king as rival husband-to-be, as an ardent and jealous lover attempting to exact a promise of love and fidelity that exceeds the bounds of a culturally acceptable father-daughter relationship. To Lear's highly unusual demand on the eve on her engagement to a French suitor, Cordelia expresses an anguished awareness of her father's unexpected role confusion:

> Good my lord,
> You have begot me, bred me, loved me; I
> Return those duties back as are right fit,

> Obey you, love you, and most honor you.
> . . . .
> Haply, when I shal wed,
> That lord whose hand must take my plight shall carry
> Half my love with him, half my care and duty.
> (1.1.94–97; 99–101)

Notable here is Cordelia's attempt to reposition herself and her father within accepted familial roles, to nudge Lear from an incomprehensible rivalry that threatens the most fundamental notions of appropriate parent-child relationships. The incestuous undertones of the play have been discussed at length within recent scholarship. Stanley Cavell, for instance, has suggested that "what Lear is ashamed of is not his need for love and his inability to return it, but of the *nature* of his love for Cordelia. It is too far from plain love of father for daughter." Might we not also read Lear's disturbingly sexualized rivalry as the desperately irrational response of a father attempting to retain that which proves the source of his identity. And Lear's identity, as the text will make clear, is inextricably linked to the land he is on the verge of giving away. Indeed, as Kathleen McLuskie has noted, "Cordelia's notion of love gained precedence in modern ideology but it seriously disrupts Lear's discussion of property and inheritance. When Lear responds with 'Nothing will come of nothing' (1.1.89) his words need not be delivered as an angry reaction to an inappropriate idea." The division scene, which begins as a routine cultural performance, quickly devolves into a threatening social drama.[19]

Anthropologist Victor Turner's theoretical model of the social drama provides insight into the nature of the crisis that grips *Lear* from the beginning. Turner defines the social drama as a communal response to an event that has shaken the public consciousness, one that demands immediate attention if the group is to return to a state of order. Turner calls the social drama "processually structured," identifying four stages that the community must go through before the crisis can be resolved. In the first stage, there is "*breach* of regular norm-governed social relations made publicly visible by the infraction of a rule ordinarily held to be binding."[20] In the case of *Lear*, the breach involves the rules governing the assignment of inheritance and dowry. Because Lear has no son, he has a perceived cultural obligation to name his three daughters as equal heirs to his estate.[21] And Lear at least initially appears to satisfy this obligation when he calls his court together for the expected purpose of naming heirs and assigning dowries.

Yet as Turner also notes, the cultural performance is by its very nature "often a critique, direct or veiled, of the social life it grows out of, an evaluation (with lively possibilities of rejection) of the way society handles history." Lear's ritualized division, in other words, signifies from the very beginning that a problem exists regarding the impending division, one which this ritualized performance will attempt to resolve. As Turner further notes, those instituting the cultural performance hold up "'magic mirrors' which make ugly or beautiful events or relationships which cannot be recognized as such in the continuous flow of quotidian life in which they are embedded." In the case of *Lear*, these "magic mirrors" both reflect and distort the impact of female entitlement on the established social system. Lear's unexpected behavior not only challenges ritual practice; it forces his audience to evaluate, perhaps for the first time, the ultimate cost of endowing daughters, what Lawrence Stone and Jeanne Fawtier Stone have termed "the hazards of biological failure."[22]

Stanley Cavell has suggested that it is Lear's feeling of powerlessness "to *appoint* his successor, recognized as the ultimate test of authority" which begets Lear's love test, enabling the crisis to subsequently ensue.[23] To this I would add that Lear expresses a sense of powerlessness to appoint a *male* successor, a feeling shared by virtually all within his community. The opening dialogue between Kent and

Gloucester, it will be recalled, noticeably excludes mention of female heirs in regard to the impending division. Instead the two puzzle over which son-in-law will enjoy the bulk of Lear's estate. In short, a female heir is essentially equivalent to no heir at all.

The breach stage of the social drama is followed by what Turner calls *crisis*, "when people take sides, or rather, are in the process of being induced, seduced, cajoled, nudged, or threatened to take sides" (34). Crisis occurs when Lear inexplicably institutes the love test as a necessary criterion for the attainment of dowry and inheritance. Goneril and Regan, of course, give appropriate responses to Lear's test and are correspondingly rewarded for their performance. Cordelia's flat "Nothing, my lord" (1.1.85) falls far short of the desired response, setting in motion the crisis stage. Lear's sudden disinheritance of this youngest daughter draws mixed responses from those present. Goneril and Regan, of course, read this unexpected event as opportunity and at least initially appear to support their father. Kent, perhaps, best represents that public opinion which expresses outrage at the violation of a routine cultural ritual. He would rather face exile, or even death, than remain silent on what he considers a critical cultural matter. Others such as Gloucester and Albany mostly exhibit confusion; as mystified as they are by this turn of events, they nonetheless express continued, open support of the king.

The third stage of the social drama involves what Turner calls "the application of *redressive or remedial procedures*." During this stage, the community "bends, even throws itself back upon itself, to measure what some of its members have done, and how they have conducted themselves with reference to its own standards" (34). In the case of *King Lear*, this stage of the social drama is most vividly seen through the figure of Kent, who will, throughout the course of the play, repeatedly challenge the behavior of a society which commits increasing violence against itself. His astounded, insistent plea following Cordelia's disinheritance is representative of his stage three role as mediator:

> Kill thy physician, and thy fee bestow
> Upon the foul disease. Revoke thy gift
> Or whilst I can vent clamour from my throat
> I tell thee thou dost evil.
>
> (1.1.160–63)

Kent functions here as Turner's "reasonable man" (35), one who assumes the onerous responsibility of calling attention to a dangerous departure from a communal standard of behavior. Not only does Lear err in denying Cordelia a dowry and an inheritance, but even worse he denies her paternity, thereby condemning her to a kind of illegitimacy: a violence against not only his daughter, but to the communal conception of kinship which should unconditionally support and protect its own.[24] Indeed, as Gayle Whittier has noted, illegitimacy condemns "the child to a legal nonexistence, perpetual confinement to the mother's body of flesh rather than endowment with the father's body of social identity and land."[25] In the case of Cordelia, disinheritance means not only a loss of dowry and inheritance; it ultimately constitutes a kind of bastardy which places this daughter, arguably yet loved above all the rest, in a position akin to that of the despicable Edmund.

During the fourth and final stage of Turner's social drama, an order of some sort is restored to the community in crisis. This restoration can take one of two forms: either there is a "*reintegration* of the disturbed social group" or a "*recognition and legitimation of irreparable schism* between the contending parties" (35). This stage of the social drama is complexly manifested in *King Lear*. While a measure of resolution is achieved by the end of the drama, it is in many ways an unacceptable one. Not only is resolution achieved through the senseless death of Cordelia, it ultimately does violence to established rules governing female entitlement within the community. While Lear's sins are fully acknowledged by play's end, Cordelia's dowry and inheritance are never restored; instead, this last surviving daughter, arguably most entitled heir to her father's fortunes, is inexplicably killed. Lear's estate is quickly and quietly transferred to a collateral male — first to Albany, the surviving son-in-law, and then to the legitimate Edgar who, as Ian Kirby has noted, comes to represent "the restoration of temporal order."[26] The issue which incited this communal crisis, female entitlement, is irreparably undercut by play's end.

It is, perhaps, the impending marriage of Cordelia that proves the single most threatening event within the text of *King Lear*, for a proposed contractual alliance with either France or Burgundy, indeed with any husband, carries with it a threat to the patrilineal order. For with her marriage, Cordelia carries away English land and with it obscures Lear's patrilineage. John Roland Dove and Peter Gamble have suggested that before Lear's formal announcement to the contrary, his court naturally assumes that Cordelia will receive a cash settlement in lieu of an equal share of her father's lands. Kent and Gloucester's opening dialogue would seem to support such a premise, for while the two discuss an equal division between the two eldest daughters, no mention is made of Cordelia. And as Jack Goody has noted, such a practice was, in fact, routine in early modern England in the case of "out-marrying" daughters — those who married into families outside defined community boundaries. Funding a cash settlement rather than transmitting a landed estate enabled the bride's parents to secure a suitable marital alliance while at the same time preserving familial lands. Indeed, as Margaret Cavendish, the Duchess of Newcastle, somewhat coolly observed, daughters "are but branches which by marriage are broken off from the root from whence they sprang, and ingrafted into the stock of the other family . . . daughters are to be accounted but as moveable goods or furnitures — that wear out." Ideally, at least, they are not to take away estate lands. That Lear endows all his daughters with land rather than cash means a breakup not only of the family estate, but of the kingdom as well, or what David Cressy has termed "the family writ large."[27] In short, although Lear endows all his daughters through their respective husbands, a proposed union with either Burgundy or France represents an especially significant threat to Lear's already imperiled patrilineage, for such an endowment enables a foreign power to assume at least partial control of a divided and, suddenly, visibly weakened English state.[28]

In his discussion of the functions of kinship, Pierre Bourdieu has argued that the political marriage represents symbolic capital to the woman's family, a means that both secures an alliance and brings honor to it. Certainly, the fact that Lear plans to marry his youngest and most favored daughter to either a French duke or king would seem to suggest that at least one of the purposes of the union is to secure an advantageous political alliance. The "third more oppulent" (1.1.84) portion that Lear has planned for Cordelia takes on added resonance when read as political leverage. Indeed, as Gayle Whittier has noted, Lear's daughters represent "dynastic chattel and verbal coinage" to their aging father, a means by which he can purchase added prestige within the larger world. Moreover, as Bourdieu further notes, "marriage to a stranger living at a distance is prestigious because it bears witness to the extent of the lineage's prestige." Cordelia is, in essence, offered up as a gift to the foreign power that would receive her, creating future obligations to Lear and England. Since failure to reciprocate inevitably dishonors the receiver, the exchange would serve to create or stabilize relations between England and France. For Lear, such a union would serve as a public proclamation of his self-inflated net worth — notice to the world that a mighty king wields power and influence well beyond national boundaries. Yet, as he is quick to deduce,

Cordelia's proposed marriage also comes to signal a corresponding division of affections as well as lands and property. As this youngest daughter candidly declares, "haply when I shall wed / That lord whose hand must take my plight shall carry / Half my love with him, half my care and duty" (1.1.98–100). I think we have to read this division of affections as a division of loyalties as well, in both a political and kinship sense: an idea with chilling implications, her loyalties divided not only between father and husband, but between England and France. As Barbara Millard has argued, Cordelia's "ascension to the throne of France completes an emblem of a most highly charged and threatening political meaning for British kings and subjects. Cordelia's role as Queen of France becomes a part of her identity which no one in the play can afford to forget." In the end, Cordelia's politically advantageous marriage signals a dangerous and irrecoverable loss of potentially staggering emotional as well as economic and political proportions. As Bourdieu concludes, receiving a man from the outside is different from receiving a woman from the outside. A woman brings; a man takes.[29]

Lear's unexpected and ultimately disastrous love test during the course of the ritual division can thus be read as a futile attempt to reconcile the threat that female entitlement presents to a patrilineage on the verge of extinction. Indeed, the test itself becomes a kind of oath of loyalty, not only to Lear and his prior kinship claims, but to an English state suddenly teetering on the brink of dissolution. It is interesting that when Cordelia fails to give the correct response, fails to flatter, coax or in some way appease her father's barely suppressed anxiety, Lear does not simply back out of the political alliance he has planned for this youngest daughter. Instead, he removes the economic incentives enabling such an alliance in the first place. I concur with those, including Stanley Cavell and Lynda Boose, who have suggested that Lear purposely disinherits Cordelia, less to publicly disgrace one who will not yield to his obsessive demands than to keep her and his property within England and under his control. Indeed, as Dove and Gamble have observed, as reprehensible as Cordelia's disinheritance has been to centuries of audiences, "even more abhorrent would be the idea of the divided British kingdom being ceded by way of dowry to a French ruler."[30]

Lear's failure to quash the soured marriage negotiations results not only in a father's anguish and a king's madness (which can itself be viewed as the most extreme state of anxiety), but in the increasing vilification of all three heiresses. Indeed, the text itself ultimately argues against the wisdom of female entitlement to the survival of the social order. Goneril and Regan systematically strip their father of his knights, and in so doing remove all traces of his parental/political authority and thus his identity, for Lear's identity is inextricably linked to his role as father and king. They blind a bewildered old man simply for offering shelter to his king; they seek a father's death by forcing him out into a violent storm and when Lear refuses to die they conspire with a vicious, vengeful bastard to commit murder. Although Cordelia, now Queen of France, does not participate directly in their villainy, she too, in the end, must inevitably commit violence against England. Her introduction of invasionary foreign forces onto native soil to rescue her imperiled father threatens not only life and property, but a badly shaken national psyche as well. And even this bold and controversial measure is not enough to save him; her ineffectual leadership abilities become painfully apparent as she is captured alongside the childlike Lear and led off to prison where she will shortly meet her death. Ultimately, it falls on Edgar's legitimate authority to best the upstart Edmund and return order to a badly managed English state.

The dowry scene of *King Lear* can thus be read as a routine early modern English cultural performance gone horribly awry, where the problem of female entitlement is contained only at the conclusion of a social drama that culminates in the deaths of all three heiresses and the restoration of male authority. Social dramas, as Turner has observed, "may often contain episodes of purification and sacrifice, both of which aim to remove the pollution of self-serving or factional conduct and restore, sometimes in the image of an ideal or mythical past, a pure state of relations among its members." There is little doubt that an arrogant King Lear bears direct responsibility for the widespread human suffering that prevails by the end of the play. Yet, it is only with Cordelia's death that this social drama finds resolution. As Leonard Tennenhouse observes, "were Cordelia rather than Albany and Edgar to remain at the end of the play, the crown would descend to her upon Lear's death; either that or the play would challenge the metaphysics of blood all over again in giving the crown to a male."[31]

In Geoffrey of Monmouth's *Historia Regum Britanniae* and Raphael Holinshed's *Chronicles of England, Scotland, and Ireland,* in fact, the much-maligned Cordelia does survive her sisters' reign of terror and is restored as rightful heir to Lear's lands and office, where she undertakes, alongside her husband, a peaceful, if short-lived reign of England. Five years later France is dead and Cordelia's two nephews, disdainful of female rule, gather forces against her, inflicting great catastrophe upon the land. Unlike the gritty Anne Clifford, who survived two exploitive (if not abusive) husbands, systematically adding to her Clifford inheritance and dying at the age of 86 a respected, generous patron both to her sex and to her community, this Cordelia proves inherently incapable of sustaining her inheritance.[32] When captured and imprisoned by rebellious forces, Cordelia *takes* her own life, making a strong case for the ineffectiveness of female authority to the maintenance of the social order.[33]

Barbara C. Millard has suggested that Cordelia's death results "from her decision to invade Britain; a preemptive attempt to reverse the effects of her rebellion in the first scene of the play."[34] Indeed, as long as female heirs threaten the world of *King Lear*, only discord is seen to prevail. The evil Goneril and Regan wreak havoc virtually unchecked on their community, while the wronged Cordelia threatens the state with foreign troops. It is only with the death of the last surviving female heir to Lear's estate that order is finally restored. The legitimate Edgar emerges as the sole and rightful heir to an ancient estate, emphasizing with his succession the perceived importance of male inheritance to the preservation of the social order.

8 • Multiple Parenting in Shakespeare's Romances

Marianne Novy

In early modern England, parenting was often multiple, reaching beyond the nuclear family (though in very different ways than we might imagine it today).[1] Not only was there a high parental death rate and frequent remarriage, but there were many other institutions that involved children's presence in households outside their birth families. Many infants were sent away to wet nurses for several years; older children were often sent away to apprentice in other households, and aristocratic families practiced informal exchanges of children, partly as a way of reinforcing their alliances.[2] Unlike modern England and America, early modern England had no formal laws regulating adoption — the institution that today most clearly raises questions about multiple parenthood — but informal adoption of various kinds frequently appears in the theater as well as in the prose romances that were the popular fiction of the time.[3] Today, practices of multiple parenting sometimes raise questions of how parenthood should be defined — by genetics or by active nurturing. I am interested here in whether early modern literature imagines anything like this debate.[4]

In three of Shakespeare's last plays, *Pericles, Winter's Tale* and *Cymbeline*, children are relinquished, abandoned or taken from their parents and raised by others. Each play ends with the reconstitution of the family of birth.[5] These are all plays in which the emphasis on the similarity of long-separated relatives is strong, and in which the separated children are noticeably different from others in their surroundings. I here consider these plays in relation to the evidence of multiple parenting of the time and show that, while their plots are determined by a mythology of blood, they also contain some tribute to the effects of nurture and some emphasis on the family as a construction. So, for instance, although the plots always define the birth parents as the real parents, and some foster parents in *Pericles* and *Cymbeline* are murderous, the plays all present alternative images of foster parents as actively benevolent.[6] Specifically, I want to compare these plays with regard to four closely intertwined aspects of their treatment of multiple parenting: the degree of splitting of parents into good versus evil; the discussion of heredity versus environment, or, in the plays' terms, nature versus nurture; the emphasis on physical resemblance in the birth family; and modes of recognition by separated members. These comparisons show that each of these plays emphasizes heredity, but each complicates the mythology of blood to some degree. A belief in "blood" was part of the Renaissance worldview, even though there were conflicting views about how heredity worked.[7] But it was accompanied by a recognition that, on the one hand, children were often very different from their parents, and, on the other hand, good or bad nurture had a significant impact on how children developed.[8] Nurture was most often discussed with regard to wet nurses (who were thought to transmit moral qualities very literally with their milk) and teachers, but the concept is clearly relevant to the foster parents of these plays.[9]

The relative benevolence of the foster parents in comparison to the biological parents increases from the first of these plays to the third. *Pericles*, written first, clearly poses evil foster parents against good biological parents. Thinking his wife Thaisa is dead, Pericles gives the newborn Marina to his friends Cleon and Dionyza to raise — emphasizing that they should give her education according to her noble rank; because she outshines their daughter in weaving, sewing and singing, Dionyza plots Marina's murder, and only the chance kidnapping by pirates saves her — to be sold to a brothel. She is talented enough to escape the brothel by her persuasion to chastity, sewing and singing, and at the end of the play she is reunited first with her father and, finally, with her mother, who turns out to be still alive in a temple of Diana.

In spite of the polarization between good parents and evil foster parents, there is a good foster parent for Marina in this play — her nurse, Lychorida. The murder plot is hatched after Lychorida's death; Dionyza tries to gain Marina's confidence by offering herself in Lychorida's place: "Have you a nurse of me."[10] Lychorida is a shadowy figure, who appears only in the scene where Marina is an infant, but it was she who passed on to Marina the story of her birth and an admirable image of her father's courage and patience:

> My father, as nurse says, did never fear,
> But cried, "Good seamen!" to the sailors,
> Galling his kingly hands, hailing ropes;
> And clasping to the mast, endured a sea
> That almost broke the deck.
>
> (4.1.55–59)

Furthermore, Lychorida's importance in transmitting memories is explicitly honored in the recognition scene, when Marina says,

> My mother was the daughter of a king,
> Who died the minute I was born,
> As my good nurse Lychorida hath oft
> Delivered weeping.
>
> (5.1.162–65)

In *Cymbeline*, the distribution of good and evil between biological and surrogate parents is somewhat more ambiguous. Imogen has a wicked stepmother, who begins by denying that she is "After the slander of most stepmothers, / Evil-ey'd unto you" (1.1.71–72). But is Cymbeline, Imogen's father, good or bad as a parent? He has brought up the orphaned Posthumus in his household, but upon Posthumus's marriage to Imogen, and his own to his new wife, Cymbeline banishes him and rages at this daughter. Is Belarius, who has been raising Cymbeline's sons (Imogen's brothers) as his own in the pastoral setting of Wales, good or bad as a foster parent? Belarius criticizes the insincerity of the court world and gives them training in religion and morality. But he is a kidnapper. On the other hand, his kidnapping is in retribution for Cymbeline's injustice to him, and in general he seems to be portrayed as morally superior to Cymbeline in spite of that misdeed. At the end, the wicked queen dies, Belarius is reconciled to Cymbeline and his sons return to him, and Posthumus, who has, in disguise, fought bravely on the king's side, is reconciled both to Cymbeline and to Imogen, whom (in a familiar Shakespearean motif) he has planned to kill because he suspected her — without cause — of adultery.

The Winter's Tale is ambivalent about the adoptive father, referred to only as "Shepherd," in a different way, and it is even more ambivalent about the birthfather, Leontes, who, unlike any other father in the romances, threatens his child with death and commands her to be abandoned because of his suspicion about her parentage. When the shepherd enters the play, he is highly preferable to Leontes. Unlike his counterpart in the source, Greene's *Pandosto*, the shepherd at once decides to take up the abandoned babe, Perdita, even before he knows that gold has been left with her. As Carol Neely notes, he seems admirable in his lack of possessiveness of his children, accepting Perdita's teenage sexuality as he encourages her romance with Florizel, disguised as a shepherd, but obviously high-born.[11] His pastoral world seems, emotionally, a better environment for childrearing than the cold and suspicious world of the court, and this helps to present his nurturing of Perdita as an act of nature as well as of adoption.

His evocation of his dead wife, Perdita's adoptive mother, shows an appreciation of her energy and sociability that is especially remarkable because of Leontes's suspicion of his own wife's friendliness to others:

> When my old wife liv'd, upon
> This day, she was both pantler, butler, cook,
> Both dame and servant, welcom'd all, serv'd all,
> Would sing her song and dance her turn; now here,
> At upper end o'th'table, now i'th'middle;
> On his shoulder, and his; her face o'fire
> With labor, and the thing she took to quench it
> She would to each one sip.
>
> (4.4.55–62)

This figure is far from the wicked stepmother; nevertheless, the shepherd evokes her explicitly only as a hostess, and Perdita does not follow him in evoking this adoptive mother as a precedent for her behavior. Unlike Desdemona, who speaks of doing "such duty as my mother show'd" (1.3.199), Perdita says, "It is my father's will I should take on me / The hostess-ship o'th'day" (4.4.71–72).

Thus, imaginatively, the play makes very tenuous the role of the shepherd's wife in nurturing Perdita; Hermione's place is to be left unfilled until the very end. And the shepherd's benevolence to Perdita seems to disappear when he sees that Florizel's father is angry about the apparently cross-class betrothal. He calls Perdita a "cursed wretch" (4.4.458); perhaps a relic of the belief in a curse on adoption and/or on bastards, a category in which he places Perdita. He plans to protect himself by telling Polixenes that Perdita is none of his "flesh and blood" (4.4.692). He shows the birth tokens he found with Perdita, and this fear-motivated virtual disowning brings about the happy ending, as Polixenes recognizes Perdita as Leontes's lost daughter and sends word to him. The shepherd, his son, Polixenes, Florizel and Perdita all meet at Leontes's court, and Leontes and Perdita, and eventually Hermione, are reunited.

Critics have seldom noted that in the report of the recognition between Perdita and her father we hear that Leontes "thanks the old shepherd, which stands by like a weather-bitten conduit of many king's reigns" (5.2.55–57), and that, after this depersonalizing image, there is a brief dialogue between the shepherd and his son after this scene, suggesting utopian possibilities of an extended cross-class family of biological and adoptive parents: the son says, "the King's son took me by the hand and call'd me brother; and then the two kings call'd my father brother; and then the Prince my brother and the Princess my sister called my father father; and so we wept" (5.2.141–45). But clearly Perdita has been restored to Leontes as *his* daughter, and in the next scene, as he discovers that his wife is still alive, Perdita's other family is lost from sight. The characterization of the old shepherd, at this point, is designed to reduce interest in him and to focus attention instead on the reunion of Leontes, Hermione and Perdita. Leontes is regenerated and his family reconstituted; when Hermione asks her daughter, "Where has thou been preserv'd? Where liv'd?" (5.3.124), the questions are generally taken as a sign of her love, but they can also be taken as questions whose answers would bring several different characters into the charmed circle of the family.

Heredity is dominant in these plays, but environment is not as weak an influence as generalizations sometimes assume. In *Pericles*, nature and nurture, one could infer, combine to contribute to Marina's superlative musical skills: Cleon teaches her, but when her achievements far surpass those of his daughter, one might remember that Thaisa's father, Simonides, had, after all, called Pericles "music's master" (2.5.30) and had said, "my ears were never better fed / With such delightful pleasing harmony" (27–28).[12] More importantly, one might read the supremacy of nature over nurture in the way Marina's goodness escapes the bad influence of Cleon and Dionyza, as well as in the way she shows the courage and patience that the nurse has told her her father exemplified, but one could also credit Lychorida's influence. None of these points is explicit — the spectators can analyze Marina's virtues and talents however they wish.

In the other two plays, characters are more emphatic on the issue. Belarius believes that his sons' true identity appears in their ambition and desire to fight. "How hard it is to hide the sparks of nature! . . . [T]heir thoughts do hit the roofs of palaces, and nature prompts them / In simple and low things to prince it much / Beyond the trick of others" (3.3.79, 83–86). As Susan Baker has noted, however, the fact that Belarius himself knows they are princes can be seen as influencing his upbringing of them, and so one can argue that it is he who so prompts them, not nature — just as one could argue that Lychorida's image of Pericles's courage is more important in influencing Marina's courage than her heredity.[13] Similarly, descriptions of Perdita by observers suggest that she is superior to her surroundings: Florizel's father, himself a king in disguise, says, "Nothing she does or seems / But smacks of something greater than herself, / Too noble for this place" (4.4.157–59), and Florizel himself tells an aristocratic friend, "She's as forward of her breeding as / She is i'th'rear 'our birth" (4.4.581–82). Baker has pointed out that the shepherd knows about her aristocratic birth because of the clothes and gold left with her, and though he has not told her, he might have influenced her by having higher expectations of her; nevertheless, although in other plays of Shakespeare it is clear that aristocratic heredity does not inevitably produce intelligence or moral nobility, the standard reading of this scene stresses the influence of Perdita's heredity over her environment.

Many other speeches in *Winter's Tale* explicitly emphasize heredity in commenting on physical resemblance — and while the issue of marital fidelity is in *Pandosto*, this emphasis on resemblance is not.[14] After Leontes is first reunited with Perdita, but before he knows that she is his daughter, he says that he thought of Hermione, "Even in these looks I made [admiring Perdita]" (5.1.228). When the old shepherd produces the tokens he found with the child, observers who describe the achieved certainty that the lost daughter has been found stress "the majesty of the creature, in resemblance of the mother" (5.2.36–37). In several other comments, Leontes makes father-child physical resemblance the test of a mother's fidelity to her husband. At the beginning, he is worried about whether his son looks enough like him to prove Hermione's faithfulness. "[T]hey say we are / Almost as like as eggs. Women say so, / That will say anything" (1.2.129–31). He greets Florizel for the first time by saying, "Your mother was most true to wedlock, Prince, / For she did print your royal father off, / Conceiving you" (5.1.124–26). Similarly, when Pericles is unknowingly reunited with his daughter, he comments on how similar she is to his wife: his daughter has "[m]y queen's square brows; / Her stature to an inch; as wandlike straight; / As silver-voic'd; her eyes as jewel-like / And cas'd as richly" (5.1.111–14), and he says he will believe her because "thou lookest / Like one I loved indeed" (127–28).

A textual emphasis on physical similarity has a complicated effect in the theater; Anne Barton remarked of Shakespeare's *Twelfth Night* that it would be an extremely rare theater company that would have two characters as similar as Viola and Sebastian are supposed to be; so, in many cases of family resemblance in these plays, the play's language is in tension with the stage picture in which the actors are not really identical.[15] Given this problem, it is interesting that Shakespeare sometimes added such emphasis on resemblance to his source. Perhaps the issue is analogous to how the Elizabethan audience reacted to boy actors as female characters: most of the time the audience would focus on the female characters; but some of them (most of the time) and most of them (some of the time), cued by textual self-consciousness, would see the actors more as boys than as women. The plays provide much material for reflections on family relationships as well as gender constructions. The audience, guided by the dialogue and the plot, will want Marina to look like Thaisa and will probably imagine that they look similar. Sometimes these mothers and daughters are doubled in performance, which means that the experience of the hereditary resemblance in the reunion scene between Pericles and Marina is less of an imaginative construction; but then the audience would still have to use their imagination about the similar appearance of the figure who is brought into the play to perform the mother in middle age.

One moment in *The Winter's Tale* particularly exemplifies the ideology of resemblance as a sign of family relationship: the moment when Paulina, to prove Hermione's faithfulness, enumerates all the details in the baby girl's face that are like Leontes's. When Paulina refers to the baby as having "the trick of's frown, his forehead, nay, the valley, / The pretty dimples of his chin and cheek, his smiles, / The very mould and frame of hand, nail, finger" (2.3.101–03), she is describing details that the audience must find impossible to see; indeed, most likely the baby would have been "played" by a doll, not a live baby at all. At the same time as it suggests the image of Leontes as an infant (there is no other passage I know of in Shakespeare where the "pretty dimples" of an adult male are mentioned), this passage evokes the still enduring tendency to *look for* details of resemblance between family members — and to imagine them into existence — especially in relation to babies. The question of whom the audience members would believe about the similarity between the baby and Leontes recalls the analogous uncertainty about whether to believe Gonzalo's description of the island at the beginning of *The Tempest*. Paulina may be credible in her description to the extent that she seems to be morally reliable in general; yet even in Jacobean times, it must have been obvious that, even if the baby were not as identical to Leontes as she claimed, it would not necessarily have meant that Leontes did not beget her. Some might well consider any exaggeration on Paulina's part to be justifiable as an attempt to save the baby and Hermione from Leontes's rage. This would then suggest how the desire to preserve a child may generate the ability to imagine resemblances between child and parents. Ultimately, Leontes's recognition of Perdita as his daughter takes place offstage, and, in the end, the play subordinates the question of whether Perdita looks like him: the emphasis on her resemblance to her mother, which has nothing to do with fidelity in marriage, testifies to the fact that Leontes has regained his belief in Hermione.

In all three plays, there is a complicated tension between recognition and lack of recognition of family members, which puts the audience at the edge of their seats waiting for signs of the characters' discoveries. When Pericles's ship accidentally arrives in the same city as the daughter he thinks is dead, she is sent for, with no knowledge of their relationship, in the hope that she will cheer him out of his paralyzing melancholy. The dejected Pericles, unresponsive to anyone else, resists speaking to her at first — perhaps even pushes her away — and then begins to talk to her slowly and with rather incoherent echoes of her words: "My fortunes — parentage — good parentage — / To equal mine" (5.1.100–01). After a few more questions, he says, "My dearest wife was like this maid, and such a one / My daughter might have been" (110–11). He asks questions about her origin and education, to which she replies enigmatically. When she says she thinks her story is too improbable to tell, he says, "I will believe thee, / . . . for thou lookest / Like one I loved indeed" (125, 127–28). But if he does guess who she is, he does not acknowledge it for many lines and many questions after this point. Even when she says, "My name is Marina" (145), when she reveals that she was born at sea and names her dead nurse, Lychorida, he cannot acknowledge that she is really his daughter.

At various places in this long dialogue, he wonders if she is flesh and blood or if this is a dream. When she finally identifies herself as daughter to King Pericles, he does not respond directly to her until he has consulted with Helicanus; then, finally, almost 100 lines after the first hint that he recognizes her, he welcomes her as "Thou that beget'st him that did thee beget" (5.1.200) and, even after that, wants confirmation about her mother's name. For the audience, his caution dramatizes not only his melancholy but also the importance of her return to him, on which the play focuses for this long poetic scene. As Pericles says, "truth can never be confirm'd enough" (206). The spectators know that his sense of Marina's similarity to his lost wife is indeed a true guide to her identity, but the plot, in a sense, stops to maintain suspense about whether he will trust this partial recognition and when the questions that he asks will lead him to security about it.[16]

No line in this scene hints at Marina's reaction to her discovery that Pericles is her father or describes her reunion with him. Instead, the scene is written to make us imagine his point of view much more than hers; critics seldom even discuss the question of when she recognizes him. Terence Cave argues that she "believes that she is healing a disturbed mind, so that his agitation as the truth gradually sinks in seems to her only a symptom of that disturbance."[17] This is the most likely interpretation, since she has not seen him since her infancy and asks him his name after he greets her as his daughter. On the other hand, I could imagine a Marina who has been told that this is Pericles and who deliberately takes her time in leading him to this recognition, who has a purpose in introducing herself by talking about her ancestry and the loss of her parents. This is not, after all, the inevitable way to assuage the grief of a melancholy stranger. She hints at the connections that Pericles will eventually trace out: "She speaks, / My lord, that, may be, hath endured a grief / Might equal yours [,] / . . . ancestors / Who stood equivalent with mighty kings" (5.1.89–91, 93–94). His echoes of her words, "My fortunes — parentage — good parentage — / To equal mine" (5.1.100–01), make his suggestion of their relationship more explicit than hers, though it takes him many lines to acknowledge it. These two different versions of Marina, ironically, might well appear the same on stage, for her consciousness is not explored in the dialogue as is Pericles's.

The final scene is particularly notable for the way in which the embraces of the family reunion are evoked in imagery that both emphasizes the familial physical connection and pictures family members as losing their identitites in each other. In the language of the scene, first Pericles disappears in Thaisa, then she disappears in him, and then Marina merges back into Thaisa, reversing Lychorida's early description of her as "this piece of your dead queen" (3.1.17–18):

> *Per.* You [the gods] shall do well
> That on the touching of her lips I may
> Melt and no more be seen. O come, be buried
> A second time within these arms!
> *Mar.* My heart
> Leaps to be gone into my mother's bosom.
>
> (5.3.42–46)

These images of death and disappearance in reunion reenact and reverse the earlier apparent deaths of Thaisa and Marina.[18] Pericles continues the physical imagery of family connection while returning all to visibility by saying, "Flesh of thy flesh,

Thaisa, / Thy burden at the sea, and call'd Marina / For she was yielded there" (47–49).[19]

This play began with a scene in which Pericles, in his first quest for a bride, discovers that the princess he seeks is living in incest with her father; the ending transforms this malignant mingling of identities in the family to a benign version. Physical ties are emphasized — flesh of flesh, heart and bosom, lips and arms. At the same time, the ending occurs in the temple of Diana. Both Marina and Thaisa are emphatically chaste, and the night oblations that Pericles promises to Diana in thanksgiving sound to at least one critic, Janet Adelman, like a disturbing attempt to erase sexuality from the reunited family.[20] Marina's ancestry is now confirmed as noble, and, accordingly, she is married to Lysimachus (who was impressed with her purity when they met in the brothel), but there is little emotional weight given to their relationship. The heart of the play is with the parent-child bond, emphasized as a bond of flesh and blood, and yet the parents and their daughter, Marina, are to be separated again at the end, when she and Lysimachus are to rule in Tyre, while Pericles and Thaisa are to go to her family home in Pentapolis. However joyful a parent-child reunion is, however long delayed, in this play it is still fragile. None of the other romances of family reunion is so emphatic that the family is again separated at the end. Perhaps this is another way to measure the strength of the threat of incest in *Pericles*.

The final scene of *Cymbeline* is extravagantly full of many different kinds of partial, incomplete recognitions. As Ann Thompson writes, this play allows "the audience to savour the recognitions and reversals at more than naturalistic length. . . . The pleasure we take . . . depends on our anticipation of the characters' pleasure."[21] But, she notes, precisely because there are so many reunions and recognitions in this scene, *Cymbeline*'s ending is in many ways funny. No matter how forceful the sense of some connection with another, characters often fail to recognize exactly what that connection is. Because there are so many characters to follow, the effect (in contrast to that in *Pericles*) is somewhat distancing.

When Guiderius and Arviragus, kidnapped since very early childhood, meet Imogen in her masculine disguise, all three at once feel a strong, though unclear, connection. Guiderius says that if Fidele (Imogen's name in her boy disguise) were a woman, he would woo her in marriage; Arviragus says, "I'll love him as my brother" (3.6.72), and Imogen, guessing better than the others, says to herself, "Would it had been so, that they / Had been my father's sons!" (76–77). In the last scene, Cymbeline is slow to recognize the children who have been separated from him, but he does have the excuse that his sons have been raised without knowledge of him, and his daughter is pretending to be a boy. Introduced to Imogen in her disguise by the Roman she has been serving as Fidele, he says, "I have surely seen him: / His favor is *familiar* to me. Boy, / Thou hast looked thyself into my grace / And art mine own" (5.5.93–96, emphasis mine; note the etymological connection between "familiar" and "family"). The play provides another example of mysterious affinity stemming from "blood." He goes on to emphasize that he is offering this page life and a boon not because of the pleas of Lucius but for some other, unexplained reason: "I know not why, wherefore, / To say 'Live, boy.' Ne'er thank thy master" (96–97).

However, family affinity does not by itself dispel confusion. Although Belarius and Arviragus do recognize the disguised boy Fidele as the same Fidele they thought was dead, they and their father don't recognize this page as Imogen until other characters guide them. The one character who does recognize Fidele as Imogen is not a relative of Imogen's but rather her servant Pisanio, who is, after all, the one who gave her the disguise to wear in the first place. After Posthumus strikes her, thinking she is an unrelated boy intruding on his grief for Imogen, Pisanio finally names her, and the revelation proceeds.

Belarius eventually confesses his kidnapping to Cymbeline. When he says, "First pay me for the nursing of thy sons" (5.5.324), he alludes to the practice of requiring the father of an exposed child to pay the expenses of the parents who had raised the child before returning him to the original family.[22] To prove that they are really the king's sons, he calls on such tokens as are found in many classical recognition stories. Arviragus, he says, was wrapped in a "curious mantle, wrought by th' hand / Of his queen mother" (363–64). Cymbeline remembers, "Guiderius had / Upon his neck a mole, a sanguine star" (365–66), and Belarius, the adoptive parent paying reverence to nature, says, "This is he, / Who hath upon him still that natural stamp. / It was wise nature's end in the donation / To be his evidence now" (367–70). Nevertheless, relations of adoption are given some tribute in the conclusion: Belarius's wrong in kidnapping the children is easily forgiven; Cymbeline says to him, "Thou art my brother" (401), and Imogen echoes, "you are my father too" (402). As in *Pericles*, the "blood" tie does not lead to clear recognitions without additional evidence, and the adoptive relations are not erased.

The recognition scenes of these plays in general tend to develop the perspective of the genetic fathers much more than the perspective of anyone else in the large family constellation. We see the anxieties of Pericles and Leontes, and we hear their joys. The fathers' words at recovering their daughters sometimes suggest an intensity of joy that brings them close to death — Cymbeline says, "If this be so, the gods do mean to strike me / To death with mortal joy" (5.5.236–37), and Pericles says to his friend Helicanus, "Give me a gash, put me to present pain; / Lest this great sea of joys rushing upon me / O'erbear the shores of my mortality, / And drown me with their sweetness" (5.1.196–99). These lines, suggestive of the characters' old age and evocative of Gloucester's death at Edgar's self-acknowledgment, have no parallel in the children's speeches. And while the plays do present the children as happy to be reunited with their parents, there is little attention to how Perdita, Guiderius and Arviragus feel about discovering a different set of parents or how they come to terms with those they earlier thought of as their only parents.[23] (In his rewritten last act of *Cymbeline,* George Bernard Shaw imagines that Guiderius would say, "We three are fullgrown men and perfect strangers. / Can I change fathers as I'd change my shirt?" — and then refuse to inherit the throne.) Nor are they much concerned with the feelings of the foster parents, though the foster fathers receive somewhat more attention than the foster mothers. With the exception of the shepherd's wife and Euriphile (significantly, both deceased), the foster mothers are characterized in a way congruent with the general cultural prejudice against stepmothers.[24] And although birthmothers are recovered in two of these plays, the final reunion is clearly seen from their husbands' point of view, not theirs.

Many of Shakespeare's plays can be discussed with reference to an absent mother. Romance is the genre in which he gives mothers, comparatively, the most attention, and an idealized image of motherhood is evoked most vividly in the return of Hermione in *The Winter's Tale.*[25] Her silence to Leontes may be, as Gail Paster suggests, a sign of her diminishment by patriarchal discipline (she would be justified in reproaching him, as she does at the beginning of the play for lesser faults); yet in her words of affection and attention to Perdita, suggesting that it is through concern for her daughter alone that she has preserved herself, she is the mother that any separated daughter would want.[26] The fact that Hermione speaks only to Perdita and, indeed, says that it was because of hope to see her daughter that she remained alive, appeals to the fantasy that any child might have — that she was the one her mother loved best after all.

The idealized birthmothers Hermione and Thaisa contrast sharply with the evil foster mothers, Dionyza and Cymbeline's nameless queen. While Stephen Collins relates the negative view of stepmothers in the Renaissance to a general misogyny, these plays show that misogyny could be part of a polarized view of women.[27] Hermione and Thaisa, in their returns, are as idealized as a dead or absent mother is likely to be by a child who lives with an unsatisfactory substitute. And, indeed, they are accompanied in the romances by a third idealized birth mother, appearing only in a dream vision, Posthumus's mother, who died at his birth.[28] Perhaps the point is to focus dramatic attention on the birth mother (recovered at the end of *Pericles* and *Winter's Tale*) by removing motherly competition from her. When women do foster maternally in Shakespeare, as Lychorida and Paulina do, they are no threat to the prerogatives of the birth mother — indeed, they present her or her memory to the daughter.

The recognition scenes of all these plays emphasize bodily connections in the family. Embraces are indicated by the characters' words. Refound characters are introduced to each other as "Flesh of thy flesh" (Pericles says this of Marina to Thaisa, 5.3.47) or "the issue of your loins . . . and blood of your begetting" (Belarius thus returns Cymbeline's sons, 5.5.332–33). The plays are full of the imagery of birth, pregnancy and conception, most often in literal references to characters' origins.[29] This imagery reinforces the plays' "mythology of blood" and their emphasis on biological relatedness. But it is often used metaphorically, and sometimes the point of the metaphor is to make the reunion of parents and children into a rebirth or a reconception. Pericles, seeing Marina, says, "I am great with woe, and shall deliver weeping" (5.1.109). Cymbeline, recognizing his sons upon Belarius's proof, says, "O, what am I / A mother to the birth of three? Ne'er mother / Rejoiced deliverance more" (5.5.370–72). And Pericles welcomes Marina as "Thou that beget'st him that did thee beget," using a word typically descriptive of male action to describe her generative power. These images stand out because of the intense moments in which they are uttered, but birth/

pregnancy imagery is also used at other times. Camillo alludes to folklore about pregnancy when he describes his desire to see "Sicilia" (a name that refers to both his king, Leontes, and his country) as "a woman's longing" (4.4.671), and Imogen describes her desire to see Posthumus by saying, "ne'er long'd my mother so / To see me first, as I have now" (3.4.2–3). Though good mothers here are largely absent or dead, imagery of biological maternity is frequent in the words of both male and female characters.[30] Concern with the link between generations is so strong that images of pregnancy and childbirth appear frequently partly because they are the most vivid way to picture that link: occasionally, images of begetting also occur. But the plays also show, and use for images, child rearing as well as child bearing. A memorable line when the young Pericles declares his love for Thaisa puts "fostering" and "blood" together and suggests fostering may be seen as just as basic:

> *Sim.* What, are you both pleased?
> *Thai.* Yes, if you love me, sir.
> *Per.* Even as my life my blood that fosters it. (2.5.88–90)

The family separations and reunions in Shakespeare's plays have many possible relations to early modern family psychology. They glamorize the shorter-term family separations common in his culture: the wet nursing of baby aristocrats, their later exchange between households to learn manners and bond dynasties, and the training of children of other classes for work are transformed into the more dramatic separations of abandoning, kidnapping and shipwrecking.[31] Gail Paster writes that Perdita's experience is "a version, romantically heightened, of what happened soon after birth to countless babies in the wet-nursing culture . . . [:] inexplicable extrusion from the birthing chamber, enforced alienation from the maternal breast, and a journey to the unknown rural environment of a foster family lower in station than its own. Even though the birth parents knew where they had placed their baby and occasionally visited it, the physical and social separation of the two environments was virtually as complete as it is here."[32] A similar analysis could be made, though with more qualifications, of Marina's, Guiderius's and Arviragus's experiences. These romance plots also provided a fantasy compensation for the more permanent separations caused by frequent mortality, which was much higher than ours for both parents and children, and highest, it seems, in London, where the plays were performed. At the beginning of the seventeenth century, the life expectancy at birth in London was only 22.3, and "by age 20, 47 percent of women born in London had suffered the death of their fathers."[33] Furthermore, infant and child death rates were, in general, high in early modern Europe. "An infant in the first four months of life had in general a 20 to 40 percent chance of dying before his or her first birthday. . . . [T]he chances of surviving to age 20 were in general no better than 50/50."[34]

Members of the original audiences in different family circumstances probably differed to some extent in their responses to these plays, just as members of the audience in different circumstances do today. Paster has argued, for example, that the emphasis on the difference in behavior between Perdita and her foster family and on characters' identification of her with nobility "offers a powerful counter-narrative for the specific fears and repressed anxieties of the wet-nursed child."[35] In the same way, the play could also soothe anxieties of parents of wet-nursed children. Similarly, the emphasis on resemblances between biological family members might have reinforced the sense of solidarity for parents of wet-nursed children and for those who had been wet-nursed in childhood, as well as for families involved in the exchange of children in fostering out.

On the other hand, what of the many audience members whose parents had died early and who had been raised by stepparents? How important was it to them to emphasize their connections with their deceased parents? How much did their stepparents take on parental roles in their imagination? The orphaned Posthumus, who has been raised by Cymbeline, is left without a household again when he is banished for marrying Imogen; in absence from her, his suspicion of women alienates him from her as well as the memory of his parents: "That most venerable man which I / did call my father was I know not where / when I was stamped" (2.5.3–5).[36] How much does this dramatize anxieties of the time? For some members of the audience, who could never hope for a reunion in life, Posthumus's dream vision of his family could have served as a reassurance of their continued connection with their family, but Posthumus's marriage to Imogen reconnects him with his foster father Cymbeline as well as with her.

Adults raised by stepparents could have enjoyed the wish-fulfillment of the reunions with birthparents presented in these plays, but they might also have drawn another kind of satisfaction — as could parents who were raising step-children — from the fact that actors seldom have as much similarity as the characters they are playing are supposed to have. The doubleness of effect — characters are biologically related, and the text tells us to see them as similar, actors are not related, and probably don't look very similar — is analogous to the doubleness in the meaning of family terms such as "father" and "mother" that stepfamilies and adoptees have to deal with.[37] In ordinary language today, the term "role" is used in connection with parenthood almost as much as it is used in relation to sex and gender. Is there a theatrical aspect to parenthood? Or is this usage a sign of inauthenticity? What are the strengths and limitations of the formulation "The real parents are those who act like parents"? Leontes does not act like a parent when he commands Perdita to be exposed; does Pericles, when he leaves Marina at Tharsus? For much of the rest of both plays, penance is the only form available to these fathers for acting like a parent, a role that Pericles has never played with his daughter until their reunion.

The plots of these plays — somewhat like contemporary

American adoption law — are largely structured to limit a family to one "real" set of parents, male and female, and the conclusion of *Pericles* — following the play in which the good foster parent, Lychorida, appears only briefly, and the wicked foster parents are more vivid — stays closest to this model. But knowing something about the frequent uses of wet nursing, fostering out and other varieties of child care beyond the nuclear family in Renaissance England may help to explain one of the most vexed aspects of this play: why is Pericles not only grief-stricken but virtually immobilized and apparently in need of prolonged penance after he hears about his daughter's death from Dionyza, since he acted in good faith when he believed that she and Cleon were responsible people?

With infant and child death rates so high, it may well be that parents whose children died while in someone else's house had a particularly complicated sense of self-blame. They were following the accepted pattern in their society, but was that why their child had died? Within England, Gottlieb notes, while wet nursing was often criticized, sending children away when young was not openly questioned, but at least one Italian observer felt that this showed "the want of affection in the English."[38] Pericles, concerned about returning to Tyre in time to get its crown, assumes that he must give Marina to others to raise in their home instead of taking her and Lychorida or another nurse with him. The years he stays away pass quickly in Gower's act 4 chorus; perhaps those whose children had died (or who feared their children might) while away from them had particular reasons for interest in his story. Both the death of children and their boarding out might have been especially frequent in 1608–1609, the probably first year of *Pericles*'s performance; plague closed the theaters part of that time.[39] Perhaps it was because the occasion for disaster seemed such ordinary behavior — rather than the insane jealousy of Leontes, for example — that *Pericles* was one of the most popular of Shakespeare's plays in its day.[40]

9 • Profitable Children

Children as Commodities in Early Modern England

Claire M. Busse

> A great deal of capital, which appears today in the United States without any birth-certificate, was yesterday, in England, the capitalized blood of children.
>
> — Karl Marx

Commenting on the drastic shifts in the enforcement of morality in Vienna, Pompey, servant to a bawd and rampant rogue in Shakespeare's *Measure for Measure*, asserts: "'Twas never merry world since of two usuries the merriest was put down and the worser allow'd by order of law" (3.2.5–7).[1] To the twentieth century reader, Pompey's comments about two usuries may at first appear cryptic — after all, how many types of usury can there be? And, what exactly is the "merriest" form of usury to which Pompey refers? Editorial notes in the Riverside and Norton Shakespeares provide some helpful hints, the usury "allowed by order of law" is financial usury, or in layman's terms, moneylending at interest. The "merriest" form of usury is either "fornication" (Riverside) or "prostitution" (Norton).[2] While the analogy between prostitution and usury makes some sense in that both are economic practices considered morally questionable, the links between usury and fornication are less obvious. However, for at least one writer, the sixteenth century definition of usury contains a surprising amount of flexibility. Indeed, in a 1591 treatise usury is described as an empty signifier that can be employed to address any subject: "If it be Usury to take any thing more than the principal, who is not a Usurer? . . . for Usury extends not only to money, but also to meat, or any thing that is put forth?"[3] All individuals participating in various types of exchanges can be identified as usurers; all they need is something to put forth which functions in excess of direct exchange.

Yet, what is the thing put forth for notions of fornication? And, what is the excess that can mark fornicators as usurers? There can only be one answer: children. After all, the only *thing* possible as the material signifier in excess of sexual exchange is the progeny that can result from sexual relations. Indeed, connections between children, sexual relations and economic transactions have been considered significant enough to be addressed in introductory material found within a major edition of Shakespeare's works. In his introduction to *The Sonnets* in *The Norton Shakespeare*, Walter Cohen posits that textual links between beauty and usury in Shakespeare's *Sonnets* present usury "as the economic equivalent of human reproduction" with the child functioning as the material gain of sexual transactions.[4] In focusing on the child as the primary material result of sexual transactions I do not mean to appear puritanical in my failure to acknowledge the exchange of pleasure that is also implicitly at stake. Rather, I am interested in the necessity of *thing* for understanding exchanges figured as usury: a *thing* which indicates a material gain. An emphasis on material indicators of sexual encounters appears at the very heart of *Measure for Measure*; while the laws of Vienna attempt to limit sexual pleasures, they are only effective when material evidence, such as a child (or the money that changes hands in cases of prostitution), reveals the transaction.

The early modern association of children and usury arises from a tradition that can be traced back to Aristotelian conceptions of usury as a form of unnatural reproduction.[5] In a discussion of household governance that appears in book 1 of *The Politics*, Aristotle delineates acceptable and unacceptable means of gathering wealth to manage the household. Acquisition as preparation for future needs is acceptable, accumulation of wealth without limits is not. Usury is "the most hated sort" of such accumulations, Aristotle offers, for it "makes a gain out of money itself, and not from the natural object of it. For money was intended to be used in exchange, but not to increase at interest. And this term interest, which means the birth of money from money, is applied to the breeding of money because the offspring resembles the parent." Aristotle's depiction of usury as a form of monetary reproduction is later employed by Aquinas who, in justifying the prohibition of usury, argues that money can only "reproduce naturally" through exchange. The distinctions drawn by Aristotle and Aquinas between what is natural and unnatural provide an interesting dilemma: for that which is considered unnatural is nevertheless possible. Just as illicit human relationships can result in children, so can illicit monetary transactions result in profit. Ann Louise Kibbie qualifies this by offering that "the argument against usury in the *Politics* revolves not around the natural sterility of money but rather around its threatening capacity to reproduce itself from itself" in an "incestuous" form of increase. Usury is an illicit and problematic transaction which is, nevertheless, possible. The impact of this classical and religious tradition against the practice of usury on an early modern society increasingly dependent on interest meant that, according to E. Pearlman, the "idea that usury is unnatural was deeply imbedded in Elizabethan awareness."[6]

Shakespeare was not the first early modern author to invoke the Aristotelian links between children and usury. On the contrary, he was only one of a number of authors who depicted a quality of early modern childhood that has often been overlooked by twentieth century critics, the notion of a child's status as a thing which held economic value. Yet despite recognition of the material value of England's youth in works that range from representations of children as exchangeable goods in John Lyly's plays, to the attempts of treatise writers John Stockwood, Charles Gibbon and Henry Smith to interrogate designations of children as properties, to Shakespeare's metaphorical figurations in the sonnets, such acknowledgment did not necessarily signify acceptance.[7] Many of these authors found themselves grappling with inconsistencies caused by the clash of what were considered traditional definitions of children as parental property with emerging conceptions of an individual's moral agency and independent choice. Late sixteenth century writers questioned whether children should hold positions within the family that were either autonomous or economically determined. When traditional definitions of children as their parents' possessions began to conflict with more modern concerns about moral responsibility, writers were forced to reconsider the position of the child within the family and to consider the following questions: If children are fundamentally property, can they possess free will?[8] And, if children indeed have free will, must they obey their parents to the extent that they function as their property? I wish to argue that the writers of the late sixteenth century began to dispute cultural perceptions of children as commodities and exchangeable property. Such challenges, however, ultimately proved futile. Despite these authors' attempts to imagine possible scenarios where children were not commodities, the economic realities of the late sixteenth century forced them to identify such scenarios as fictions and fantasies.

While Stockwood, Gibbon, Smith and Lyly limited their

discussions primarily to consideration of *parental* commodification of children, they could not isolate notions of the youths within the family from the greater economic status of other juveniles such as wards, orphans, apprentices and vagrants. For children were frequently moving outside of familial boundaries to participate in the larger social milieu. Any reconsideration of the child's role in the family would have implications for early modern English society as a whole. Redefinition of children's status would force a reexamination of well-established institutions that relied upon the mandatory labor of child servants and apprentices.

The link between children and the profits of usury highlights the very uncertainty caused by the material values inscribed upon children. More than other types of exchange or monetary transactions, usury posed a particular moral dilemma for sixteenth century Englishmen. The practice which had once been abhorred as corrupt and immoral was becoming more necessary in an economy increasingly reliant on financial transactions that did not involve the direct exchange of goods. Consequently, throughout the late sixteenth and early seventeenth centuries, restrictions on usurious practices were reconsidered, forcing early modern Parliaments to find a balance between upholding moral laws and addressing increasing economic needs. Interestingly, one of the most difficult "moral" issues faced by Parliament arose from the conflict between idealistic laws prohibiting usury and the usurious practices considered necessary to support the City of London's orphans. Indeed, the Usury Act of 1552 and those that followed had to be amended to allow the transactions deemed necessary for the support of orphans.[9]

Concepts of children and usury, then, as disparate as they may seem, occupied analogous positions in early modern English logic, for both invoked images of profitable yet questionable economic practices. Not surprisingly, early modern texts that connect usury and childhood also consider issues of salvation and damnation. For instance, as the central and pivotal question of the "five profitable and pithy questions" debated in Charles Gibbon's 1591 treatise *A Work Worth the Reading*, the concern "Whether a reasonable allowance may be taken for lending of money" moves the reader from consideration of child-centered debates of "Whether the Election of Parents is to be preferred before the affection of their Children in Marriage," and "Whether the Father may lawfully disinherit his first born," to the more spiritual discussions of "Whether the Rich or Poor are to be accounted most blessed," and "Whether there be degrees of glory in heaven, or difference of pains in hell." The rhetorical structure of the treatise suggests a connection between usury and children: from children one moves to usury and from usury to discussions of salvation in relation to wealth.

Henry Smith's amalgamation of treatises, sermons and prayers, *A Preparative to Mariage. The summe whereof was spoken at a contract, and inlarged after. Whereunto is annexed a Treatise of the Lord's Supper: and another of Usurie*, printed in 1591 (the same year as Gibbon's *Work*), reveals further links between children and usury in terms of morality.[10] Smith's discussions of children and usury present logics that are strikingly similar to each other. In the "Preparative," Smith warns parents to be careful not to overvalue their children for fear of offending God: "before we teach parents to love their children, they had need be taught not to love them too much . . . for the giver is offended when the gift is more esteemed then he" (77). Overinvestment in the gift of children is an insult which may anger the giver, God. Similarly, usury is defined as a "sin" that places love of money before love of God: "Usury is the sin which God will try now whether you love better than his word: that is, whether you will leave it if he forbid it, for if he flatly forbid it, and yet you willfully retain it, then you love Usury better than God's word" (198). Usury and parent-child relations are similar concerns in that both can lead one to hoard one's love from God.

Profits from the Past

The family may have been where the debate about commodifications of children found the most expression; however, in order to understand the concerns underlying the debate we must look outside of the family to the place of children in society. The family was a space where discussions of parental concern and affection often obfuscated the pecuniary issues involved. Rather than immediately turning to family structures to explain the context of debates about children's status within the family, then, I will first turn outward to examine children's status independent of (and in circumstances external to) familial structures. While the family was one space or "market" in which children functioned as economic resources in the late sixteenth century, it was a peculiar and distinct microcosm of a social system of child commodification. Removed from the more affective relationships of the family, the child becomes more openly a valuable *thing* to be exchanged and profited from. Children were, in short, economically essential to early modern England's society. A significant portion of the English workforce was composed of children who worked as apprentices, servants and farm laborers.[11] Children were also a major source of revenue for several state and city institutions. The Court of Wards was authorized to sell an orphan's wardship, while London's Court of Orphans, run by city leaders, took advantage of its controls and (temporarily) pooled orphans' monies into London's city coffers.[12] These institutions, it should be noted, were not new to the late sixteenth century; rather, they had been in place for years, and in some cases centuries. Profiting from children had become a tradition, accepted and rarely questioned — at least until the late sixteenth century.

In the Royal Court of Wards, and the urban Courts of Orphans, individuals and local governments profited from children who openly functioned as commodities and sources of revenue. The Court of Wards officially placed funds acquired from the sale of the wardship into the queen's coffers while providing the orphan with a stable guardian. Unofficially, the Court of Wards secured a living for a number of men involved in the "speculative market" of buying and selling wardships (Pinchbeck and Hewitt, *Children*, 60–61). Parentless children of the gentry became valuable properties with "guardians" who often functioned as much as the minors' realtors (selling rights to possession and marriage of the children) as their surrogate parents. Although London's Court of Orphans eliminated the market aspect of the Royal Wards, it did not completely eliminate the economic benefits that could be gained from children. Town orphans were placed under the control of London's Court of Orphans where, in most circumstances, their inheritance would be placed in the City Treasury to be "protected" and returned to the children when they reached their majority or married.[13] The court then appointed guardians who received expenses for the upbringing of the wards but did not have control of the ward's estate (80). While the child's body did not readily function as a commodity on the open market, the money entailed in a wardship was essential for borough governments. The orphans' fund (the largest of the funds in the "floating balances" of the City of London's treasury) provided a means for the city to pay off other debts and mask financial difficulties, at times depleting resources necessary to provide the children's inheritances when they came of age (which complicated Parliament's attempts to prohibit usury) (81). The city may not have openly traded its children for profit, but it was taking advantage of its power over their bodies and their possessions.

Such uses of the child for profit were matched by written sixteenth century legislation regulating the employment of children, such as the 1563 Statute of Artificers and poor laws enacted in 1535, 1547, 1549, 1572, 1576 and 1597, which upheld the child's status as property. Those laws varied in their severity, ranging from attempts to provide employment to poor children who were considered "needy" to punishment of vagabond children. While the laws were framed as attempts to improve the lot of young workers while preserving social order by "banishing idleness" and "advancing husbandry," they also denied these young workers any choice in the terms of their employment. Early modern children, in short, had no power to protest mandatory employment. And while they might be paid a fair wage they also became a part of their masters' holdings.

Poor Laws enacted throughout the sixteenth century, which simultaneously worked to aid the plight of poor children and orphans by placing them in apprenticeships and service positions and to punish children who resisted such employment, most clearly reveal instances where we can see children as possessions.[14] For while the poor laws of the 1530s mandated a forced apprenticeship for idle and begging children, the Act of 1547 took this forced labor to its logical conclusion. Vagabond children who ran away from their apprenticeship more than once were to become "slaves" throughout their childhood. The act states: "It shall be lawful for every such master to take the said child again and to keep and punish the said child in chains or otherwise, And use him or her as his Slave in all points for the time before rehearsed of the age of such child that is to say 'till twenty the woman child and the man child twenty-four."[15] The enslavement of children was to last for the time of the apprenticeship. Yet in many ways it was no different from forcible apprenticeship. In fact, the master of an apprentice had the same powers over the child that the master would have over a slave: "Any master either of the men or of the women so adjudged Slaves *or of the children adjudged apprentice or servant* may let set forth sell bequeath or give the service and labour of such Slaves or Servants so adjudged as it is aforesaid to any person or persons to whom so ever he will . . . after such like sort and manner as he may do of any other his movable goods or Cattle" (1 Edward VI c. 3; my emphasis). While adult *slaves* could be sold as if they were "movable goods or Cattle" *all* children who were forcibly apprenticed could function as such goods. As slaves or as servants they could be sold or traded along with the rest of their master's possessions (Pinchbeck and Hewitt, *Children*, 96). That commodification of children was substantiated by a later clause in the act, which legislated that parents who attempted to take their child from their apprenticeship could actually be prosecuted for theft. While its effects were more or less temporary, the Act of 1547 revealed the material realities behind children's apprenticeships. It openly established that children were indeed property in that they essentially belonged to their masters, and commodities in that their master had the right to exchange them as he wished.

This open assertion that children were guaranteed possessions and able to be sold was quickly revised in later legislation that moved away from the severity of these laws. Enforced slavery was revoked in the Act of 1549, which removed the clauses concerning slavery from the punishments for runaway apprentices with no explanation for this removal. The repeal of the law occurs in a small section buried in the middle of the act with no apparent indication of the motivations or legal reasoning for this repeal: "And be it further enacted by the the authority aforesaid, that all and every Statute and Act of Parliament, made for punishment of vagabond slaves aged or impotent parsons or any of them . . . shall be from henceforth utterly void repealed and of none effect of force" (3 and 4 Edward VI c. 16). Suggesting that popular reaction against the severity of the law may have worked to undermine the policy of forcible slavery, Pinchbeck and Hewitt provide the rather ambiguous explanation that "this ferocious legislation defeated its own ends and was withdrawn two years later. . . . Compulsory apprenticeship continued, but the taint of slavery was removed" (96). I argue, however, that the law could be easily repealed because, at least in the case of children, it was entirely unnecessary.

The repeal of this law made little difference for children since the system of apprenticeship in which these children were placed had already defined them as the possessions of their respective employers. With permission of the guild involved, apprenticeships could be sold if the master chose (Pinchbeck and Hewitt, *Children*, 228). Since the Act of 1549 did not change its call for mandatory apprenticeship, there was no need for a slavery clause to commodify children. Later laws, such as the 1563 Statute of Artificers, reconfirmed the ideological connection of children and commodities. The Statute of Artificers mandated apprenticeship for all youths between the ages of 12 and 30 who were not already employed or were in a class status that placed them outside of these regulations. The reality of this legislation was that while apprentices were workers, their labor was a commodity owned by their masters.

Enforced or not, these laws and their prescriptions about childhood served as a basis for determining the status of children in early modern society. While examination of the rhetoric of these laws can lead to claims that the laws disempowered children, such analysis does not address recent historical claims, such as Ilana Krausman Ben-Amos's, which indicate that, in many cases, children were very much involved in arranging the terms and conditions of their apprenticeship. Yet despite such indications that children did hold some autonomy in determining their futures and presents, sixteenth century authors of laws, treatises and plays continued rhetorically to construct and thus define children as commodities. Whatever the particular realities of orphans, wards, vagrant children and apprentices, designations of children as property were considered significant enough by treatise writers and authors throughout the late sixteenth and early seventeenth centuries to be questioned and challenged, not only in the public realms of local and royal governments, but also in the more privatized realms of the family.

Good or Goods?

Complications with conceptions of children as disposable goods arose even in arguments advocating these conceptions. For instance, in the 1591 treatise, *A Bartholomew Fairing for Parentes*, John Stockwood describes children as belongings in order to explain why they could not marry without their parents' consent. In a moment of wishful thinking, Stockwood imagines this to be an easy solution to the problem of rebellious children. Since children are their parents' property, he argues, they are not individuals who can use their free will to rebel. "Children," Stockwood avows, "are worthily to be reckoned among the goods and substance of their fathers." Therefore, Stockwood continues, it "stands with great reason, that the owner dispose of the goods, and not contrariwise the goods of the owner, which were indeed a thing very absurd or contrary to all reason."[16] That is to say, it would be absurd for children, as property, to disobey their parent-owners.

Despite the backdrop of laws and institutions supporting definitions of children as possessions, Stockwood's argument does not work and even Stockwood knows this. Children might be considered a part of their parents' estate, but, unlike the rest of their parents' assets, they have agency. While the idea of an article of clothing or a section of land rejecting its owner and choosing its own fate does seem absurd, the analogy cannot effectively extend to human beings. A child who decides to reject his or her parents may be rebelling against the conventions of social practice, but would not necessarily be acting "contrary to *all* reason." Even as he advocates children's status as property, Stockwood seemingly was unable to deny the instability of his assertion, implicitly acknowledging that children do have agency in his later suggestion that, as "their father's riches," children "must not bestow themselves but must be bestowed of their parents, whose goods they are" (23). Stockwood, it becomes clear, finds himself with no choice but to address these children and command them to allow themselves to be "bestowed" by their parents. His charge that children "must not bestow themselves" affirms the very thing Stockwood once hoped to deny: children *do* have agency and must be *convinced* to follow their parents' wishes.

Stockwood's dilemma emphasizes the fact that, despite traditional and contemporary assertions that children could — or should — be perceived as property, there were increasing difficulties in arguing for these beliefs. Issues concerning children's agency became more problematic to writers such as Stockwood and Charles Gibbon as they were forced to accommodate criticisms that parents were increasingly perceived to be profiting from their children, much to the moral and social detriment of the children. The issue came to a head for both Stockwood and Gibbon in discussions of marriage as the writers attempted to resolve the question: can children choose their own marriage partners, or are they obliged to follow their parents' wishes? The answers to that question varied from firm support of parental authority to ambivalence, with Stockwood determining that children must obey their parents and Gibbon presenting arguments for and against the commodification of children. Yet despite differences in content, Stockwood and Gibbon's arguments are similar in their inability to advocate the position that children must obey their parents because they are their parents' property.

In *A Bartholomew Fairing*, John Stockwood attempts to perpetuate what he perceives as traditional relationships between parents and children. Claiming that children "must to their very utmost seek to make them recompense and requital of some part of those unrequitable pains the which their loving parents have taken with them, and make some amends for the unconterveraillable kindness that they have showed towards them," Stockwood thus establishes the parent-child relationship as one of exchange: Parents give their children love and kindness; children repay and return this love through their obedience (27). Stockwood's argument, however, is riddled with contradictions. Drawing upon historical and religious traditions that classify children as property, Stockwood asserts that children were morally obligated to obey their parents and that children, as their parents' possessions, had no legitimate power to disobey their parents.

Additionally, Stockwood's discussion was limited by his claims that children, as property, should be denied the ability to choose their marriage partners. If children are indeed a part of their parents' estates, Stockwood asserts, then they should behave like controllable property. Children's refusal to accede to their parents' wishes, he determines, is more than bad behavior, it is practically unthinkable: "in seeking to betroth themselves at their own pleasures, not regarding to have the good will and leave of their parents, [children] deal, as preposterously, and overthwartly, as if the goods should go about to dispose the owner and possessor of the same, and not be disposed and ordered by those unto whom the possession and property of the same does by right and equity belong and appertain" (22). Children, as the "possession and property" of their parents, are to be disposed of according to the desires of their parents to whom they belong "by right."

The tradition Stockwood invokes in order to support his claim that children are their parents' property proves to be outmoded — or so the early modern printer of his treatise suggests in a peculiar marginal gloss which appears to undermine one of Stockwood's strongest statements: "By right," Stockwood asserts, children are the "goods" of their parents. Interestingly, Stockwood avoids directly referring to more recent English laws in which children were determined to be property that could be bought and sold. Rather, he points to extreme, and perhaps questionable, examples from cultures far removed from his present-day England. The "right" that Stockwood invokes to justify this claim is a product of a brutal past that, while not disturbing to Stockwood, does disturb the printer of his tract. Citing Mosaic and Roman law, Stockwood attempts to establish that children are the property of their parents and thus can be disposed of in cases of necessity. Children's status as goods was established by: "the great sovereignty, rule & power that by the law of Moses was given unto the Jewish fathers over their children, and by the ordinances of the Romans to the parents over their sons and daughters, by virtue *whereof the one in cases of necessity might sell their children for bondslaves to relieve themselves, and the other might kill them in revenge of their own private injuries done unto themselves or public enormities offered unto others*" (my emphasis). The brutal nature of this claim that parents have the right, under certain conditions, not only to sell, but to kill their children does not go unnoticed. The marginal gloss, most likely added by a concerned printer, attempts to soften the impact of Stockwood's argument. The commentary adds the provision that this custom is "not simply to be allowed" but is being used "to prove their [parents'] sovereignty in other matters" (21). In a possible attempt to undermine Stockwood's arguments, the author of the marginal gloss suggests that the past, in which children could be freely sold by their parents, was only to be used as an extreme foil against which the present rights of parents should be compared, not as a justification for the commodification of children.

While Stockwood does not modify his stance on the commodification of children, he is forced to acknowledge the problems that arise when this theory is put into practice. Since successful marriages depended upon reasonable decisions made by the parents, he argues, parents should not bargain away their children's futures for greed. Unfortunately, some early modern parents were doing just this. Recognizing that his contemporaries were guilty of reasoning that "if they [prospective mates for their children] be rich enough, they be both fair, well favoured, yea and also godly and virtuous enough," Stockwood amends his policy, recommending that parents, when arranging marriages, should "be free from all sinister and corrupt affection, and . . . for lucre and covetousness . . . seek not to thrust such matches upon their children, as they cannot brook, nor like well of" (80–81). It is the parents' responsibility to be reasonable in determining their children's future, he asserts. Unfortunately, as he points out, parents were not fulfilling their duties.

Stockwood attempts to resolve the problem of materialistic parents with the qualification that though children were commodities, they were not commodities that should be sold on an open, unregulated market. Unable to disregard the apparent greed of his peers completely, Stockwood suggests that, when necessary, there should be social controls to regulate the exchange of children. If a child objected to a marriage prompted by his or her parent's greed, then the case could be taken to the "sovereign authority" of the "goodly magistrate" (81). Yet, Stockwood is forced to acknowledge, there are limitations to this solution; for it is ultimately impossible to guarantee this type of state intervention in all cases.

Stockwood's argument is further troubled by other inconsistencies as well. When Stockwood suggests that disobedient children will be punished for breaking God's commandment to honor their father and mother, he is, at the same time, forced to admit that many of the parents he writes of had disobeyed their parents by arranging their own marriages. Interestingly, even Stockwood seems unconvinced by his response to this problem: these people may seem secure for the moment but eventually they will "go unto the Devil" for their sins (82–83). Even this threat, however, does not seem to be convincing enough for Stockwood (and his imagined readers). Rather than concluding his discussion with this damning statement, Stockwood proceeds to offer a more immediately threatening response to the issue by once again returning to the original assertion that children are to be treated as the goods of their parents. Stockwood asks his readers whether it is "not theft to steal away men's children by enticing them unto marriage?" (89). He proposes, in a more brutal extension of the biblical tradition of "an eye for an eye" that if one is punished for stealing property from a man, then this theft of property deserves a punishment that fits the crime. This "notorious kind of shameless thievery," Stockwood announces, "doth far better deserve to be punished with death" (88). The immediate threat of physical retribution for an economic crime by man on earth is invoked to replace the threat of God's punishment in heaven and perceived as a more persuasive deterrent.

Despite the problems inherent to his argument, Stockwood seems to perceive the designation of children as property to be the most effective support for his position that children must obey their parents' decisions in choosing a marriage partner. In Stockwood's logic, an argument based on property takes precedence over morally based arguments which suggest that children must obey their parents because God has ordained it. Certainly, fear of God's law may have been recognized as a powerful motivation for obedience, but it was, at least for Stockwood, not as seemingly persuasive as economic examples. Whether Stockwood found these economic persuasions to be more convincing than morally based arguments, or whether he was convinced that they would be more persuasive for his readership is unclear. However, it is clear that Stockwood posited the strength of his argument in his invocation of economic examples. Not only did he give precedence in his treatise to persuasions based on images of the market, he also names it after one of the most important markets of the sixteenth century, *Bartholomew Fair*. Worried that his treatise on parental control of marriageable children — although useful for "the Church and commonwealth . . . and many private families" — might not be a bestseller, Stockwood spiced up his title, admitting to his readers that he had used the title "A Bartholomew Fairing for Parents" in hopes of enticing a readership through the promise of a "Bartholomew

Fairing," a souvenir brought back from the ever-decadent and exciting fair ("Epistle Dedicatorie"). Once again disclosing the limitations of his argument, Stockwood admits to utilizing this shrewd marketing technique to ensure that, even if his argument is found to be unconvincing, his treatise will nevertheless be sold.

Stockwood's contemporary, Charles Gibbon, on the other hand, suggested that arguments like Stockwood's, as enticing as they might be, created more problems than they resolved. Rather than determining whether children were property, Gibbon concerned himself with the moral implications of determinations of children as property: Could the child-property be held responsible for his or her actions? Gibbon considered these issues in *A Work Worth the Reading*, a dialogue published in 1591 (two years after Stockwood's treatise) in which five "profitable and pithy questions," including "Whether the Election of Parents is to be preferred before the affection of their Children in Marriage," are debated by the fictional "lovers of learning," Tychicus and Philogus.[17] In the treatise the character Tychicus argues a position similar to that argued by Stockwood: children are their parents' goods and thus should obey their parents. Philogus, on the other hand, challenges the definition of children as property, arguing instead that children are consumers within the marriage market and are morally obligated to consume wisely, even if it means disobeying their parents in order to avoid immoral marriages (13–14). Through this dialogue, Gibbon places a discussion of the market at the center of his debate by shifting its terms from a discussion of whether children are moral agents or property to a consideration of the morality of exchanges within the marriage market, and the morality of the market itself.

Although Gibbon never directly links his treatise to Stockwood's, it seems likely that Tychicus's arguments in the marriage section of the tract were modeled on Stockwood's treatise.

For Tychicus rearticulates Stockwood's argument that children are in fact their parents' goods — if not to be sold, to be "bestowed." Tychicus thus asserts: "If a man may give his goods to whom he will, he may as well bestow his children where he think best, for Children are the goods of the Parents . . . If you look into the old law, you shall find that Parents might sell their Children to supply their necessity" (7). Like Stockwood, Tychicus points to an ancient law that lays the groundwork for parental control of children. Yet, unlike Stockwood, Tychicus distances himself from the past in which these traditions originated. Like the printer of Stockwood's text, Tychicus suggests that these laws should be used, not as guidelines to follow, but as justifications for the less extreme actions of the present. Marriage transactions are something akin to, but not the same as, the sale of property: "Therefore if Parents had this great privilege then (which is almost importable) why should they be barred of this benefit now, not in selling them but in bestowing them (which is so reasonable)" (8). Perhaps what is most interesting about Tychicus's statement is the implicit suggestion that the "selling" of children is "unreasonable" while the "bestowing" of children is not. Tychicus labels children as property, yet in this case they are possessions which may be distributed but never sold.

Through Gibbon's representation of Tychicus, readers become unable to overlook the flaws of the system Tychicus supports, for Tychicus acknowledges that profit is the force controlling contemporary marriage arrangements. Marriages are being arranged for material reasons which are, at times, immoral both in their inception and their consequences: "And yet is nothing respected in these days, for in marriages amongst us, we make no regard of godliness, but goods, of righteousness, but riches, how well, but how wealthy, they be made: be he Atheist, be he Papist, be he Neuter, we respect not the man, but his money, not his life, but his living, not his profession, but his promotion" (12). Parents, Tychicus recognizes, are greedily arranging marriages irrespective of religion — essentially condemning their children to marriages with "idolators." As in Stockwood, market forces prevail over fear of God.

Despite the presence of such immoral practices, Tychicus, unwilling to compromise his position, asserts that the maintenance of social hierarchies (father above child) is more important than attempts to challenge the pervasive greed that motivates marriage negotiations. Tychicus argues that this desire for "goods" rather than "goodliness" is an "idolatry" that pervades his society, and is thus inescapable (12). It is not surprising, therefore, that marriages are being fashioned as *exchanges* in which the children are like goods. Since marriages are no longer based on a foundation of explicit moral considerations, there is no moral reason for children to rebel. Instead, Tychicus places the burden of moral responsibility on the parents. He asserts that the "fatherly . . . property of parents" is to "bestow [the children], not as they desire, without discretions, but as is most expedient: with circumspection" (9). Parents must submit their self-interest to what is morally "circumspect," not what is economically advantageous. If society is to be reformed, Tychicus posits, the reform should not happen at the expense of familial hierarchies. Children should not respond in kind to their parents' actions: "that parents be sometime perverse, shall children be pernicious, or (as we commonly say) drive out one nail with another?" (10).

Tychicus's opponent Philogus, on the other hand, questions the designation of children as property. Through Philogus, Gibbon offers an argument that acknowledges that marriage may duly be considered a type of market but asserts that children are not the passive items of exchange, but active consumers who must "make their own bargain": "Marriage is of great moment, not for a month but a whole life time, there is no reason, but he or she that enters into that bond, should make their own bargain: because it is they that must abide by it" (7). Rather than denying or concealing the images and characteristics of the market that underlie marriage negotiations, Philogus confirms them in order to redefine children as the consumers in these markets. Since the children, not the parents, must live with their marriages, they should choose their partner. Like the customer buying shoes, it is important that the child finds the right "fit" in a marriage partner: "She that matches her self after anothers mind, is like him that fits his foot by anothers last: one is often wrong with his shoes in the wearing, the other often vexed with her husband after wedding" (5). The parents may be responsible for providing proper matches for their children, Philogus notes, but more importantly, the children hold the responsibility for assessing the propriety of these matches.

By stipulating that children are consumers and not goods, Philogus endows children with agency. And with this agency, children become morally culpable. While parents "have government of [children's] bodies," they are overruled by "our celestial Father, which preserves both body and soul, and is able to cast them (the children) into hell fire" if they participate in immoral actions, such as immoral marriages (13). Children can rebel in these situations and stay "within the bounds of obedience" because the rebellion is done, not in "contempt of . . . parents, but in regard of God's glory to avoid the occasion of evil" (14). By shifting the terms of the debate and making God the final authority, Philogus creates a space in which children can rebel without undermining social hierarchies.

Through this redefinition of the child as commodity to the child as consumer, Gibbon's Philogus shifts the debate from discussion of traditional hierarchies to one of contemporary markets and contemporary notions of property. For Philogus, the problems between parents and children present themselves as a microcosm which is indicative of a larger problem in society — the importance given to the possession of goods. In the opening speech of the treatise Philogus cites "an old verse which retains his old virtue being as credible for antiquity as truth":

> When Adam dig'd and Eve span
> who was then a Gentleman?
> Then came a rich churl and gathered good,
> and so came in the gentle blood.
>
> (1)

Philogus begins his argument by undermining the importance of class and possessions. Yet although he begins the treatise by asserting that gentility is arbitrarily based on ownership of goods, he subsequently undermines the legitimacy of any possession of property: "Goods are the gift of God, and he hath appointed us, not to do as we list with them, like Lords, but to dispose them well, as his Stewards" (24).[18] This fundamental denial of proprietary rights nullifies the legitimacy of parents' demands that children, as property, must obey.

So which argument did Gibbon ultimately support? It is difficult to tell, for while Gibbon assigns the first word in this debate to Philogus, he gives the last to Tychicus. Yet in doing this, he chooses not to present Tychicus as solidifying his position. While the reader might expect Tychicus to use this moment to respond to and refute Philogus's final support for his claims that children should not be forced to follow their parent's wishes — delivered through the example of a bad marriage caused by a young girl being forced to marry a wealthy old man — Tychicus instead fails to address the concerns raised by Philogus. Rather than responding directly to Philogus, Tychicus instead considers the negative impact such a marriage would have on the man's heirs. He shifts the focus of the argument from children's will to a discussion of legal wills, a move which represents Tychicus as a figure who, while refusing to retract his arguments, remains unable finally to support his position. Gibbon, therefore, ends his treatise in rhetorical uncertainty with neither position on children's obligations to their parents confirmed nor discredited.

The lack of resolution in Gibbon's text is indicative of late sixteenth century writers' attempts to determine children's status. In the end, neither Stockwood nor Gibbon is successful in his attempt to assert claims in favor of or against what can be perceived as commodifications of children. Rather than attempting to discredit counterarguments to his position, Stockwood requests that his readers stop trying to reason their way out of their social obligations. "Seek not how to be wise and witty," Stockwood counsels, exhorting his readers not to "devise windlesses and starting holes to shroud and hide themselves in" (*A Bartholomew Fairing*, 82). Unable to address discrepancies in his argument, Stockwood instead insists that his audience accept his authority on the subject. And while Stockwood's abandonment of reasoned argument in favor of claims for his own authority undermines the effectiveness of his argument, the dialogic form used by Gibbon prevents resolution — for Gibbon's dialogue fails to resolve in favor of either speaker, or even end in compromise. Rather, he presents his readers with characters unable to find common ground in the issues they address. For both Stockwood and Gibbon, the question "whether the election of the parents is to be preferred before the affection of their children in marriage" remained unanswered.

Gilding the Lyly

While early modern treatises that addressed issues of child commodification were, for the most part, unable to offer any sense of resolution about the status of children, we might expect to find something more conclusive in staged fictional representations of these concerns. The dramatic plot, at least, could be resolved in some form or another — and if the plot was one that presented or depicted contemporary problems of parent-child relationships we might expect at least a gesture of narrative resolution. Not surprisingly then, in the plots of *Mother Bombie* (ca. 1588–1591) and *Love's Metamorphosis* (ca. 1590), John Lyly attempted to offer resolutions of parent-child conflicts similar to those described by the treatises. Although the topicality of Lyly's plays — and indeed most of Lyly's plays — has for the most part been ignored in recent criticism, the plays can be seen as clearly participating in debates about at least one topic: children's status as property. Writing contemporaneously with Gibbon and Stockwood, Lyly also considers the problems of children's status, employing the fictional world of the theater to explore possible resolutions to the contradictions created by the commodification of children. Yet despite his ability to create fictional solutions, like Gibbon and Stockwood, Lyly seems unable to resolve the problem of the status of children, for *Mother Bombie* and *Love's Metamorphosis* advocate opposing sides in this debate. *Mother Bombie* seems to criticize parents' attempts to profit from their children's marriages while *Love's Metamorphosis* points to the advantages of such a system. *Mother Bombie* critiques the materialistic desires of the parents and endorses the children's position, while *Love's Metamorphosis* suggests that children should willingly and happily sacrifice themselves to the needs of their parents. Nevertheless, although the endings of the plays present different resolutions, the individual narratives are able to reconcile the conflicts between parents and their children.

These conflicts dominate *Mother Bombie,* a play written and performed sometime during the late 1580s and early 1590s. The entire first act of the play depicts parents scheming, purely for profit, to marry their children to unacceptable marriage partners. The act culminates with a confrontation between the characters Prisius and Sperantus, two "citizens of modest means," and their children, Livia and Candidus. In this confrontation the parents and children articulate two sides of the debate about children's agency, using terms and claims strikingly similar to those articulated by Stockwood and Gibbon. On the one hand, this is a discussion about competing hierarchies; the parents take a traditional view, arguing that their children are obligated to obey them unquestioningly. In contrast, the children argue that their parents' failure to arrange marriages responsibly nullifies their obligation to follow their parents' wishes. On the other hand, the debate is a discussion about individual responsibility. While Prisius and Sperantus claim that their children's actions have implications for their parents' moral and spiritual well-being, the children contend that such claims wrongly disregard their rights to free will and serve to commodify them. And while the fathers lament their offspring's lack of gratitude and obligation, the children criticize their parents' desire to turn marriage into a "market."

Like Stockwood, these fathers expect their relationship with their children to be one of obligatory exchange — they have supported their children and their children must now follow their wishes as a sign of their support. Sperantus's and Prisius's overall willingness to articulate their mercenary motivations for choosing their children's marriage partners does not stop them from claiming victim status when their children rebel. A child's refusal to participate in this exchange is a moral injustice that apparently brings pain to the parent. A child's rebellion, the father's argument goes, is like the rebellion of one's own body, one so powerful as to be torturous. It is, Prisius suggests, as if "the collop [offspring] of thine own bowels . . . be the torture of thine own soul" (1.3).[19] The multiple use of the possessives "thine" and "own" in this statement serves to emphasize parental ownership of children. Since children are their parents' creations, their actions are significant primarily in relation to their effects on their parents' "souls." Children's moral independence is denied — they are not criticized for their own immoral actions but for the effect of their actions on their parents' moral status.

Furthermore, while Sperantus and Prisius advocate a position that greatly resembles that of Stockwood, their children take up a debate much like that of Gibbon's Philogus. The basic issue at hand, the children claim, is not one of obligation. What is at stake are the ethical implications of the motivations behind these marriage negotiations. Accusing the fathers of inordinate greed, Candidus justifies his rebellion: "let our fathers lay their purses together, we our hearts. I will never woo where I cannot love" (1.3). Candidus's statement reconfigures the debate about children's obligations, prioritizing the issue of free will and moral obligation to one's self over obligation to one's parents. Implicit in this rebellion is the suggestion that children's overall value is not material but is to be measured by their ability to act morally. When the children are driven by heartfelt desires and the parents by greed, the argument suggests, there is no contest about whose desires should be prioritized.

Rejecting notions that she is her father's property, Prisius's daughter Livia also draws a sharp distinction between her obligations as her father's child and the possibility that she is, in fact, her father's possession. Denying the latter she invokes the right to choose her own marriage partner: "I will measure my love by mine own judgement, not my father's purse or peevishness. Nature hath made me his child, not his slave" (1.3). Like Candidus, Livia asserts her inclination and overall ability to judge for herself. Her obligation to her father, in the final analysis, simply does not include the resolution of his financial need. In their attempts to force their children to marry, she argues, parents hypocritically deprive children of their rights as individuals: "Indeed, our parents take great care to make us ask blessing and say grace when we are as little ones; and growing to years of judgement, they deprive us of the greatest blessing and the most gracious things to our minds, the liberty of our minds" (1.3). Livia's mutinous statements suggest that materialistic considerations and treatments of children do more than annoy children; they deprive them of their moral rights to free agency, self-determination and happiness. For, if children are really their parents' goods, they can no longer be moral agents and are thus deprived of the graces their parents had attempted to instill in them during their infancy.

While the children acknowledge the economic metaphors that make them their parents' goods, they challenge the values placed upon them by these economies. Commodification of their physical bodies, the children fear, is also a commodification of their will. They question the morality of their parents' actions arguing that, by treating them as commodities, their parents have failed in their obligations to their children:

> Parents in these days are grown peevish. They rock their children in their cradles till they sleep, and cross them about their bridals till their hearts ache. *Marriage among them is become a market.* "What will you give with your daughter?" "What jointer will you make for your son?" *And many a match is broken off for a penny more or less, as though they could not afford their children at such a price, when none should cheapen such ware but affection, and none buy it but love* (1.3; my emphasis).

Candidus complains that parents treat children as commodities to be exchanged when they should be placing emotional value on their children instead.

Lyly's play presents both sides of the larger debate on children that we saw in the treatises. The force of the narrative, however, points to conclusions that are absent in Gibbon and Stockwood. The narrative of the play reveals that the materialistic desires of these parents lead to problems and complications with potentially dire consequences. Prisius's and Sperantus's self-serving desires for their children's marriage are mirrored by the actions of Memphio and Stellio, two "wealthy landowners" who also choose to marry off their children for their own profit. In all four situations the planned marriages, if enacted, will end disastrously. The marriage partners the fathers have chosen for their children, Selina (the "supposed daughter of Stellio") and Accius (the "supposed son of Memphio"), are "idiot children," the simple-minded offspring of a common woman who switched her children with Memphio and Stellio's children while they were in their infancy. If the marriages of Candidus to Silena and Livia to Accius were to occur they would be economically unsuccessful (the children really aren't the heirs to wealthy men) and morally problematic (Livia and Candidus would be trapped in marriages to inferior partners). The intended marriages of Memphio and Stellio's supposed children would lead to the moral peril of incest. The possibility of such dangerous consequences would, no doubt, leave the audience with little choice but to dismiss the validity of the parents' position. The play thus ultimately appears to support the side of the debate that holds that children are persons.

While throughout *Mother Bombie* Lyly engages in the lively debate about children's status as exchangeable property, in *Love's Metamorphosis* he interrogates the implications of the commodification of children as an accepted practice. In the subplot of *Love's Metamorphosis*, Erisichthon, the ruler of the forest, is punished by Ceres for cutting down a tree that was actually the metamorphosed form of one of Ceres's nymphs. Unable to endure the hunger caused by his punishment (famine "gnawing" on his bowels), Erisichthon determines to sell his daughter Protea to a wealthy merchant so that he can afford to buy more food. While it is not clear that this transaction is a marriage negotiation, the very issues raised by Lyly's play are strikingly similar to those debated by Gibbon and Stockwood — similar enough, that is, to consider this text as part of the continuing dialogue about children's rights.

In *Love's Metamorphosis* Lyly depicts the child's relationship to the parent as one of willing obligation and exchange. Protea agrees with Erisichthon's claims that her submission to his needs is both "necessary" and "natural": "Necessity causes thee to be sold; nature must frame thee to be contented" (3.2). Obviously willing to sacrifice her happiness for her father's benefit, she responds to her father's request by expressing a desire to go to almost sacrificial extremes for him: "Dear father, *I will obey both sale and slaughter*, accompting it to the only happiness of my life, should I live an hundred years, to prolong yours but one minute. *I yield father; chop and change me; I am ready*" (3.2; my emphasis). By claiming that she will accept not only being sold but even the brutal extreme of slaughter, Protea calls to mind the ancient laws of the Romans and Jews invoked by Stockwood and Gibbon — laws where parents, "in cases of necessity might sell their own children for bondslaves to relieve themselves and . . . might kill them in revenge of their own private injuries done unto themselves, or public enormities offered unto others" (Stockwood, *A Bartholomew Fairing*, 21). Through Protea's willingness to sacrifice herself for her father — whether through death or submission to sale — Lyly offers his audience a scenario where concerns about children's agency and free will are no longer at issue. In doing this, he forecloses critiques of the laws that were depicted as problematic by Gibbon's and Stockwood's editors.

This reading of *Love's Metamorphosis*, however, is not intended to argue that Lyly himself advocated such beliefs — indeed, the coexistence of *Mother Bombie* indicates that Lyly's plays merely serve to present the two sides of the debate, much as Gibbon's dialogue did. Lyly's shift away from the question of whether children should be treated as commodities — clearly in this play they should be — enables him to consider the ethical problems that arise when children actually *are* commodities. The prominent question at issue is not whether the child has rights to his or her physical body; in this play she does not. Instead, Lyly considers the extent to which this child must submit her will to the owner of her body. Although she is willing to be sold to the merchant, Protea fears that the merchant's impiety will lead to a greater commodification of her: "if he find[s her] beauty worth one penny, [he] will put it to use to gain ten, having no religion in his mind, nor work in his mouth, but money" (3.2). This anxiety about her future causes Protea to discuss with her father exactly how much of her is up for sale. Erisichthon provides a vexed answer: Livia's body can definitely be sold but he is unclear about whether her mind is actually included:

> *Pro.* Father, hath this merchant also bought my mind?
> *Eri.* He cannot buy that which cannot be sold.
>
> (3.2)

Protea debates the terms of the sale with the merchant, who argues that the material realities of the sale will limit the moral freedoms which Erisichthon had seemingly promised. The merchant-buyer, on the other hand, argues that his possession of her body, by limiting her ability to act freely, will enable him to control her will. Protea counters this by arguing that her free will empowers her:

> *Mer.* You are now mine Protea.
> *Pro.* And mine own.
> *Mer.* In will, not power.
> *Pro.* In power, if I will.
>
> (3.2)

This debate recontextualizes Erisichthon's assertion that "he cannot buy that which cannot be sold." For at the end of this discussion it is unclear whether or not the will can be sold; however, the conclusion of the play suggests that it cannot be. Protea emerges from the transaction free in both body and mind. In what seems to be a handy solution to the crisis facing the treatise writers, Lyly momentarily suggests to his audience that children who willingly allow themselves to be commodified by their parents can somehow still retain their free will. Thus, in *Love's Metamorphosis*, Lyly presents the possibility that the difficulties with the commodification of children are not located in the commodification of their wills, but in the children's willingness to submit.

Through *Love's Metamorphosis* and *Mother Bombie*, Lyly offers his audience parallel yet competing conceptions of parent-child relationships. Yet, in the end, Lyly's attempts to offer stable resolutions for the problems inherent in each argument produces only uncertainties. In *Mother Bombie*, attempts at resolution are undermined by the play's treatment of parental actions in the past that were not "unnatural" and "materialistic" but "overnatural." While Lyly's play seems to criticize the "unnatural" greed of the fathers that led to commodification of children, it is equally critical of the "overnatural" actions of Vicinia, the mother who, in loving her children too much, switched her "idiot children" with Memphio and Stellio's children in order to give them a better life. Vicinia's actions cause her to be as (if not more) responsible as the materialistic fathers for the threat of incest that hovers over the play.

Thus *Mother Bombie* ends ambiguously and ironically. If parents are to be criticized for acting *against* the best interests of their children, they are also to be criticized for acting *for* the best interests of their children.[20] The rebellions of the children in this play are not to be interpreted as affirmation of their rights to free will, but as a restoration of order disturbed by a parent who was, in the end, too loving. And, if this is not sufficient to undermine any moral the play might impart, the servant Riscio undermines the legitimacy of the children's rebellion against their parents by arguing that it has all been a game of wits. The children's rebellion, he argues, occurred primarily "to show that old folks may be overtaken by children" (5.3). Lest we take this play too seriously, Riscio's remarks attempt to convince us that this has all been an insignificant game.[21] Interestingly, this representation of a game of wits encompasses the complexities of Lyly's play. For by depicting the children as successfully matching wits in a game of wills with the adults of the play, the concept of the jest invokes the youth's moral agency at the same time that it dismisses it as a mere frolic.

The jest that undermines the viability of the resolutions offered in *Mother Bombie* finds its counterpart in the mythical setting of *Love's Metamorphosis*, a setting removed from the realities of sixteenth century life. This setting undermines the play's suggestion that the commodification of children does not necessarily deprive the child of free will. Protea is willing to be sold by her father *because* the god Neptune, with whom she has had a sexual relationship, will transform her and enable her to escape. Before being sold to the merchant, Protea entreats Neptune to help her to remain a source of revenue for her father without becoming a source of revenue for the merchant. She prays to Neptune: "Let me, as often as I be bought or pawned for meat, be turned into a bird, hare, or lamb, or any shape, wherein I may be safe" (3.2). Neptune obliges and creates a system where Protea can continually aid her father while avoiding the degradations she faces as purchased property: "My father cannot be miserable if Protea be happy, for by selling me every day he shall never want meat, nor I shifts to escape" (4.2). In the happy world of *Love's Metamorphosis* the commodification of children becomes a profitable game played by father and daughter that has no repercussions for either. In fact, Protea's willingness to be sold for her father is a display of love that convinces Ceres to remove the curse from Erisichthon. In this mythical world children become commodities who also retain the liberty of their minds.

Protea's willing submission is based on her ability to escape from this distasteful situation — an ability that comes from a relationship to which the ordinary English child would not have access. Indeed, when this fictional child participates in her own commodification — an instance of the moment

Stockwood dreads when the goods manage to "dispose" themselves — the transaction is figured in a way that invokes images of that ever-controversial, morally questionable form of exchange: usury. Just as money lent by a usurer returns with a profit, Protea returns to her father with the money paid for her. She takes advantage of her relationship with Neptune to create a system where her father can "sell" her every day for a profit yet have her return to be sold again. In the one instance where a child is depicted as accepting of her status as property, this acceptance is undermined by its figuration as usury.[22] Hierarchical orders are disrupted (Protea arranges her own exchange), economic transactions fail (the merchant never receives what he paid for), and a child's obedience to her father leads to immoral practices.

Even in the fictional world of the stage, Lyly remains unable to take a position on whether or not children should be defined as commodities. While he presents two sides of the debate — in *Mother Bombie* he argued that children should not be commodities, in *Love's Metamorphosis* they were happily commodified — the playwright seems unwilling (or unable) to endorse either. The fact that Lyly attempts to argue both sides of the debate but, in the end, undermines both arguments reveals the intensity of the problem of children's status in early modern England.

Conclusion: Commodities out of Control

Stockwood's, Gibbon's and Lyly's inability to resolve debates about commodification of children in familial settings, even when (as in Lyly's plays) this resolution occurred in a fictional space, reveals powerful anxieties about children and commodities in the late sixteenth century. On the one hand, these debates depict an anxiety about the effect of economic systems on individuals. Commodification of children calls into question concepts of free will. On the other hand, the debates reveal an increasing anxiety about the power of commodities to act autonomously. Writers of the late sixteenth century faced a dilemma when they wrote about children. There were two possible conclusions they could make, but both positions were, in the end, untenable. If they rejected the tradition that had defined children as commodities, they challenged the legitimacy of powerful institutions that relied on the material values of children such as the apprenticeship system, the Court of Wards and London's Court of Orphans. However, if they defined children as commodities, they would need to redefine their conceptions of commodities. If children were commodities, then commodities could have agency and could no longer be controlled by organized market systems.

It is not surprising that writers began to reevaluate the economic status of children. Anxieties about commodities out of control were indicative of larger anxieties about changing economic systems. As trade routes reformulated systems of exchange and the increasing use of money dematerialized exchange transactions, English citizens were forced to rethink and retheorize economic systems, including ones that involved children.[23] At the same time, as usury became a more acceptable practice, money became something that could be perceived to "act" on its own — going out into the world and creating its own offspring. The connections between children and usury became even stronger, for conceptions of both raised anxieties that commodities could not always be controlled by regulated markets, for in usury money reproduced itself outside of systems of exchange. The amount of money lent increased indefinitely without further transactions. Similarly, the child commodity also had the power to maneuver outside of controlled markets. Children reaffirmed anxieties that commodities could escape market controls.

It is also not surprising that John Stockwood invoked Bartholomew Fair to name a treatise that attempted to define children's status. For, as Peter Stallybrass and Allon White argue, the fair served as an undefinable space of confusion — one in which economic concerns intermingled with pleasurable entertainments.[24] This type of "inmixing" was troubling to early modern individuals' desires for separation of the commercial and pleasurable and led to "competing, conflicting, and contradictory definitions" of the fair.[25] Children presented a similar but perhaps even more troubling dilemma for early modern theorists. For children were a space where agency became inseparable from economy. The child commodity was doubly disruptive. Its presence undermined conceptions of free will and beliefs in the stability of economic systems. If commodities could act, then they could not be controlled.

Yet if debates about children were part of a larger cultural problem, why turn to the family to work through the problem? For late sixteenth century authors, the family served as an easily representable fictional space through which they could attempt to avoid the very real complications created by children's dual status as individuals and commodities. While it is unlikely that state systems would change their treatment of children, it would be possible for individual parents to choose to do so. Thus, the family was envisioned as an entity that was removed from economics, one where the commodification of children became a choice rather than a necessity — an issue of familial affections rather than social economies. By moving to the fictional realms of the family, writers could offer the possibility of resolution for the concerns raised by the commodification of children (and through this, more general concerns about commodities). Unlike the fair that was perceived as a space of uncontrollable excesses, the family served as a fictional construct in which parental control of children could be imagined to regulate the disruptive nature of commodities. Yet even in this fictional realm, the success of such regulation was unimaginable.

10 • Cockering Mothers and Humanist Pedagogy in Two Tudor School Plays

Ursula Potter

There was a familiar tale in Renaissance England that held cockering (pampering) mothers responsible for their children's later crimes. In George Whitney's 1586 book of emblems the tale is headed *Indulgentia parentum, filiorum pernicies* ("the indulgence of the parents leads to the destruction of the child"), but, despite this inclusive gesture toward both parents, a mother is featured in the emblem and in the accompanying story. The story tells of a young thief on his way to the gallows and of his anguished mother tenderly kissing him. As she embraces him, and to the horror of those standing by, he bites off her nose. When challenged over this, he responds that if she had been more rigorous in his childhood he would not now be going to his execution, and he ends with an address to the assembled crowd: "I hope my facte shall mothers warne, that do behould this sighte."[1]

Juan Luis Vives had used the same anecdote in his *De institutione Christianae feminae* to give the same warning. In a sweeping claim, he accuses mothers of being "the cause of most part of [ev]illness among folks" and goes on to recount the tale to illustrate his point (REW, 129).[2] His version is tailored to the pedagogue's values: "For if she, said he, had corrected me for stealing my fellow's book out of the school, which was my first theft, then had I not proceeded unto these mischievous deeds" (REW, 130). By choosing the theft of a schoolbook as the first crime, Vives places the story's moral within a parent-school context. If the standards at home do not match those taught in schools, the civilizing aims of education will fail, and the loss will be not just to the parents but also to the nation. The Tudor interlude, *Nice Wanton*, is a variation on this familiar story and betrays the same pedagogical bias, tracing the prodigal children's turning point back to school crimes of truancy and the tossing away of schoolbooks, and to a mother who does nothing to correct them. As in the emblem tale, the cockering mother of this play is forcefully confronted with her own guilt for the crimes and deaths of her children.

Vives was just one of many pedagogical authors to lay the blame for the failure of children at school on mothers; Erasmus is equally outspoken about the lifelong corrupting effects of cockering mothers on the moral development of children. This hostility directed toward mothers in the pedagogical treatises reflects more than humanist understandings of female nature, it is also indicative of the tendentious relationship that existed between pedagogues and parents. Rebecca Bushnell has explored the tensions besetting this relationship, primarily in regard to tutors and fathers and their competing authorities in Tudor England, and she has used her findings to explicate a range of Tudor texts dealing with education. This essay follows

Bushnell's theory and methodology to suggest that the scapegoating of mothers was a rhetorical strategy by the pedagogical authors, who used it as an oblique means of targeting paternal resistance to their education programs, as suggested by the following criticism by Erasmus, ostensibly directed to women: "You ought not to pay attention to those silly women, or to men very much like women save only for their beards, who maintain out of a false spirit of tenderness and compassion that children should be left alone until early adolescence, to be pampered in the meantime by their dear mothers and spoiled by nurses" (DPI, 299).[3] Under the guise of the "silly women," it is in fact fathers whom Erasmus is addressing. Much in this essay will be familiar in terms of Renaissance dichotomies between male and female qualities; I focus on the application of this theory in relation to Tudor schooling.

With the growth of local grammar schools in Tudor England, more families in provincial towns were likely to have had sons staying at home and under their mother's supervision longer than was the case with apprenticeships or the traditional chivalric household training away from home. The school timetable encouraged contact with mothers, as most children who lived close enough returned home for breakfast early in the morning and again for lunch at noon. Under these conditions, logic dictates that mothers were more likely to be familiar with their child's schooling than were fathers, and therefore more likely to determine the children's schooling. The two plays analyzed here suggest that mothers were the more immediately involved parent with their children's schooling, and that the schools had to deal with the mothers, while the pedagogical treatises insisted it should be the fathers. By drawing on the public school culture of the period, I will demonstrate that there existed a body of support for maternal authority, which stemmed from within the school system and which sought to repudiate popular images of damaging maternal authority as illustrated in the emblem tale and in the education treatises.

Not all pedagogical authors are as dismissive of maternal qualities vis à vis schooling as Vives and Erasmus. Richard Mulcaster, headmaster of Merchant Taylors' school, shows less hostility toward mothers and women in general. He demonstrates an awareness of the potential scapegoating of women for male failure when he argues that those who "blame silly wymen as being the onely cause why they went awrie" have some private error of their own. Maturin Corderius, who wrote a series of Latin dialogues used extensively in Tudor schools, also shows more support for mothers than is usual in pedagogical texts from this period. Both these authors were practitioners, as opposed to Erasmus and Vives who are generally regarded as education theorists.[4]

This essay compares the treatment of mothers in the treatises and school dialogues of Erasmus, Vives and Corderius with the dramatic treatment of mothers in two mid-sixteenth century plays dealing with schooling, *Nice Wanton* and *July and Julian*. These two plays stand out for their interest in parents and for their contrasting views of maternal authority in relation to schools. *Nice Wanton* exemplifies the negative maternal images projected by education theorists such as Vives and Erasmus, and *July and Julian* supports the positive image of a practitioner such as Corderius. Where both works concur is in the depiction of absent or inadequate paternal involvement in the education of children.

Mothers were commonly blamed for their children's undoing. Fond mothers were likened to Aesop's ape, crushing their children to death, or, as Robert Burton puts it, "pampering up their bodies to the undoing of their souls. . . . Who is he of so little experience that knows not this . . . to be true?" Biblical wisdom was cited to the same end, such as "The rod and correction give wisdom, but a child set at liberty maketh his mother ashamed. *Prov. 29.15*," as William Kempe states on the title page of his *Education of Children* (1588).[5] To pious scholars such as Vives, indulgent mothers represented a significant impediment to learning and to virtue: "I have seen very few men come to great proof of either learning, wit, or virtue, that had been daintily brought up, nor can the bodies come to their due strength, when they be feebled with delicate [en]keeping. And so when mothers think they save their children, they lose them; and when they go about to keep them in health and strength, they foolishly minish both their health and their life" (REW 128). By "dainty upbringing," Vives means a pampered existence, a lack of moral rigor and a mother who shows too much affection for her children and too little respect for schooling, all faults embodied by the mother in *Nice Wanton*. He cites the example of his own mother as the ideal and writes approvingly of how she showed so little affection toward him as a child that he held her in awe and fear: "No mother loved her child better than mine did; nor any child did ever less perceive himself loved of his mother than I . . . and therefore there was nobody that I did more flee, or was more loath to come nigh, than my mother, when I was a child" (D, ix). It was only when he was an adult and his mother dead that he revered her memory. The implication is that his success as a scholar may be attributed to her rigor and distance in his upbringing. Few authors share Vives's deep anxiety about mothers, but even the more worldly Erasmus is severe toward them: "What kind of maternal feeling is it that induces some women to keep their children clinging to their skirts until they are six years old and to treat them as imbeciles? If their love of play goes this far, why do they not procure for themselves a monkey or a Maltese puppy? 'They are only children,' they argue. Quite true, but even so, one cannot emphasize too strongly the importance of those first years for the course that a child will follow throughout his entire life" (DPI, 309). "Imbeciles" and the animal analogies here betray the perceived dichotomies of maternal versus pedagogical values. The educator's desire to separate children from the "maternal feeling" which so threatens humanist values can be read behind the polemic of both Erasmus and Vives. Erasmus resorts to the language of the law to distance the values of the nursery from those of the school: "Hard and unbending before his teacher is a child that is the product of such a soft and permissive upbringing — gentleness is their word for it, but its effects are totally corruptive. Should mothers of this type not be prosecuted for maltreatment of their children?" (DPI, 309). As in the emblem tale, a mother's cockering is seen as a public crime rather than a private and domestic affair.

The School Texts

Tudor schoolboys were introduced early to contemporary pedagogical theory on parents through their Latin dialogues, giving them the occasion to consider and compare domestic reality with schoolbook theory. Erasmus and Vives both wrote collections of Latin dialogues for use in grammar schools; Erasmus compiled his *Colloquia* and Vives wrote the *Linguae Latinae Exercitatio* (*Dialogues*). The *Colloquia* were in use in various schools in London, including Saint Paul's School and Westminster School, but also in many provincial schools which adopted the curriculum set out by Saint Paul's (for example, Bruton in Devon, Guildford in Surrey). The *Dialogues* of Vives, which were first published in 1539, were known to have been required reading in such popular schools as Eton, Shrewsbury and Rivington (D, xxxiv). These dialogues generally commenced in second form, when the boys were about ten or 11. The statutes for Ruthin Grammar School, for example, which are based on those for Westminster School, stipulate that the usher was to read "to the 2nd Class Erasmus his Colloquies."[6]

Vives's *Dialogues* were dedicated to the 11-year-old Prince Phillip of Spain. The simplicity of the early dialogues, their separation into short narratives, and the thematic material dealing with the very young schoolboy learning his alphabet and moving on to advanced material all attest to youthful readers. Mothers rarely feature in them (presumably they were not an appropriate subject for intellectual activity); when they do, however, their representation echoes the prejudices and stereotypes cited above. As they learned to privilege Latin over the mother tongue, schoolboys studying Vives's dialogues would also learn to privilege male over female values. In one of the early dialogues, "Morning Greetings," this dichotomy between school and domestic life is rendered through opposing maternal and paternal representations.

Mother and father are clearly delineated in characterization, in function and in literary treatment. The dialogue opens with conventional daily blessings from parent to child. The father stands silently by as the mother questions her young son on how he slept, her detailed questioning punctuated with such endearments as "my light," "my darling," and she fusses inordinately over a headache experienced by the child: "It grieves me sorely to hear that!" she exclaims, and breathes a sigh of relief to hear it is gone: "Now I breathe again; for you took away my breath" (D, 6–7). The mother's part, which dominates this first narrative, is characterised by melodrama and emotional expression and by shallowness of matter. Its juxtaposition with the father's part reinforces her intellectual limitations. The narrative moves from mother to father through a brief passage entitled "Playing with the Dog," in which Vives introduces the commonplace Renaissance beast versus rational man analogy as a precursor to discussion on schooling; he uses the puppy to symbolize childish behavior. This is the same image Erasmus drew on when conceptualizing mothers: "If their love of play goes this far, why do they not procure for themselves a monkey or a Maltese puppy?" he demands (DPI, 309). Vives's dialogue separates maternal and paternal functions through this animal imagery, and the narrative moves to "The Father's Little Talk with his Boy." Now the father takes control, even to the point of choosing what the child will eat. The dialogue illuminates the beast analogy, equating the separation of the boy from home with his intellectual development. The father contrasts the puppy's life with that of his son, and asks the boy what differentiates him from the dog:

> *Boy.* But I am a man.
> *Fath.* How do you know this? What have you now more than a dog? But there is this difference that he cannot become a man. You can, if you will.
> *Boy.* I beg of you, my father, bring this about as soon as possible.
> *Fath.* It will be done if you go where animals go, to come back men.
> *Boy.* I will go, father, with all the pleasure in the world! But where is it?
> *Fath.* In the school.
>
> (D, 7)

Just as the father does not participate in the conversation on his son's sleeping habits, so the mother is excluded from discussions on schooling. Vives's desire to separate parental functions reflects contemporary pedagogical theory that a mother's responsibility is primarily, if not exclusively, for her child's physical welfare.

Since these narratives are largely drawn from a scholarly environment, female characters rarely occur, but when they do they tend to function as agents for highlighting vices or weaknesses the young student should avoid. The women are depicted for such stereotypical qualities as their "distaff philosophy" (D, 40). Superstition, gossip, vanity, inefficiency and extravagance are characterized through female figures, and female promiscuity is linked to a corrupted religion (D, 16). The understanding to be gleaned from these dialogues is that once a boy joins the school environment he is prompted to view women as intellectually and morally inferior, and discouraged from spending time in their company. In the words of one speaker, Vives's youthful readers learn that "in my opinion, it is a greater disgrace if men hang upon the judgments of inexperienced and stupid girls" (D, 201).

Fathers fare better than mothers in the *Dialogues*. The concern Vives shows for fathers to act as wise mentors and role models to their sons is reflected in dialogues 3 and 4, where a serious father introduces his son to school and to the principles of selecting a teacher. Vives rarely shows a father in a negative light; at the worst he is a merchant, and therefore "impervious to culture" (D, 49). In dialogue 20, where Vives lays down the precepts for good government, is found the pedagogue's vision of the ideal father, one whose love for his child is expressed not in material terms or in displays of affection, but in care for his son's education (D, 181).

Vives's *Dialogues* leave the distinct impression that their author aims to do more than educate his student in moral and ethical principles or in grammatical precepts. He is also driving a wedge of intellectual superiority between the young schoolboy and the domestic, female world of his mother. He reinforces the understanding evident in the treatises that mothers were to have little authority in the schooling of their daughters and none in that of their sons; this was to be an entirely masculine domain. This intellectual wedge was reinforced linguistically through the exclusive use of Latin in grammar schools. As Walter J. Ong has demonstrated, the "cleavage between the vernacular world and the Latin world coincided with the division between a world in which women had some say and an almost exclusively male world." The "mother tongue" was barred in most grammar schools, and Latin was the only language to be spoken both in the classroom and in recreation; punishment was meted out to those who were caught speaking English. In such isolated communities as Kirkwall in the northernmost islands of Scotland, even the Song School rules demanded that boys speak Latin in the streets, and that censors (prefects) monitor this. At Ruthin School boys were not to speak their mother tongue of Welsh, it was a punishable offense. At Aberdeen students could speak Latin, Greek, Hebrew, French or Erse (Gaelic), but never the vernacular.[7]

The *Colloquia* of Erasmus are more numerous and considerably longer and more complex than those of Vives. They stimulated much contemporary controversy with their satirical tone, their explicit material, and their attacks on certain religious orders, and there were those who considered many of them unsuitable material for schoolboys (C, 623–24). Given that the *Colloquia* were generally read in second class, as noted earlier, it is evident that pubescent boys were at times the recipients of some highly satirical and explicit images of wifely and female behavior. With two notable exceptions, mothers have no place in the *Colloquia*, which are generally more concerned with issues relevant to a young man rather than a young boy, such as courtship, marriage, prostitution, travel, government, war and religion. The two exceptions are "The Marriage" and "The New Mother," and in each of these there is an erring husband in the background. "The Marriage" is discussed here for its relevance to *Nice Wanton*.

"The Marriage" was one of the most popular of Erasmus's colloquies. As the title indicates, it is more concerned with marital relations than with mothering. Both the colloquy and *Nice Wanton* name their protagonist Xantippe, after Socrates' notoriously shrewish wife. Erasmus chose the name on the assumption that his schoolboy readers would make the connection with Xantippe's husband, and it can be argued that the playwright of *Nice Wanton* chose the name for similar reasons; he undoubtedly had the colloquy also in mind, since both the colloquy and the play feature the same wise neighbor Eulalia ("sweetly speaking"). When Corderius, for example, refers boys to the writings of Erasmus for examples of "a crafty old wife" (P, 25), it is presumably this colloquy and the wily

Eulalia's advice on marital harmony he has in mind. In "The Marriage," Erasmus presents Xantippe in an extensive discourse on marital harmony. Satire invests the colloquy with much humor, intended to amuse as well as instruct the schoolboy reader. True to her namesake, Xantippe is vocal and complaining, but in Erasmus' version her husband is a philanderer and a drinker. Xantippe tells Eulalia that he squanders her dowry:

> *Eul.* On what?
> *Xan.* On whatever he pleases: wine — whores — dice.
> *Eul.* That's no way to talk.
> *Xan.* But it's the truth. Besides, when he comes home drunk in the middle of the night, after being long awaited, he snores all night and sometimes vomits in bed — to say no worse.
> (C, 116)

Eulalia gives Xantippe advice on how to deal with such a husband, ranging from a contrived Patient Griselda approach to getting pregnant. For thousands of schoolboy readers of "The Marriage" colloquy, Erasmus wryly reduces the great philosopher to a very domestic and irreverent figure. There is nothing akin to this humor or this theme in the *Dialogues* of Vives, who is unlikely to have considered such narratives appropriate for schoolboys. Indeed, Erasmus did have to defend this colloquy, which he did by pointing out that it dealt with the failings of husbands and lauding the wisdom of wives who can overlook such failings and improve husbands' behavior (C 629).

The name Xantippe had become a cipher for disrespect for learning, and was used as such in Renaissance England by educators and preachers alike. In a Tudor homily on the state of matrimony the congregation was expected to know who was meant by "a certain strange Philosopher, which had a cursed wife, a froward and a drunkard." The relationship between Socrates and Xantippe, that is the relationship between scholarship and domestic life, was commonly proposed as a topic for debate in schools. When Vives lists subjects for debate, he naturally thinks in terms of impediments to learning and he therefore suggests that "one might for instance make a comparison in the case of the philosopher by adding the idea of his wife." When Erasmus identifies topics of humor, interest and delight to the boys, he includes the theme of: "if Alcibiades should persuade Socrates that he thrust his quarrelsome and illtongued wife from the house." Alcibiades, who was Socrates' most brilliant student, and the "object of [the philosopher's] impassioned attention," represents the antithesis to Socrates' scolding wife. Simply by using the name Xantippe in *Nice Wanton*, the playwright draws on a public debate over educational versus domestic values, and on parental authority within the family. By using the name "Eulalia," he may also be drawing attention to Erasmus's colloquy and to its theme of shared marital responsibilities.[8]

Erasmus regarded parenting as a joint responsibility, but not an equal one (C, 60, 67). It was up to husbands to supervise wives and children. In "A Pilgrimage for Religion's Sake," a colloquy published in English in 1536, Erasmus sketches a responsible father as one who monitors his family. Menedemus, a character from Terence whose name suggests "stay at home," outlines his own method of overseeing the behavior of his household: "Thus I go my stations at home, I go into thc parlour, and I see unto the chaste living of my daughters, again from thence I go into my shop, I behold what my servants, both men and women be doing, from thence into the kitchen, looking about, if there need any of my counsel, from thence hither and thither observing how my children be occupied, what my wife doth, being carefull that everything be in order" (TT, 96). A father named Menedemus makes a brief appearance offstage in *July and Julian*, and I will argue that his name prompts a satirical understanding of his paternal role.

Satire and humor should not be overlooked when dealing

with school drama and school texts. Erasmus made it evident in his defense of his colloquies that a sense of humor was a necessary reading tool: "People react differently to it. Some of my English friends, learned and sensible men, were delighted with the work; they think it helpful both for improving Latinity and for exposing popular prejudices. On the other hand, there are some who are not amused — people with no sense of humor. If your Grace will take the time to go through the book you will find that besides instruction it has much else pertinent to the sound training of youth. Entertainment is thrown in as a bait, to entice an age sooner captivated by what is agreeable than by what is good for it" (C, 623–24). Erasmus may have had religious practices in mind in his reference to prejudices, but misogyny may also be qualified or reversed by humor in school texts. In one late fifteenth century schoolbook, for example, a translation exercise depicts a mother whose son has not slept well. As the day dawns she decides to let her son sleep in, and instructs the household to be quiet. When the boy arrives late at school he blames his mother, claiming that "she wold not let me be callyd up. Therfor my mother is the cause of my late comyng and not I."[9] Rebecca Bushnell quotes this text and takes it as given that "mothers, in particular were blamed, just as any female role in the child's education was suspect."[10] For prescriptive texts by such authors as Vives she is undoubtedly right, but this is not necessarily the case with all school texts. Irony may well be intended here, schoolboys being notoriously adept at providing novel excuses for tardiness and schoolmasters entirely up to their tricks. The text may be offering a humorous image of mothers being used as scapegoats by the errant schoolboy. In the dialogues of Corderius mothers are transparently represented as dedicated supporters of schooling and as figures of authority. Here the mother figure is usually found exhorting lazy sons to get out of bed in order to arrive at school on time (P, 5, 6, 12), demanding good manners (P, 6), and more concerned with their child's attendance at school than leaving home with an empty stomach:

> *Thom.* Mother, when shall we dine?
> *Vinc.* By and by, if so be that you wait a little?
> *Thom.* I must go away forthwith. . . .
> to the very place of execution. . . .
> if you will not give me meat, I will goe away undined.
>
> . . . .
>
> *Vinc.* If thou dine not, thou wilt sup more gladly at night.
> (P, 12)

Satire plays a role in this dialogue, "the very place of execution," but it is directed at the school and not at the parental figure. Corderius had been a schoolmaster himself; he was appointed by Calvin to a school in Geneva. He chose to present his young readers with firm and positive maternal images in these exercises, aligning mothers with similar values to those of schoolmasters. One could argue that these are satirical images of preferred maternal authority, but this argument fails in its relationship to the critical paternal images in these exercises. Corderius includes no dialogues with fathers, but they do feature as background figures, and his treatment of them suggests that their authority is generally imperfect. His dialogues present schoolmasters as supporting paternal authority in public but conscious of its imperfections. This is where the dialogues support Rebecca Bushnell's findings, tacitly acknowledging the potentially conflicting values and authority that existed between fathers and schoolmasters. But these dialogues also suggest that Corderius was less ambivalent toward maternal authority and did not support a pedagogical theory that dictated that mothers should have no role in their child's schooling.

Much mid-sixteenth century drama, including *Nice Wanton* and *July and Julian*, features poor paternal authority, and this is where the drama gives evidence of a different pattern of parenting to that promoted by the pedagogical authors, or by the popular emblem tale quoted above. There is evidence behind both the dramatic representations of absolute maternal control, that the playwrights were tacitly directing criticism at fathers. By understanding these two plays as products of the Tudor school culture, the positions of their playwrights toward parenting roles become evident.

School Drama

Drama written for schools not only participates in the public education debate, but also shows evidence of engagement with the school texts. This should come as no surprise since the dialogues and colloquies were themselves written in dramatic form in order to perfect a boy's performance skills. The majority of grammar school boys did not spend their time silently writing at their desks. Writing was, in fact, regarded as a separate skill often taught at a later stage and by a separate writing master. Much of the Tudor school curriculum required reciting out loud in front of the class, sometimes with the rudiments of acting — gestures, displays of emotion, appropriate countenance. The transition from reciting the dialogues to performing in school drama would have been a natural progression, bringing with it a wealth of pedagogical and intertextual allusions. Of the two plays to be analyzed here, *Nice Wanton* (1560) was probably written for school or civic performance, and *July and Julian* (c. 1559–1571) has every appearance of being part of a larger and more elaborate sequence of entertainment performed by schoolboys or choristers. While these two plays deal primarily with maternal authority, they also show interest in popular arguments against schooling, such as public schools as common, unmasculine and unhealthy. This raises the question of whether resistance to schooling may have come from fathers concerned for their son's masculine image.

Nice Wanton is difficult to date prior to its entry in the

Stationers' Register on June 10, 1560, but can be understood against a background of increasing emphasis on schooling.[11] This is a morality play that wholeheartedly promotes schooling as both a citizenly and religious duty and renders a mother guilty for her children's lives of crime and their miserable deaths. The tone is earnest, at times zealous, and the limited humor rather labored. There is no plot as such, rather a tracing of humanity's moral decline as outlined in the prologue, and nothing is left to the audience in terms of mystery or tension. The didactic tone directs the audience straight to the moral meaning "as here in this interlude ye shall see plain" (12) supported by such loaded vocabulary as "daliance" and "wantonly" and "mischief" (15).

The concentration upon education and the upbringing of children, together with various addresses to "ye children," leads Greg Walker to consider this a school play. Michael Shapiro narrows the field to provincial grammar school boys, and his suggestion is compatible with the relatively unsophisticated audience level implied by the simple action, didactic tone, and emphasis on piety. The entertainment value of the play is secondary to the moral lesson it imparts. *Nice Wanton* is a short play that could have been part of a joint school and civic function. Most grammar schools played host to the governing authorities, together with civic dignitaries, at least once a year, when the students and masters were examined as to their competence. At King Edward VI's Grammar School, Norwich, the statutes required that "every year the High Master was to choose a 'learned dialogue' or a comedy or two to be presented by the boys. As the Mayor was to be present the Corporation was to bear the cost of the costumes."[12]

The play depicts the stock cockering mother as a hindrance to schooling and good citizenship. She has three children, two are delinquent and one is virtuous. This latter son, Barnabas, is the main voice of pedagogical and religious authority in *Nice Wanton*. His mode of counsel is through proverbial and biblical quotations, and his delinquent siblings mock him as a fool, "Master Hoddypeak" (48). The tone of his opening lines is reminiscent of a frustrated schoolmaster dealing with protective and aggressive mothers:

> they do me threat
> to complain to my mother; she for their sake,
> Being her tender tiddlings, will me beat.
> Lord, in this perplexity what way shall I take?
> What will become of them? Grace God them send
> To apply their learning and their manners amend.
>
> (33–38)

It was usually to mothers that a schoolchild would complain if severely punished. In Mulcaster's *Positions* (1581), he urges prospective schoolmasters to use their discretion when it came to corporal punishment of a child, in case of repercussions from mothers. The master ought to: "leave as little as he may to the child's report, who will alway lean and sway too much to his owne side, and bear away the bell, even against the best master, chiefly if his mother be either his counsellor, or his attorney: or the father unconstant, and without judgement."[13] The mother in *Nice Wanton* represents just such a softhearted counselor.

A number of popular arguments against schooling are introduced into the play, mediated through Xantippe's adversarial role toward school. Her resistance goes to the heart of conventional public complaints about school — the lack of physical exercise, the low quality of schoolmasters and their cruelty: "Alas, poor souls, they sit a' school all day / In fear of a churl, and if a little they play, / He beateth them like a devil" (109–11). The lack of physical exercise in public schools was one of the early arguments against schooling. This was acknowledged as a valid argument by most pedagogical authors, and one to which Erasmus responds that "even if something is lost in the way of physical robustness, this disadvantage is well outweighed by the great intellectual benefits that the child will receive" (DPI, 323). For the upper classes, the absence of physical skills training was a major impediment to schooling. Thomas Elyot's program of education, written as it was for the gentry and nobility, included wrestling, swimming, riding and other exercises appropriate to that class of society, and he emphasised that tutors should not suffer "the child to be fatigued with continual study or learning, wherewith the delicate and tender wit may be dulled or oppressed." In a 1566 letter from Sir Henry Sidney to his son, Philip, then at Shrewsbury School, the father is concerned that his son's study shall be "safe for your health" and encourages him to "Give yourself to be merry for you will degenerate from your father if you do not find yourself most able in wit and body to do anything when you be most merry."[14]

The epithet "churl" for the schoolmaster exemplifies a common image of schoolmasters as boors and of low rank, and Xantippe follows this up with commonplace assumptions of cruelty, "he beateth them like a devil" (111). She is reflecting her children's opinion, for Ismael, too, is "in fear of a churl" (60), and Dalila responds similarly, "I would sit quaking like a mome for fear" (62). All three characters reflect popular images in Renaissance pedagogical literature of schoolmasters as tyrants in the classroom.[15] This mother boasts to Eulalia that her children "go handsomely" (125), indicating it is their looks and social presence she is concerned with. In *Misogonus* (ca. 1571), another contemporary interlude promoting education, it is a father who voices similar erroneous values, as he proudly claims that his son shall learn to look big, stand stout and go brave.[16] Study was considered a threat to such masculine images. Erasmus repudiated such fears, not by dismissing their validity, but by rewriting the definition of "manly": "We are afraid of study as something that will ruin our physical attractiveness. . . . It is unmanly to let physical appearance become a matter of excessive concern" (DPI, 323).

Xantippe ignores warnings from Eulalia, her neighbour, that

her son is "light fingered" (116) and her daughter "hath nice tricks" (117). The advice of neighbors was considered almost a duty, as Mulcaster outlines in his section on "Conference between parents and neighbours."[17] But it was also shameful to need outside advice; correct parental guidance, Erasmus claims, would avoid the need for children to be "forced to beg from their neighbours advice on how to conduct their lives" (DPI, 332). When the delinquent children come home from school Xantippe hurries to feed them, "I will go get them meat to make them merry" (140). Like Sir Henry Sidney, Xantippe is concerned that her children should be lively and cheerful. By adding "to make them merry" the dramatist has identified yet another familiar criticism from the pedagogical treatises, that of giving children foods which stimulate the blood and the baser appetites. Diet is a topic dear to the hearts of pedagogues, and foods and their effects on the body are frequently discussed in school texts. Vives devotes several pages in his treatise on the education of girls to the dangers of incorrect foods which stimulate the natural heat of the bodies of children and young men and maids "in the lusty age." He uses the term "meat" to signify primarily flesh (REW, 64–65).

The children's decline into stealing and prostitution earns them early deaths. Xantippe herself is shown as shocked into recognition of her guilt, and is condemned to a life of perpetual penitence and worldly shame for her negligence as a mother. The play closely reflects pedagogical warnings. The dramatist could well have taken his synopsis from Erasmus: "Every day we have examples before our eyes of citizens who, because of their dissolute children, have been reduced from wealth to indigence, who are tormented and crushed by unbearable shame because their son has been led to the gallows or their daughter has turned to prostitution. I know eminent citizens of whose numerous children scarcely one has escaped unscathed: one child, for instance, is being consumed by that horrible affliction euphemistically called the 'French Pox'"

(DPI, 307). There is much about the dramatic treatment of Xantippe to indicate that the mother in *Nice Wanton* was little more than a personification of the complaints of educators, not a representative of mothers in general. Her characterization can be seen in terms of a catalog of common criticisms leveled at parents by pedagogues: she displays no respect for learning or schoolmasters, values looks over learning, is critical of the lack of exercise in schools and of excessive school discipline, ignores the advice of neighbors, is indulgent in the home, provides an inappropriate diet, fails to supervise her children, and shows favoritism, and she is, of course, a shrew.

Toward the end of *Nice Wanton* the audience is gratuitously reminded of Xantippe's name. Having been out of the action for most of the play, she is brought back on stage after the death sentence is passed on her son Ismael. The vice figure, Worldly Shame, who will confront her with her children's deaths and her guilt, reminds the audience of her name and her nature:

> Xantippe, a curst shrew,
> I think all the world doth her know.
> Such a jade she is and so curst a queen,
> She would out-scold the devil's dame, I ween.
>
> (445–48)

In the mouth of the vice figure, this superfluous accusation works in Xantippe's favor and this is where the play introduces new considerations. Xantippe has been so relentlessly condemned, so systematically characterized with parental weaknesses, and so isolated as the sole source of blame, that she invites sympathy in her role as a victimized figure in the community. Xantippe's vices were never vicious or malicious; she stands condemned for her ignorance and her misguided values, and as such she can be read as a scapegoat. As stage misogynist, the vice figure's accusation endorses this inference. Linda Woodbridge's argument that "the stage misogynist is a tool for overcoming prejudice [toward women] through forcing it into the open," can be applied to *Nice Wanton*. As Woodbridge explains, at the deepest level of plays with female protagonists, "Woman is on trial, as she was on trial in the writings of the formal controversy; the misogynist is her accuser." She points out that Xantippe was a favorite *exemplum* of the formal misogynist in drama, and quotes *The Taming of the Shrew*: "as curst and shrewd / As Socrates' Xanthippe."[18] The 1557 translation of Erasmus's colloquy "The Marriage" was published under the English title of *A Merry Dialogue Declaring the Properties of Shrowde Shrews and Honest Wives not only very pleasant, but also not a little profitable: Made by the famous clerk D. Erasmus Roterodamu* (TT, 245). Xantippe is indeed on trial in *Nice Wanton*, but the play also offers her some defense. The vice figure's comments merely remind the audience that the play is using a literary euphemism for opposition to learning, and that this euphemism had a husband.

As the audience would have known, mothers cannot be held entirely to blame. In Harrison's *Description of England*, he criticizes "women of the poorer sort . . . being of themselves without competent wit, they are so carelesse in the education of their children," but he adds "wherein their husbands also are to be blamed."[19] In *Nice Wanton* the audience is reminded several times of a silent and unseen father. The prologue talks only of "the mother," but early in the play Eulalia, the good citizen neighbor, draws attention three times to the responsibility of the children's "parents" or "their elders" (85, 92, 94). Twice we learn that Ismael steals from his father's purse, "By the mass, if he can get his purse, / Now and then he maketh it by half the worse" (180). In the daughter's monologue of penitence, where the play's moral is reiterated yet again, Dalilah lays blame three times on her parents, not just her mother, for their tiddling (cockering):

> Yet we were tiddled, and you beaten now and then.
> Thus our parents let us do what we would,
> And you by correction they kept under awe.

When we grew big we were sturdy and bold,
By father and mother we set not a straw.

(314–18)

This is not an impoverished family; the children "come of good kin" (357) and their father owns cattle (217). The father's existence is brought to the fore in the final lines of the play, as Barnabas exhorts his mother to repent, have faith in God's salvation and go "and thus comfort my father, I pray you heartily" (527). The epilogue, which repeats the moral yet again, has shifted from focusing on a mother's guilt, as in the prologue, to addressing parents jointly in the broader community:

Many miscarry, it is the more ruth,
By negligence of their elders and not taking pain
In time good learning and qualities to attain.
Therefore exhort I all parents to be diligent
In bringing up their children.

(533–37)

Few in the audience could have failed to understand that it is fathers as much as mothers that this interlude is addressing.

One further feature of Tudor schooling needs to be taken into account. Schoolmasters, too, were held accountable for monitoring their students' behavior, both inside and outside the school. This was particularly relevant in provincial communities. In the small community of Kirkwall high in the Orkney Islands, northernmost region of Scotland, the incumbent schoolmaster was directed to visit his students' parents to enquire of their behavior. In Aberdeen the schoolmaster was repeatedly charged with controlling the annual riotous and violent behavior of his students at Yuletide both inside and outside the school. Had Ismael, the delinquent son, been at school in Guildford in Surrey, he could have been expelled: "if any Scholar shall be a common picker, stealer, usual swearer or blasphemer of the name of God and cannot be reformed by often admonitions and moderate corrections his friends having knowledge thereof shall immediately take him from the school in peaceable manner which if they refuse to do he shall be by the Schoolmaster and the Schoolwardens or any two of them put out of the school never to be admitted thither again." And in Yorkshire, the Almondbury school statutes specifically stipulate that the master is to "take special care of the scholars not only in the school that they diligently apply themselves to their books and studies but also out of school with regard to their recreation, and to prevent all profane, idle and immoral practices, and to advise the parents to the same effect." By excluding the schoolmaster from the *personae dramatis* in *Nice Wanton*, the dramatist circumvents the delicate question of parent-school contact, but by giving the son Barnabas the voice of pedagogical authority faced with unapproachable parents, the play replicates the difficulties schoolmasters faced in confronting parental authority.[20]

Written somewhere between 1559 and 1571, *July and Julian* deals with the same childrearing theme as in *Nice Wanton* but departs from that play in terms of genre, representation of mothers, tone and purpose of performance.[21] Whereas moral and religious dogma takes precedence over entertainment in *Nice Wanton*, the reverse is true of *July and Julian.* There is no religious doctrine and the moral lessons are secondary to the play's entertainment value, which is spelled out in the prologue:

> We are come hither to trouble you as boys.
> And after sage things to shew our trifling toys.
> Pleaseth it you therefore to be so favourable,
> If we children make mirth as we be able.
> Not desiring praise but to shew our witte,
> In such exercise as for us be fit.
>
> (7–12)

"After sage things" suggests the preceding presentation of a tragedy, or declamations, or perhaps a disputation in Latin by the senior scholars. To "make mirth" and "to show our wit" are the keynotes to the performance conditions. It is clear from both prologue and epilogue that the play is only one part of a much larger program of entertainment extending over at least two days, possibly for a wedding. Following the happy resolution of the plot with an espousal, the epilogue announces that July and Julian will be married tomorrow and invites the assembled audience to return the following day (1310–13). Over 25 pieces of music are recorded in the commonplace book in which the play is written, leading John M. Ward to suggest that the author of *July and Julian* was "most likely a schoolmaster and amateur lutenist-composer, one whose tablatures may have served pedagogical ends."[22]

July and Julian is indeed a display of light wit and humor, a comedy in the Roman manner with scheming servants, a gullible master and mistress, with romantic intrigue and a happy ending. Classical comedy was familiar fare in Tudor schools, valued not just for teaching language and eloquence but also for developing performance techniques in young orators. The statutes of Ruthin School in Wales stipulate that the master "shall hear his Scholars rehearse an Act out of Terence's Comedies or Plautus whom I require to be instructed by the Master. Both in the manner of Speaking and Gesture."[23] *July and Julian* is explicitly Terentian; the dramatist names two fathers, Chremes and Menedemus, names found, for example, in *Phormio* and *The Self Tormentor*. The dramatist expected his players to understand the allusions behind these names. Menedemus, for instance, has already been referred to as the ideal father who stays at home. Apart from his naming twice as the father of Missis, Menedemus has no function in the play, but Missis, his daughter, has a brief cameo role in which she comically fends off the aggressive and bawdy servant, Ffenell, at her front door. The implication is that her "stay-at-home" father is conspicuously absent. In the case of Chremes, the playwright seems again to be playing with convention. In a discussion on the delineation of different characters developed by Terence, Erasmus describes Chremes as "polite and always calm, self-controlled on every occasion, resolving all differences as far as he can, gentle but hardly simple-minded."[24] In *July and Julian* Chremes is impulsive, simple-minded and a drunkard.

In many ways *July and Julian* is a model of family harmony and good parenting, or more accurately, good mothering, since all credit must go to the mother for her children's excellent training. She is the antithesis of Xantippe. The sole weakness in this mother is a defect in her moral judgment that may be attributed to the absence of moral guidance by her husband. So closely do the two plays work with the same material, and so contrasting is their treatment of maternal authority, that *July and Julian* could have been written as a satire of *Nice Wanton*. It treats the same pedagogical issues, it uses satire to demolish the arguments against school, and it defends the mother's controlling role from accusations of shrewish behavior by suggesting that mothers have to compensate for inadequate paternal involvement. It goes further to tacitly align schoolmasters and mothers as maligned disciplinarian figures in the training of children.

Mawd, the mother, is introduced early in act 1 where the scene heading indicates her dramatic status, "Mawd the good wife" (100). This is "a goodly household," according to the servant Wilkin, who refers to Mawd as "my old dame principall" (291–92). This may mean no more than the proper domestic hierarchies, but as the play develops it becomes clear that Mawd is indeed the principal figure within the family. In the mouth of this rancorous servant, it could well reflect Mawd's ruling role in the household. While the servants manage to fool her husband with ease, they show more respect for Mawd (1035–38). The same pedagogical issues used to demonstrate maternal negligence in *Nice Wanton* are reworked in *July and Julian* for a positive characterization of Mawd: domestic discipline, diet, favoritism and the familiar arguments of schooling as unhealthy, unmasculine and unkind to boys' buttocks.

This is a well-to-do, urban family, and the opening dialogue immediately characterizes Mawd as concerned with material status and of a utilitarian bent. The playwright introduces a sundial as a measure both of Mawd's material values and her adherence to punctuality. The sundial is a symbol of the eternal problem of getting boys out of bed and to school on time. Schools started at 6:00 a.m. in summer and 7:00 a.m. in winter. This was a familiar topic for school texts, as in Vives's dialogue, "Getting Dressed and the Morning Constitutional," which features a sundial and a clock (D, 82). Mawd is proudly showing her country brother, Pierpinte, around her garden, and the sundial alerts her to school hours. She calls to her youngest son Dick: "Here it, trip tothe [*sic*] schole qickly, or Ile twidg yor dock" (111). Mawd is threatening to "twigge" (birch) her son unless he hurries to school; it is more usual to find the schoolmaster accused of such behavior, as in *The World and the Child*, a 1522 interlude: "I will not go to school but when me lest, / For there beginneth a sorry feast, / When the master should lift my dock."[25] In upholding school punctuality Mawd aligns herself with school values. Her next lines indicate she is equally observant of her servants:

> *Mawd.* Why fenell where a bowt go yowe.
> *Ffen.* To fetch whitt poddings for your breckfast, I cold get but thes two.
> *Mawd.* Yt is well provided, geve them to Julian, mak hast
> That Dicke were had to ye schole, it is vj of ye clock, & past.
> (116–19)

Mawd instructs the servant Fenell to accompany Dick to school. Unlike Xantippe, this mother is ensuring that her child will not be given any opportunity to play truant. Likewise, Mawd's approval of white pudding informs the audience that plain and wholesome fare is served in this household, not meat to make the children merry as in *Nice Wanton*. Mawd's disciplinarian approach is given humorous emphasis by her refusal to agree to her brother's request that his nephew should have the day off school in deference to his visit. The day in question is Monday and Mawd responds decisively: "On the monday wold ye so, nay yt cannot be" (121–22). The dramatist may be flagging the uncle's awareness that Monday was the most dreaded day of the school week, or he may be indicating a country uncle's undervaluing of schooling. The difficulties of persuading rural families of the value of schooling are still humorously evident in a 1618 treatise by Nicholas Breton, "The Court and Country or A Briefe Discourse Dialogue-wise set down between a Courtier and a Countryman," where the countryman's view is put forward: "Farmers know their cattle by the heads, and Sheepheards know their sheepe by the brand, What more learning have we need of, but that experience will teach us without booke? . . . Then what should we study for, except it were to talke with the man in the Moone about the course of the Starres?" It is just as likely, however, that the dramatist expected his audience to understand Monday as the prompt for the uncle's request that his nephew be given the day off. This was the day when punishment was meted out to students for transgressions committed in church on Sunday or at school during the previous week. The 1574 statutes for Ruthin School state that: "Monday at 9 o'clock in the morning every week (unless it be a holiday) an account to be taken in order to examine into Boys faults unless the Master should see occasion to omit or overlook it. But I think it expedient that some Crimes be immediately punished according to the Discretion of the Master and not delayed until Monday."[26] Most schools tried to be strict about attendance, except for illness, allowing a child a maximum number of days absence a year. Occasionally an entire school could be granted one or two free days a year at the request of some eminent person visiting the school. Dick's older brother, July, manages this later in the play: "Master scholmaster, I pray yow lett your scholers go play." "By my troth sir," responds the grammar master, "although they have don noght to day, / Yet for yower sake, lett them go" (598–600). The following statute for Almondbury School allows us to identify July's status as a person of quality: "Special holidays may be given at the request of any neighbouring or other gentlemen or persons of quality except to scholars on the Black Bill, once only in two years by the same gentleman."[27]

The uncle persists with his request, and Mawd's response highlights two further popular complaints against schooling, that of study as unhealthy and as unmasculine. These were the arguments the ignorant Xantippe used to excuse her children from school, but in *July and Julian* Mawd satirizes them:

> *Pier.* I pray you let him go.
> *Mawd.* I be shrewe me than.
> Tutt with playinge Dicke, thow canst never be a man.
> To morowe at yower request he shall play.
> And that is twesday.
>
> . . . .
>
> Nay if boies shuld play to much, they wold be lystlys.
> *Pier.* Alas, boyes shuld be borne wythe.
>
> (120–30)

Similar irony attaches to Dick's complaint that:

> Men may do what thei lyst god wott, so cannot we.
> For if I laughe, my father a wanton calles me,
> If I be sadd, my mother saith, I am dumpish and sorlye.
>
> (147–49)

Here the dramatist turns his satire away from public theories about schooling to parody pedagogical theories about gendered values in parenting. Pedagogical theory, in general, presented fathers as the more sedate and serious parent and depicted mothers as affectionate and indulgent; the assumption was, according to one Renaissance author, that paternal austerity prepared children for adulthood, while mothers softened and spoiled them.[28] The irony of the severe Mawd and the negligent

Chremes paying lip service to such a pedagogical theory is typical of the play's humor.

On their way to school, Ffenell and little Dick have the misfortune to meet the grammar schoolmaster and the song (choir) schoolmaster, who accuse Dick of loitering. The grammar master takes his rod to Dick, prompting Ffenell to observe that "Scholmasters be findishe fellows, ye may me be live" (185–91). As the audience well knows, Ffenell is quite right: many schoolmasters were indeed fiendish fellows and motherly pleas for gentle treatment of their child often resulted in an unfortunate backlash. The following extract is from a letter written by an ex-student of Richard Mulcaster: "The prayers of cockering mothers prevailed with him just as far as the requests of indulgent fathers, rather increasing than mitigating his severity on their offending child." Mothers were even rumored to bribe schoolmasters to treat their children gently.[29]

Mawd's parenting skills contrast with Xantippe's deficiencies. Mawd has no favorites, but exacts obedience and diligence from all three children alike. At one point she canes her daughter for failing to follow instructions (194–95). This scene follows directly on young Dick's unhappy encounter with the schoolmasters on his way to school, thereby exploiting dramatic juxtaposition to align the mother with the schoolmaster. Nan complains to Ffenell, the servant, of her mother's strict treatment, providing an opportunity for the servant to undermine the mother's authority, but the daughter's sense of filial duty does not allow her to indulge in criticism of her mother's discipline. Instead, she turns her attention to her household duties, "I must go mak redy my fathers breckfast" (243). Nan is the antithesis to Dalila in *Nice Wanton* who was only seen outside the home and who spent her time in idle and wanton pursuits. Nan lists her household chores and points out that she has little time for ease (236–39). According to most authors on the education of women, a good housewife was "never to be idle, but always to be well occupied"; Thomas Becon considered this important enough to gloss in the margin with "Note well." These are clues for the audience to recognize that this is a well-trained and diligent daughter who will make a good wife; Shakespeare used similar hints to characterize Desdemona in *Othello* as diligent in household affairs: "But still the house affairs would draw her thence."[30]

Cause and effect are being established in *July and Julian*, demonstrating that strict parenting produces well-trained children. But is the mother in danger of becoming a shrew? Will the children hate their mother? In anticipation of such a reaction by some in his audience, the dramatist inserts a direct address to his audience in the mouth of the servant Ffenell:

> How say yow masters, is not my dame a shrewe,
> I dare not say it my selfe, but ile be judge by you.
> How she canvased litle Nane before your face?
> And what knaves be thes scholmasters in like case?
>
> (248–51)

Ffenell's role as stage misogynist, similar to that of the vice figure of *Nice Wanton*, undercuts his accusation and prompts the audience to recognize that the mother's ostensibly shrewish behavior has produced fine, obedient children, and she should not therefore be judged by common prejudices. In the next line, the same line of argument is applied to schoolmasters, "and what knaves be thes scholmasters in like case?" (251), thus tacitly acknowledging that mothers and schoolmasters share similar problems and similar roles. The playwright is drawing on a literary tradition in which the shrewish wife is the schoolmaster's rod, a euphemism with which schoolboys were already familiar from their *vulgaria*: "I maryed my mayster's doughter to daye full soore agayn my wyll. / My thynketh her so roughe / and soore a huswyfe yt I cared not & she were brend in the hote coles."[31]

References to Mawd as a shrew invoke humor, but invariably work in her favor. Potentially negative perceptions of her as a shrewish mother are offset by references to her good qualities. It is the servants, not the family, who label this mother a shrew, yet their complaints serve only to highlight her shrewdness, not her shrewishness:

> I durst take in hand,
> To blynd Chremes quickly, that cold I warrant.
> But when moppinge Mawd, her browes doth bend,
> Methinke the dyvell whyrles on her nos end.
>
> (1035–38)

It is not the master of this household, but the mistress, who earns the respect of the servants. Mawd is just the wife Chremes needs, shrewd, efficient and supportive. The competent housewife is a boon to her husband, as one schoolbook phrase acknowledges: "I am out of all care for gydynge of my housolde / as longe as I have suche a wyfe."[32]

Mawd follows the advice of a number of pedagogical authors. According to Erasmus there are some failings a wife ought to wink at (C, 123), and Becon likewise suggests a good wife will not only bear the incommodities, but will "dissemble, cloke, hide, and cover the faults and vices of her husband."[33] Mawd overlooks her husband's vices (swearing, drinking, fighting) as she humors him and supports his authority:

> Julye go writ yower letter your father did byd yowe.
> Wilkin wait on your master lest he ned yowe.
> Take yowe laisere, writ hit faire, hear ye?
>
> (408–10)

Her "writ hit fair, hear ye?" ensures that the audience understands how much value this mother puts on good handwriting. For many in sixteenth century England, good handwriting was seen as a clerical skill, neither appropriate nor requisite to the nobility or upper gentry. With the advent of printing, handwriting had suffered a further loss of status. Educators were often frustrated by this attitude of disdain: "But now, with the existence of printing, it has come about that some scholars never write at all. If ever they do decide to put their thoughts on paper, their artistry is so marvellous that they often fail to make out what they have written, and they have to get a secretary to read and recognize what they cannot!"[34] Brinsley devoted an entire chapter to "Directions for faire writing" in *Ludus literarius*.[35] Mawd can be seen to be supporting simultaneously the school's values and the authority of July's father. Mawd is never faulted for her discipline; it is her judgment that is in question. July, when frustrated by his mother's meddling in his romance, still acknowledges that his are good parents: "Yt is noght to have good parents, ill dysorderinge, / Ther good childrens good disposicion" (274–75). With this reference to disposition, the dramatist is engaging with yet another topical pedagogical issue. Many authors, like Vives and later Mulcaster, pointed out the need for schoolmasters to understand a child's disposition, that is, the child's nature and talents, and adapt their treatment of the child accordingly. The need for parents to take individual dispositions into account was evidently an issue in contemporary child rearing debate. It features in the educational literature and in personal notations. In a commonplace book, dating from the late 1590s, a quotation identifies the difficulty for parents of balancing discipline with disposition. Glossed in the margin as "Parents Children Disposition," is the following notation: "It is a good propertie of wisedom in parents to find out the disposition of their children, but it is a principal effect of their judgement to cut off with discipline all corners of errors that feed their natural corruptions."[36] Similar wording is evident in Peacham's *The Compleat Gentleman* (1622): "it is a principal point of discretion in parents to be thoroughly acquainted with, and observe the disposition and inclination of their children."[37] Mawd has erred on the side of cutting off with discipline not July's vices but his virtues, for which, ironically, she might take some credit. The issue opens the way for the play's main criticism of this family — that is the materialism that characterizes both parents. The parents' ambitions are threatening the welfare of their son. The potential for tragedy is averted by an anagnorisis that turns parental ignorance into self-knowledge. After a device that tricks the parents into marrying their son to Julian, the maid, the scheme is revealed and Mawd and Chremes have the grace to acknowledge their own faults:

> In ded sonne Julye thow wast in no fault
> But I my selfe and my wyffe Mawd
> Which for gaine of a little money
> Sold Julian quight owt of the contry.
>
> (1068–71)

The only explicit criticism of parenting in the play is directed against the materialism that impelled both parents to use their son and the maid, Julian, in the hope of profiting financially. The dramatist puts this mercenary philosophy in the mouth of Mawd: "at no time, is any time to refusse money" (701). The play's main moral thus treats avarice as the fault both parents share, a fault common to both Terentian comedies and to Elizabethan domestic drama, and often invoking in the latter the dramatic irony that parents who bring their children up virtuously put them at risk through their own vices. In John Lyly's *Mother Bombie* (ca. 1594), one virtuous daughter comments of her covetous father's plans for her, that "[parents] studie twentie yeeres together to make us grow as straight as a wande, and in the ende by bowing us make us crooked as a cammocke." In *The Second Maiden's Tragedy* (1611), the daughter, refusing to prostitute herself to aid an aspiring father, comically points out to him that "I happened righter than you thought I had." As these two examples suggest, it is usually fathers not mothers who are prone to such faults.[38]

In the final analysis, it is the father's values that are being criticized. The name "Chremes" calls attention to the fact that this Chremes is not a reflection of his classical predecessors. He not only curses but he does so within his younger son's hearing (324). He lies (820–21), he has been fined for fighting over land (705), and he is repeatedly mocked for his drunkenness, "thou knowest my master Chremes can tippel well" (1041). Such paternal role models are abhorrent to Erasmus, who despairs of households where "a youngster . . . continually sees his father intoxicated and uttering streams of profanities" (DPI 308). Chremes is also comically simple-minded. After Mawd outlines her scheme to trap the maid to him, he feels compelled to give Mawd the gratuitous advice to "tell [the maid] thereof nothing" (448). He is, in Ffenell's words, the proverbial "old man twice child" (1117), and is possibly characterized as illiterate since he relies on his son's literacy skills, "July read thou and I'll drink" (1119). A more serious fault, however, is revealed in one of Dick's complaints over the mishandling he receives from school:

> *Dick.* Of all man kind, boyes be lest at easse.
> Of all boyes, I dare say, none can be worse then I:
> Both my parents, & masters, handle me so shrewdly.
> *Ffen.* In ded your ij masters play with yow to lewdly.
> *Dick.* My father doth worse to suffer them verely.
>
> (151–55)

The subject of parental responsibility for overseeing treatment at school is the topic in question here. "Lewd" is a term commonly applied to schoolmasters and usually pertaining to vulgar and ignorant behavior. The bawdy punning, however, which frequently marks Ffenell's language, introduces the possibility of sexual abuse. Ffenell is an unreliable character and the audience can discount his words, but it allows the issue of paternal duty of care toward a child's schooling to be raised. Throughout the play, there is an underlying sense of criticism directed toward paternal behavior: in the representation of Chremes, in the Menedemus reference, in the above allusion to treatment by schoolmasters, and in four lines from Julian, the maid. Chremes and Mawd hand Julian over to a stranger with no thought for her welfare, leaving her to give voice to parental duty, "I wold I wer wythe my father at whome, / He wold not lett me be led so fare" (879–80). These lines highlight both parents' responsibility in their *in loco parentis* roles toward the maid. What we have in *July and Julian* is a strong, positive image of mothering, and one that consciously shares many of the values of schoolmasters. Where the image fails is in its relationship with paternal authority and values. In providing no moral guidance to his wife, Chremes is putting in jeopardy the profits of her diligence and good qualities as a mother.

July and Julian offers a refreshingly different perspective of mothers in control, and one that refutes contemporary pedagogical stereotypes. Seen against *Nice Wanton,* which was published about the time *July and Julian* is thought to have been composed, this latter play seems to have been written as a witty and entertaining satire on such didactic educational interludes. *Nice Wanton* follows the line of reasoning found in such authors as Vives, who value education predominantly for moral and academic development and who fear mothers as impediments to a good education. However, as this essay has argued, the playwright undermines this simplistic approach by directing attention toward absent paternal authority. Seen from within the Tudor school culture, there is evidence to suggest *Nice Wanton* is primarily a rhetorical exercise in the debate over public schooling and a strategy for critiquing male disregard for schooling. *July and Julian* takes the more utilitarian approach found in Corderius, who represents schooling in terms of secular skills and values mothers for their authority within the household and for their support of schools. It introduces the notion that schoolmasters and mothers occupied similar problematical territories in the exercise of their authority over children, and aligns this unlikely partnership against a male sector of the population yet to be persuaded of the value of public schooling.

Notes

Notes to Introduction/McBride

1. Susan Dwyer Amussen, *An Ordered Society: Gender and Class in Early Modern England* (London: Basil Blackwell, 1988), 2.

2. On the *annales* school, see Marc Bloch, *The Historian's Craft*, trans. Peter Putnam (Manchester: Manchester University Press, 1954), for a classic apology for that methodology, and *The Annales School*, ed. Stuart Clark (London: Routledge, 1999), for a recent assessment of its impact.

3. On the theory and methodology of women's and/or feminist history (and some influential examples of their practice), see Joan Kelly-Gadol, "The Social Relations of the Sexes: Methodological Implications of Women's History," *Signs* 1 (1976): 809–24; Laurel Ulreich, *A Midwife's Tale: The Life of Martha Ballard, Based on Her Diary, 1785–1812* (New York: Knopf, 1990); Kim F. Hall, "Reading What Isn't There: 'Black' Studies in Early Modern England," *Stanford Humanities Review* 3 (1993): 23–33; Natalie Zemon Davis, *Women on the Margins: Three Seventeenth-Century Lives* (Cambridge, Mass.: Harvard University Press, 1995); Joan Wallach Scott, *Feminism and History* (Oxford: Oxford University Press, 1996); Diane Purkiss, *The Witch in History: Early Modern and Twentieth Century Representations* (London: Routledge, 1996); Moira Donald and Linda Hurcombe, *Gender and Material Culture in Historical Perspective* (Houndsmills, England: Macmillan Press; New York: St. Martin's Press, 2000); Linda K. Kerber and Jane Sherron de Hart, *Women's America: Refocusing the Past*, 5th ed. (New York: Oxford University Press, 2000).

4. See Alice Clark, *Working Life of Women in the Seventeenth Century* (London: Routledge; New York: Dutton, 1919); Gladys Scott Thomson, *Life in a Noble Household, 1641– 1700* (New York: Alfred A. Knopf, 1937); Ruth Kelso, *Doctrine for the Lady of the Renaissance* (Urbana, Ill.: University of Illinois Press, 1956); Philippe Ariès, *Centuries of Childhood: A Social History of Family Life* (New York: Knopf, 1962); John Summerson, *Architecture in Britain 1530-1830*, rev. 7th ed.

(Harmondsworth: Penguin, 1986); Lawrence Stone, *The Family, Sex and Marriage in England, 1500–1800* (New York: Harper & Row, 1977), and his books on marriage and divorce, including *Uncertain Unions: Marriage in England 1660–1753* (Oxford: Oxford University Press, 1992); Alan Macfarlane, *The Origins of English Individualism* (New York: Cambridge University Press, 1979) and *Marriage and Love in England: Modes of Reproduction, 1300–1840* (New York: Blackwell, 1986); and Mark Girouard's many studies on noble households, including *Life in the English Country House: A Social and Architectural History* (New Haven, Conn.: Yale University Press, 1978) and *Town and Country* (New Haven, Conn.: Yale University Press, 1992). Virginia Woolf's *A Room of One's Own* (London: Hogarth Press, 1929) and her *Three Guineas* (London: Hogarth Press, 1938) have perhaps inspired more research on women's history and women writers than any other work.

5. Antonia Fraser's work is often dismissed as overly popular, but *The Weaker Vessel: Woman's Lot in Seventeenth-Century England* (London, England: Weidenfeld and Nicolson, 1984) brings together an impressive assemblage of information on early modern, intelligently organized and presented. See also Suzanne Hull, *Chaste, Silent, and Obedient: English Books for Women, 1475–1640* (San Marino, Calif.: Huntington Library, 1982); Margaret Ferguson, "A Room Not Their Own: Renaissance Women as Readers and Writers" in *The Comparative Perspective on Literature: Approaches to Theory and Practice*, ed. Clayton Koelb and Susan Noakes (Ithaca, N.Y.: Cornell University Press, 1988), 93–116; and Peter Stallybrass, "Patriarchal Territories: the Body Enclosed," in *Rewriting the Renaissance: The Discourses of Sexual Difference in Early Modern Europe*, ed. Margaret Ferguson, Maureen Quilligan and Nancy Vickers (Chicago: University of Chicago Press, 1986), 123–42, and "The World Turned Upside Down: Inversion, Gender, and the State," in *The Matter of Difference: Materialist Feminist Criticism of Shakespeare*, ed. Valerie Wayne (Brighton, Sussex: Harvester Press; Ithaca, N.Y.: Cornell University Press, 1991), 201–20.

6. See especially Jonathan Goldberg's *Desiring Women Writing* (Stanford, Calif.: Stanford University Press, 1997).

7. Patricia Fumerton, "Introduction: A New New Historicism," in *Renaissance Culture and the Everyday*, ed. Patricia Fumerton and Simon Hunt (Philadelphia: University of Pennsylvania Press, 1999), 1–17. See also Jean E. Howard's early critique, "The New Historicism in Renaissance Studies," *English Literary Renaissance* 16 (1986): 13–43.

8. Carole Shammas has contributed scores of articles to the topic, but among the most influential are the much-reprinted study of "The Domestic Environment in Early Modern England and America," *Journal of Social History* 14 (1980): 1–24, and *The Pre-Industrial Consumer in England and America* (Oxford: Clarendon Press, 1990). See Kim F. Hall, *Things of Darkness: Economies of Race and Gender in*

Early Modern England (Ithaca, N.Y.: Cornell University Press, 1995).

9. See Joy Wiltenburg, *Disorderly Women and Female Power in the Street Literature of Early Modern England and Germany* (Charlottesville, Va.: University Press of Virginia, 1992). Alice T. Friedman, *House and Household in Elizabethan England: Wollaton Hall and the Willoughby Family* (Chicago: University of Chicago Press, 1989) "attended to women" in the early modern household as no previous study had. James A. Schultz's study of *The Knowledge of Childhood in the German Middle Ages, 1100–1350* (Philadelphia: University of Pennsylvania Press, 1995) challenged Ariès's contention that childhood was an invention of the early modern world.

10. See especially Marjorie Garber, *Vested Interests: Cross-Dressing and Cultural Anxiety* (New York: Routledge, 1992), and Stephen Orgel, *Impersonations: The Performance of Gender in Shakespeare's England* (Cambridge: Cambridge University Press, 1996).

11. Margaret Ezell, *The Patriarch's Wife: Literary Evidence and the History of the Family* (Chapel Hill, N.C.: University of North Carolina Press, 1987); Patricia Parker, *Literary Fat Ladies: Rhetoric, Gender, Property* (London and New York: Methuen, 1987); Heather Dubrow, *A Happier Eden: The Politics of Marriage in the Stuart Epithalamium* (Ithaca, N.Y.: Cornell University Press, 1991), and *Shakespeare and Domestic Loss: Forms of Deprivation, Mourning, and Recuperation* (Cambridge: Cambridge University Press, 1999); Lorna Hutson, *The Usurer's Daughter: Male Friendship and Fictions of Women in Sixteenth-Century England* (London: Routledge, 1994); Diane Purkiss, *The Witch in History: Early Modern and Twentieth-Century Representations* (London: Routledge, 1996); Susan Dwyer Amussen, *An Ordered Society*, and Amussen's collection edited with Adele F. Seeff, *Attending to Early Modern Women* (Newark, Del.: University of Delaware Press); Lena Cowen Orlin, *Private Matters and Public Culture in Post-Reformation England* (Ithaca, N.Y.: Cornell University Press, 1994); Richard Helgerson, *Adulterous Alliances : Home, State, and History in Early Modern European Drama and Painting* (Chicago: University of Chicago Press, 2000).

12. For a full elaboration of this thesis, see my *Country House Discourse in Early Modern England: A Cultural Study of Landscape and Legitimacy* (Aldershot: Ashgate Press, 2001).

13. Andrew McRae, "Husbandry Manuals and the Language of Agrarian Improvement," in *Culture and Cultivation in Early Modern England: Writing and the Land*, ed. Michael Leslie and Timothy Raylor (Leicester: Leicester University Press, 1992), 35.

14. Michael Bush, *The English Aristocracy: A Comparative Synthesis* (Manchester: Manchester University Press, 1984), 4. This landed elite and their characteristics and attitudes were referred to as "gentry" in the period under discussion here; only later are the gentry distinguished from the most wealthy and powerful landowners.

15. Hutson, *The Usurer's Daughter*, 35, 34.

16. Ibid., 96. Similarly, the *OED* defines "tillage" (1.d.) as "sexual intercourse (with a woman)," citing Shakespeare's *Sonnet 3*: "For where is she so fair whose uneared womb / Disdains the tillage of thy husbandry."

17. William McClung, *The Country House in English Renaissance Poetry* (Berkeley: University of California Press, 1977), 92. For a helpful discussion of the changes in class alliance during this period, see Lawrence Stone, "The Decline of Kinship, Clientage and Community" in his *Family, Sex and Marriage in England 1500–1800*.

18. P. W. Fleming, "Household Servants of the Yorkist and Early Tudor Gentry," in *Early Tudor England: Proceedings of the 1987 Harlaxton Symposium*, ed. Daniel Williams (London: Boydell, 1987), 19.

19. P. J. P. Goldberg, "Female Labour, Service and Marriage in the Late Medieval Urban North," *Northern History* 22 (1986): 21. Town servants typically "entered service at about twelve years and might remain in service until their mid-twenties." Goldberg further notes that these servants tended to be "of a similar social class as their employers" (23).

20. Kate Mertes, *The English Noble Household 1250–1600: Good Governance and Politic Rule* (Oxford: Blackwell, 1988), 58.

21. Girouard, *Life in the English Country House*, 28.

22. Friedman, *House and Household in Elizabethan England*, 47, 49. Gentlewomen made up a greater percentage of the females in the household than did gentlemen of the total males, as many of the women were "gentle" companions to the lady of the house.

23. Mertes, *The English Noble Household*, 197.

24. Goldberg, "Female Labour," 35, 19. See also Peter Earle, "The Female Labour Market in London in the Late Seventeenth and Early Eighteenth Centuries," *Economic History Review*, 2nd ser., 42 (1989): 328–53.

25. Goldberg, "Female Labour," 35. See also Peter Earle, "The Female Labour Market in London."

26. Merry E. Weisner, *Women and Gender in Early Modern Europe* (Cambridge: Cambridge University Press, 1993), 85.

27. Mary Prior, "Women and the Urban Economy: Oxford 1500–1800," in *Women in English Society 1500–1800*, ed. Mary Prior (London: Methuen, 1985), 95. Prior connects women's "duty" to Eve's curse, which put her under obedience to her husband.

28. Ben Jonson, "To Penshurst," in *Ben Jonson, Vol. VIII: The Poems, The Prose Works*, ed. C. H. Herford and Percy and Evelyn Simpson (Oxford: Clarendon Press, 1947), lines 48–56. Jonson's inspiration for this portion of the poem is Martial's Epigram 3.58. The complex politics of gender represented here has a long history.

Notes to Chapter 1/Ray

1. Robert Cleaver, *A Godlie Forme of Householde Government: For the Ordering of Private Families, according to the direction of God's Word* (London: Thomas Man, 1598), sig. G2. Though it is standard practice to attribute authorship of this tract to both Robert Cleaver and John Dod, Dod seems only to have collaborated as editor on some of the later editions. See *The Dictionary of National Biography*, Sir Leslie Stephen and Sir Sidney Lee (Oxford: Oxford University Press, 1917), and *A Short-Title Catalogue of Books Printed in England, Scotland, and Ireland*, ed. A. W. Pollard, et al., 2nd ed., 2 vols., (London: Bibliographical Society, 1976–1986), 1:242.

2. I use the term "Puritan" to describe the authors of the marriage tracts, though most of them sympathized with the Church of England, were trained for the clergy at Cambridge and Oxford, and were recognized as preachers by the Crown. None of these authors was a radical Puritan; they therefore should not be confused with the Roundheads of the English civil war.

3. Heather Dubrow asks the central question about how the marriage tracts were interpreted: "to what extent were readers actually influenced by the pronouncements on marriage they encountered? The Short-Title Catalogue can demonstrate that many of the conduct books sold well; but the number of editions does not indicate how thoroughly or how impartially they were read. When we apply the questions that reader-response critics have taught us to the texts of social history, we may come to wonder if some readers at least perused these treatises selectively, searching out the passages that supported their preconceptions." See *A Happier Eden: The Politics of Marriage in the Stuart Epithalamium* (Ithaca, N.Y.: Cornell University Press, 1991), 12. For more on the problem of interpreting the marriage tracts, see Kathleen Davies, "Continuity and Change in Literary Advice on Marriage," in *Marriage and Society: Studies in the Social History of Marriage*, ed. R. B. Outhwaite (New York: St. Martin's Press, 1981), 58–80; Mary Beth Rose, *The Expense of Spirit: Love and Sexuality in English Renaissance Drama* (Ithaca, N.Y.: Cornell University Press, 1988), 2–4; Valerie Wayne's introduction to her edition of Edmund Tilney's *The Flower of Friendship: A Renaissance Dialogue Contesting Marriage* (Ithaca, N.Y.: Cornell University Press, 1994), 1–37; and William and Malleville Haller, "The Puritan Art of Love," *Huntington Library Quarterly* 5 (1941–1942): 235–72. For further analysis of the marriage tracts, see L. T. Fitz, "'What Says the Married Woman?': Marriage Theory and Feminism in the English Renaissance," *Mosaic* 13, no. 2 (1980): 1–22; Constance Jordan, *Renaissance Feminism: Literary Texts and Political Models* (Ithaca, N.Y.: Cornell University Press, 1990), 286–97; Karen Newman, *Fashioning Femininity and English Renaissance Drama* (Chicago: University of Chicago Press, 1991), 7–31.

4. Kathleen Davies, "The Sacred Condition of Equality—How Original Were Puritan Doctrines of Marriage?" *Social History* 5 (1977): 565. Mary Beth Rose agrees: "It is crucial to assert at the outset that the importance of English Protestant sexual discourse in the Renaissance lies not in its originality, but in its proliferation, elaboration, and wide accessibility to a variety of social groups, as well as in its attempt to construct marriage as a concretized relationship enacted in social life" (3).

5. See David Underdown, *Revel, Riot, and Rebellion: Popular Politics and Culture in England 1603–1660* (Oxford: Oxford University Press, 1985), 36–40, and Marjorie Keniston McIntosh, *Controlling Misbehavior in England, 1370–1600* (Cambridge: Cambridge University Press, 1998), 1–6.

6. George Puttenham, *The Arte of English Poesie*, facsimile edition (Kent, Ohio: Kent State University Press, 1988), 166.

7. Thomas Wilson, *Arte of Rhetorique*, ed. Thomas J. Derrick (New York: Garland Publishing, 1982), 27.

8. Desiderius Erasmus, *On Copia of Words and Ideas*, trans. Donald B. King and H. David Rix (Milwaukee: Marquette University Press, 1963), 29.

9. Lena Cowen Orlin, *Private Matters and Public Culture in Post-Reformation England* (Ithaca, N.Y.: Cornell University Press, 1994), 85–86.

10. Thomas Pritchard, *The Schoole of the Honest and Vertuous Lyfe* (London: Richard Johnes, 1579), sig. F4. The title comprises two discrete tracts published together: an epistle, *A Laudable and Learned Discourse, of the Worthynesse of Honorable Wedlocke*, and *The Glasse of Godly Love, wherein All Maried Couples May Learne Their Duties, Each Toward Others, According to the Holy Scriptures.*

11. "Wedlock" is conventionally substituted for the word "marriage" in these tracts, and though it appears to relate intrinsically to other marital figures like "yokefellows" and "tying the knot," its etymology does not support the association. "Lock" operates as a suffix and derives from the Anglo-Saxon "lac," meaning "the sport of." However, the modernized spelling of the suffix does pun on the bondage connotations of other figures.

12. Juan Luis Vives, *The Office and Duty of a Husband*, trans. by Thomas Paynell, in *Daughters, Wives, and Widows: Writings by Men about Women and Marriage in England, 1500–1640*, ed. Joan Larsen Klein (Urbana, Ill.: University of Illinois Press, 1992), 134. William Whately, *A Bride-Bush: Or, a Direction for Married Persons* (London: Thomas Man, 1619), sig. C3 and sig. Ee3. Cleaver, *A Godlie Forme*, sig. L5v.

13. Henry Smith, *A Preparative to Mariage* (London: Thomas Man, 1591), 32, 53. H. C. Agrippa, *The Commendation of Matrimony*, trans. David Clapham (London: Thomas Bertheleti , 1540), sig. B1v; Desiderius

Erasmus, *In Laud and Praise of Matrimony*, trans. Richard Taverner (London: Robert Redman, 1536?), in Klein, *Daughters, Wives, and Widows*, 73; William Heale, *An Apology for Women, or An Opposition to Mr. Dr. G. his Assertation . . . that it was Lawfull for Husbands to Beat their Wives* (Oxford: Joseph Barnes, 1609), 10; William Gouge, *Of Domesticall Duties* (London: William Bladen, 1622), 115, 111, 114, 110, 214; Thomas Gataker, *A Good Wife Gods Gift: and A Wife Indeed, Two Marriage Sermons* (London: Fulke Clifton, 1623), 5, 7; Cleaver, *A Godlie Forme*, sig. K6; Whately, *A Bride-Bush*, sig. H2v.

14. Robert Snawsel, *A Looking Glasse for Maried Folkes* (London: Henry Bell, 1610), sig. G7. For example, Snawsel's character "Abigail" defines a good husband as one "which should be my partner, and helper, not onely in bodily and worldly things, but especially in spiritual and heavenly, that we might draw Christs yoke *equally* together that so in and through Christ wee might be glorified together" (sigs. B1v–B2). In *A Discource of Marriage and Wiving: And of the Greatest Mystery. Therein Contained: How to Choose of Good Wife from a Bad* . . . (London: Leonard Becket, 1615), Alexander Niccholes writes that the husband should "increase [his wife's] knowledge in good things, and give her certain assurance and testimony of thy love, that she may with hers againe the more *reciprocally equall* thy affection" (35–36). Thomas Taylor in *A Good Husband and a Good Wife: Laid Open in a Sermon* (London: William Sheffard, 1625), also describes the "*equall* yoke" of marriage. Gouge, *Of Domesticall Duties,* confuses distinctions between "equality," "mutuality" and "equity" when he says, "in many . . . respects there is a common equitie betwixt husbands and wives; whence many wives gather that in all things there ought to be a *mutuall equality*." He later adds, "Even in those things wherein there is a common equity, there is not an equality: for the husband hath ever even in all things a superiority" (271–72). All emphasis is mine.

15. Fitz, "What Says the Married Woman?," 5.

16. According to the *OED*, "ox" refers to the castrated male bovine, primarily a work animal. Shakespeare adopts the ox as a metaphor for impotence and cuckoldry in *The Merry Wives of Windsor* when Falstaff says, "I do begin to perceive that I am made an ass," and Ford answers, "Ay, and an ox too" (5.5.119–20). Shakespeare quotations follow the Riverside edition, ed. G. Blakemore Evans (Boston: Houghton Mifflin, 1974).

17. William Perkins, *Christian Economy: Or, a Short Survey of the Right Manner of Erecting and Ordering a Family According to the Scriptures*, trans. Thomas Pickering (London: Edmund Weauer, 1609), in Klein, *Daughters, Wives, and Widows*, 157.

18. Catherine Belsey, *The Subject of Tragedy: Identity and Difference in Renaissance Drama* (London: Methuen, 1985), 159.

19. Whately, *A Bride-Bush*, sig. N; Smith, *Preparative*, 66.

20. See Robert J. Steinfield, *The Invention of Free Labor: The Employment Relation in English and American Law and Culture, 1350–1870* (Chapel Hill, N.C.: University of North Carolina Press, 1991), 25–26.

21. T. E., *The Lawes Resolutions of Women's Rights: or, The Lawes Provision for Woemen* (London: John Grove, 1632), sig. J8v.

22. Qtd. in Haller, "The Puritan Art of Love," 249.

23. For a discussion of exegesis and the difference between literal and mystical meanings, see Frank Kermode, "The Plain Sense of Things," in *Midrash and Literature*, ed. Geoffrey H. Hartman and Sanford Budick (New Haven, Conn.: Yale University Press, 1986), 184–92.

24. Gouge emphasizes the importance of the analogy between husband and wife, Christ and church: "But because he propounded to husbands and wives the examples of Christ and the Church as patterns and motives to them, to doe their dutie, he applieth that which was first spoken of man and wife, unto Christ and his Church, to show that there being so fit a resemblance betwixt these two couples, the pattern propounded is the more pertinent to the purpose, and the reason enforced from thence the more forcible" (110).

25. Heinrich Bullinger, *The Christen State of Matrimonye . . .*, trans. Miles Coverdale, preface by Thomas Becon (London: John Gough, 1543), sig. A7v.

26. Plutarch, *Moralia*, trans. Philemon Holland (London: Arnold Hatfield, 1603), sig. Dd2v.

27. This quotation from Heywood, *A Woman Killed with Kindness*, follows *Drama of the English Renaissance I: The Tudor Period*, ed. Russell A. Fraser and Norman Rabkin (New York: Macmillan, 1976).

28. Becon, for example, notes that "Marriage is called an halter, but whoredome is recountyd a pleasure" (Bullinger, *Christen State*, sig. A5). Note also that in Webster's *The Duchess of Malfi*, Cariola's executioner calls the hangman's noose "your wedding ring" (4.2.248). This quotation follows *The Duchess of Malfi*, ed. John Russell Brown for the Revels Plays (Manchester: Manchester University Press, 1974).

29. The tracts claim that the wife should be always subordinate to the husband, even when she is richer, higher in rank or older. As Perkins sees it, "The female is woman of an inferior sex, fit to conceive and bear children" (*Christian Economy*, 161). Perkins derives this definition from 1 Corinthians 11:7, which states that man "is the glory and image of God; but woman is the glory of man," and 1 Timothy 2:12, in which Paul declares, "I permit no woman to teach or to have authority over men; she is to keep silent." All the tract writers defer to scriptural formulations.

30. Torquato Tasso, *Of Marriage and Wiving*, trans. R[obert] T[ofte] (London: John Smythicke, 1599), sig. B2. Tasso's diatribe against marriage is characterized by the following sentiments: "Let us not marry, except we will martyre ourselves forever" (sig. Bv).

31. For a thorough discussion of the woman on top topos in early

modern literature, see Natalie Zemon Davis, *Society and Culture in Early Modern France: Eight Essays* (Stanford, Cal.: Stanford University Press, 1975), 124–51.

32. Davis writes, "The lower ruled the higher within the woman, then, and if she were given her way, she would want to rule over those above her outside. Her disorderliness led her into the evil arts of witchcraft, so ecclesiastical authorities claimed; and when she was embarked on some behavior for which her allegedly weak intellect disqualified her, such as theological speculation or preaching, that was blamed on her disorderliness, too" (*Society and Culture*, 125).

33. Tasso, sigs. B3v and F4. He attributes the image of the tyrant wife to the philosopher Secundus and the image of the bound husband to the Egyptians.

34. *A Discourse of the Married and Single Life Wherein, by Discovering the Misery of One, is Plainly Declared the Felicity of the Other* (London: Jonas Man, 1621), sig. Bv.

35. Smith, *Preparative*, 54–55. Edmund Tilney expresses similar sentiments: "The office of the husbande is to go abroad in matters of profite, of the wyfe, to tarry at home, and see all be well there. The office of the husbande is to provide money, of the wife, not wastefully to spend it. The office of the husband is, to deale, and bargaine with all men, of the wyfe, to make or meddle with no man. The office of the husband is, to give, of the wyfe, to keepe. The office of the husbande is to apparell him as he can, of the wyfe, to go as she ought." See *The Flower of Friendship: A Renaissance Dialogue Contesting Marriage*, ed. Valerie Wayne (Ithaca, N.Y.: Cornell University Press, 1993), 120.

36. William Vaughan, *Golden Grove, Moralized in Three Books* (London: Simon Stafford, 1600), sig. Nv. Vaughan claims to be a "Master of Artes" and a student in the civil law; he is not a Puritan minister like most of the others.

37. Francis Dillingham, *A Golden Keye Opening the Locke to Eternall Happiness, Containing Seven Directions to a Christian Life* (London: John Tapp, 1609), 19.

38. Aristotle writes, "A good wife should be the mistress of her home, having under her care all that is within it according to the rules we have laid down. She should allow none to enter without her husband's knowledge, dreading above all things the gossip of gadding women, which tends to poison the soul." See *Oeconomica and Magna Moralia*, trans. G. Cyril Armstrong, Loeb Classical Library (1936), 401.

39. Robert Burton, cited in Carroll Camden, *Elizabethan Woman* (Houston: Elsevier Press, 1952), 125.

40. E. J. Burford and Sandra Shulman, *Of Bridles and Burnings: The Punishment of Women* (New York: St. Martin's Press, 1992), 163–85, 170.

41. See Burford and Shulman, *Of Bridles*; Davis, *Society and Culture*;

Alice Morse Earle, *Curious Punishments of Bygone Days* (1896; rpt. Detroit: Singing Tree Press, 1968); David Underdown, "Taming the Scold: The Enforcement of Patriarchal Authority in Early Modern England," in *Order and Disorder in Early Modern England*, ed. Anthony Fletcher and John Stevenson (Cambridge: Cambridge University Press, 1985), 116–36; Lynda E. Boose, "Scolding Brides and Bridling Scolds: Taming the Woman's Unruly Member," *Shakespeare Quarterly* 42 (1991): 179–213.

42. Cleaver, *A Godlie Forme*, sig. B3; Whately, *A Bride-Bush*, sig. Dd3; *A Discourse*, sigs. Ev–E2. Patricia Parker has observed links between female garrulity and unconfined sexual expression, and Boose, "Scolding Brides," has argued that "as illogical as it may initially seem, the two crimes — being a scold and being a so-called whore — were frequently conflated" (195). The marriage tracts support Parker's link and Boose's conclusion. Whately labels verbose women "twatling gossips" (sig. M3), a phrase that may explain the importance placed on wifely silence in household governance. See Parker, *Literary Fat Ladies: Rhetoric, Gender, Property* (London: Methuen, 1987), 8–35.

43. This concept derives, no doubt, from the juridical distinction between *corpus verum* — the physical body of a person — and *corpus fictim* — the spiritual body of the collective, the latter being a legal fiction. Here is an example of the Puritans appropriating concepts and metaphors from jurisprudence and using them inaccurately and inappropriately in marital rhetoric. See Ernst H. Kantorowicz, *The King's Two Bodies: A Study in Medieval Political Theology* (Princeton: Princeton University Press, 1985), 193–232, esp. 209.

44. See Nancy Vickers, "Diana Described: Scattered Woman and Scattered Rhyme," *Critical Inquiry* 8 (1981) (265–79), and "'The blazon of sweet beauty's best': Shakespeare's *Lucrece*," in *Shakespeare and the Question of Theory*, ed. Patricia Parker and Geoffrey Hartman (London: Methuen, 1985), 95–115.

45. Thomas Becon, *The Worckes of Thomas Becon, Whiche He Hath Hytherto Made and Published, with Diverse Other New Bookes Added*, 3 vols. (London: John Day, 1564), sig. XX4.

46. Niccholes writes, for example, that when a man marries he "hath his Rib again with interest and increase, branched into many Veines and ribs, and Bones, and Arteries, of wonderful use, and admirable quality" (*Discource*, 2). Gataker says that woman "was at first taken out of man; and is therefore by Creation as a limbe reaft from him. And she was afterward joyned againe in Marriage with Man, that by Nuptiall conjunction becoming one flesh with him, she might be as a limbe restored now and fastened againe to him" (*A Wife in Deed*, 9).

47. Smith, *Preparative*, 88; Whately, *A Bride-Bush*, sigs. N and Dd4; Cleaver, *A Godlie Forme*, sig. M8.

48. James I, *The Political Writings of James I*, ed. Charles Howard McIlwain (Cambridge, Mass.: Harvard University Press, 1918; rpt., New

York: Russell and Russell, 1965), 272. Use of the marriage analogy to describe the monarch's relationship to the people did not originate with James. See Kantorowicz, *The King's Two Bodies*, 210–19.

Notes to Chapter 2/Smith

1. Most contemporary criticism examines Cavendish's elaborate theories of natural philosophy and positions her work in the context of celebrated seventeenth century male intellectuals like Descartes and Hobbes. See Lisa T. Sarasohn, "A Science Turned Upside Down: Feminism and the Natural Philosophy of Margaret Cavendish," *Huntington Library Quarterly* 47 (1984): 289–307; John Rogers, *The Matter of Revolution: Science, Poetry, and Politics in the Age of Milton* (Ithaca, N.Y.: Cornell University Press, 1996); Eve Keller, "Producing Petty Gods: Margaret Cavendish's Critique of Experimental Science," *English Literary History* 64 (1997): 447–71; Jay Stevenson, "The Mechanist-Vitalist Soul of Margaret Cavendish," *Studies in English Literature 1500–1900* 36 (1996): 527–43; and Sophia Blaydes, "Nature Is a Woman: The Duchess of Newcastle and Seventeenth-Century Philosophy" in *Man, God, and Nature in the Enlightenment*, ed. Donald C. Mell Jr. (East Lansing, Mich.: Colleagues Press, 1988), 51–64. For the duchess's conflicted feminism, see Virginia Woolf, *The Common Reader* (New York: Harcourt, Brace, 1925); Sara Heller Mendelson, *The Mental World of Stuart Women: Three Studies* (Amherst, Mass.: University of Massachusetts Press, 1987); Hilda Smith, *Reason's Disciples: Seventeenth-Century English Feminists* (Urbana, Ill.: University of Illinois Press, 1982); James Fitzmaurice, "Fancy and the Family: Self-Characterizations of Margaret Cavendish," *Huntington Library Quarterly* 53, no. 3 (1990): 198–209.

2. See Bronwen Price, "Feminine Modes of Knowing and Scientific Enquiry: Margaret Cavendish's Poetry as a Case Study," in *Women and Literature in Britain, 1500–1700*, ed. Helen Wilcox (Cambridge: Cambridge University Press, 1996), 117–39; Delores Paloma, "Margaret Cavendish: Defining the Female Self," *Women's Studies* 7 (1980): 55–66; Sylvia Bowerbank, "The Spider's Delight: Margaret Cavendish and the 'Female' Imagination," *English Literary Renaissance* 14 (1984): 392–408; Elizabeth H. Hageman, "Women's Poetry in Early Modern Britain" in *Women and Literature in Britain, 1500–1700*, ed. Helen Wilcox (Cambridge: Cambridge University Press, 1996), 190–208.

Historically, commentators have avoided the domestic altogether in describing Cavendish's poetry. See Margaret J. M. Ezell, *Writing Women's Literary History* (Baltimore: Johns Hopkins University Press, 1993), where she describes the reception of Cavendish's poems, asserting that nineteenth century editors "resolutely chose passages that rely almost entirely on their ability to please the ear rather than tantalize the intellect. Their selections have shaped our perceptions of both her interests and her skills" (127). Virginia Woolf, writing in 1925, exclaims, "her natural gift, the fresh and delicate fancy which had led her in her first volume to write charmingly of Queen Mab and fairyland, was crushed out of existence." Woolf even imagines Cavendish as a member of fairyland: "She has the freakishness of an elf, the irresponsibility of some non-human creature, its heartlessness, and its charm" (112).

In *Margaret the First* (Toronto: University of Toronto Press, 1957), Douglas Grant, Cavendish's first modern biographer, dismisses the domestic in the duchess's early poetry by exclaiming that her method of comparison "leads to the ridiculous, especially in the verses where life or Nature is similized to a cook" (124). Another Cavendish biographer, Kathleen Jones, *A Glorious Fame* (London: Bloomsbury, 1988), observes that the poetry's homespun metaphors are "[a]lso interesting" (82), but "full of curious and bizarre conceits" (81), an idea voiced by early Cavendish editor Ernest Rhys in his introduction to Margaret Cavendish, *Margaret, Duchess of Newcastle: Life of the Duke, Memoirs of Her Own Life & Certain Sociable Letters* (London: J. M. Dent, 1916), who wonders at the "strange confectionary" (xxii) of the duchess's domestic fancies. Paloma, however, does not perfunctorily dismiss the domestic in Cavendish's work. "Significantly, moreover, Cavendish's poetry abounds in imagery drawn from the world of women . . . domesticity characterizes her portrait of the feminine" (61).

3. Margaret Cavendish, *Poems, and Fancies* (London: J. Martin & J. Allestrye, 1653).

4. Margaret Cavendish, *The Worlds Olio* (London: J. Martin & J. Allestrye, 1655). *The Worlds Olio* was actually composed before her first publication, *Poems, and Fancies* (1653), which suggests that Cavendish's emphasis on the domestic is, to some extent, strongest in her earlier work. She explains in her autobiography that she "writ most part of [*The Worlds Olio*] before I went into England" to petition the interregnum government for restoration of her husband's estate in 1652 (203).

5. According to Fitzmaurice, Cavendish consciously constructed a public persona of "happy wife, well integrated into a harmonious family" ("Fancy and the Family," 199) as a means to diffuse criticism of her literary career. Bowerbank also notes that "Cavendish resorts to spinning imagery when excusing herself for encroaching on male prerogative" ("Spider's Delight," 397).

6. Various critics note Cavendish's steadfast class alliance: Sarasohn sees the Duchess's tendency to prefer class over "gender solidarity" ("Science," 293). Keller asserts that "Cavendish was an ardent proponent of social hierarchy who routinely affiliated by class rather than by gender" ("Petty Goods," 452).

7. Margaret Cavendish, *Sociable Letters*, ed. James Fitzmaurice (New York: Garland, 1977), 72, 192.

8. Generally, conduct literature and cooking manuals of the period

label the responsibilities of both laboring class and gentrified women as "housewifery," a term which encompassed diverse household occupations, from cooking, weaving, and brewing to the domestic management of servants.

9. Edmund Tilney in Susan Dwyer Amussen, *An Ordered Society: Gender and Class in Early Modern England* (Oxford: Basil Blackwell, 1988), 44. Cavendish voices a similar sentiment in *The Worlds Olio*; the "Preface to the Reader" states: "Man is made to Govern Common-Wealths, and Women their privat Families."

10. Peter Stallybrass, "Patriarchal Territories: The Body Enclosed," in *Rewriting the Renaissance: The Discourses of Sexual Difference in Early Modern Europe*, ed. Margaret W. Ferguson, Maureen Quilligan and Nancy J. Vickers (Chicago: University of Chicago Press, 1986), 133.

11. Barbara L. Feret, *Gastronomical and Culinary Literature: A Survey and Analysis of Historically-Oriented Collections in the USA* (Metuchen, N.J.: Scarecrow Press, 1979), 34.

12. Michael R. Best, introduction to Gervase Markham, *The English Housewife* (1615; rpt. (Kingston and Montreal: McGill-Queen's University Press, 1986), xi.

13. Several critics take notice of the duke's avocation; Virginia Woolf wrote in *The Common Reader* of William's excellent abilities as a horse trainer (105–06); Rhys mentions "Diepenbeke's uncounted portraits of the Duke on horseback" (Cavendish, *Memoirs*, xxiv); see also Ruth Perry, *The Celebrated Mary Astell: An Early English Feminist* (Chicago: University of Chicago Press, 1986), which describes William as "harmlessly addicted to horsemanship" (114).

14. Grant, *Margaret*, 124; Jones, *Glorious*, 81.

15. Anna Battigelli makes a similar point in *Margaret Cavendish and the Exiles of the Mind* (Lexington, Ky.: University of Kentucky Press, 1998): "In stark contrast to other modernizers, she reveals no interest in securing a place for God in the new atomist systems under discussion. Instead, she reveals her own speculative delight with what appeared to be the infinite number of possibilities and permutations of a natural order governed by atoms" (51).

16. See Sarasohn, "Science"; Rogers, "Matter"; Battigelli, ibid.; and Stevenson, "Mechanist-Vitalist" on atheism and Cavendish's materialist atomism.

17. Blaydes, "Nature," 51. Paloma also uses the term "Mother Nature" ("Defining," 61) to describe Cavendish's characterization of Nature.

18. Fitzmaurice, "Fancy," 203.

19. See Battigelli's assertion that Cavendish's "religious skepticism was motivated, in part, by her personal experience of war" ("Matter," 55).

20. Price, "Feminine Modes," examines "A Description of the Battle in Fight" for its "analysis of the masculine" (130), arguing that for its centrality within Cavendish's poetic corpus.

21. Catherine Gallagher, "Embracing the Absolute: Margaret

Cavendish and the Politics of the Female Subject in Seventeenth-Century England," in *Early Women Writers: 1600–1720*, ed. Anita Pacheco, (London: Longman, 1998), 143.

22. Mihoko Suzuki, "Margaret Cavendish and the Female Satirist," *Studies in English Literature 1500–1900* 37 (1997): 484. Suzuki examines the satirical passage that centers on the soiled body of Bridget Greasy, a cook. Cavendish conflates Greasy's dirt with remnants of the kitchen; a steward complains that "in one place I find a piece of butter, and a greasie comb, full of nitty hairs lying by it . . . and your durty shooes (for the most part) stand upon the Dresser-board, where you lay the hot meat" (qtd. in Suzuki, 484).

23. Nancy Vickers, "'The blazon of sweet beauty's best': Shakespeare's *Lucrece*," in *Shakespeare and the Question of Theory*, ed. Patricia Parker and Geoffrey Hartman (New York: Methuen, 1985), 96.

24. Elise-Noël McMahon, "Gargantua, Pantagruel and Renaissance Cooking Tracts: Texts for Consumption," *Neophilologus* 76 (1992): 192.

25. There is also a clear invocation and resistance of Christological imagery in "A Dissert." I am indebted to Margaret R. Higonnet, University of Connecticut, for this observation.

26. Elaine Hobby, *Virtue of Necessity: English Women's Writing, 1649–88* (Ann Arbor, Mich.: University of Michigan Press, 1988), 110.

27. Cavendish's desire for fame is commonly noted in criticism. See Sandra Sherman, "Trembling Texts: Margaret Cavendish and the Dialectic of Authorship," *English Literary Renaissance* 24 (1994): 184–210; and Sophia Blaydes, "The Poetry of the Duchess of Newcastle: A Pyramid of Praise," *Bulletin of the West Virginia Association of College English Teachers* 6 (1981): 26–34.

28. Margaret Cavendish, *Observations upon Experimental Philosophy. To which is added, The Description of a New Blazing World* (London: Printed by A. Maxwell, 1666). See Keller, "Petty Gods," for a description of Cavendish's critique of experimenters. See also Frances Harris, "Living in the Neighbourhood of Science: Mary Evelyn, Margaret Cavendish and the Greshamites," in *Women, Science and Medicine, 1500–1700*, ed. Lynette Hunter and Sarah Hutton (Phoenix Mill, Stroud, Gloucestershire: Sutton Press, 1997), 198–217; Harris also reads this domestic passage satirically: "this was said in deliberate mockery not just of 'our Moderns' and 'their Experimental or Mode-Philosophy' but also of all over-elaborate and time-consuming housewifery" (210).

29. Ezell, *Writing*, 28; see also Jean I. Marsden, "Beyond Recovery: Gender and the Future of Feminist Literary Studies" (paper presented at the annual meeting of the American Society for Eighteenth-Century Studies, Nashville, Tenn., March 1997); Keller, "Petty Gods," argues that without a "feminist social agenda, Cavendish cannot be considered a feminist in any modern sense of the term" (466).

Notes to Chapter 3/Slights

1. William Shakespeare, *The Comedy of Errors*, in *The Riverside Shakespeare*, ed. G. Blakemore Evans et al., 2nd ed. (Boston: Houghton Mifflin, 1997), 1.1.3–15. All subsequent quotations of the play are from this edition and are cited parenthetically in the text.

2. It is widely accepted that Plautus's comedies *Menaechmi* and *Amphitruo* served as sources for *The Comedy of Errors*. For a full discussion of the play's sources, see R. A. Foakes, "Introduction" to *The Comedy of Errors*, in *The Arden Shakespeare*, 5th ed. (1962; rpt. London: Methuen, 1969), xxiv–xxxv, and T. W. Baldwin, *On the Compositional Genetics of "The Comedy of Errors"* (Urbana, Ill.: University of Illinois Press, 1965).

3. René Girard, "Comedies of Errors: Plautus-Shakespeare-Molière," in *American Criticism in the Poststructuralist Age*, ed. Ira Konigsberg (Ann Arbor, Mich.: University of Michigan Press, 1981), 69.

4. Gail Kern Paster, *The Idea of the City in the Age of Shakespeare* (Athens, Ga.: University of Georgia Press, 1985), 187.

5. This period of education and socialization outside the original family home extended to both men and women, and to members of all social classes. Depending on their sex and social station, young people worked, for example, as servants, farmhands, apprentices, pupils, ladies-in-waiting or pages. Ann Kussmaul estimates that as much as 60 percent of the population aged 15 to 24 was in service at any given time during this period. See *Servants in Husbandry in Early Modern England* (Cambridge: Cambridge University Press, 1981), 3.

6. John fit John, *A diamonde most precious, worthy to be marked: instructing all maysters and servantes, how they ought to leade their lyves* (London: Hugh Jackson, 1577).

7. *OED*, 2nd ed., s.v. "confound," 1, 1c, 3, 5–7.

8. The relevant passages read as follows: "Then certain of the vagabond Jews, exorcists, took upon them to call over them which had evil spirits the name of the Lord Jesus, saying, We adjure you by Jesus whom Paul preacheth"; "Many of them also which used curious arts brought their books together, and burned them before all men: and they counted the price of them, and found it fifty thousand pieces of silver" (Acts 19:13, 19).

9. Dromio's mockery is also designed to fan the flames of his master's anger, of course, but, as Ann C. Christensen has argued persuasively, the central effect of this climactic scene is to emphasize both the spiritual and the material centrality of the household. See "'Because their business still lies out a' door': Resisting the Separation of the Spheres in Shakespeare's *The Comedy of Errors*," *Literature and History* 5 (1996): 26.

10. Joseph Candido, "Dining Out in Ephesus: Food in *The Comedy*

of Errors," *Studies in English Literature 1500–1900* 30 (1990): 228. Candido's emphasis.

11. *OED*, 2nd ed., s.v. "mated," 1. "Confounded, amazed"; 2 a. "Matched; married."

12. Jonathan V. Crewe has also used "The Phoenix and Turtle" to gloss *The Comedy of Errors*, but he reads what he calls the "paradoxical formulas" of the poem as a model of the mythic golden age for which he claims the characters of *Errors* pine. See "God or The Good Physician: The Rational Playwright in *The Comedy of Errors*," *Genre* 15 (1982), 211–12. Also, cf. the Riverside's gloss on the poem's title (1891).

13. My use of the term "communitarian" invokes a notion of political agency that emphasizes the value of community to the formation of the individual self. According to philosophers as diverse as Charles Taylor, Alasdair MacIntyre and Seyla Benhabib classical liberalism's individualistic focus has promoted an atomistic view of selfhood, one that understands individuals as disassociated from the social relations that surround them. These communitarian thinkers challenge the resulting agonistic view of society by arguing that its emphasis on individual rather than communal rights is predicated on a fundamental misreading of the nature of community. For a discussion of communitarianism and its quarrels with liberalism, see Charles Taylor, "Cross-Purposes: The Liberal-Communitarian Debate," in *Liberalism and the Moral Life*, ed. Nancy L. Rosenblum (Cambridge, Mass.: Harvard University Press, 1989), 159–82; Alasdair MacIntyre, *After Virtue: A Study in Moral Theory* (South Bend, Ind.: University of Notre Dame Press, 1981); and Seyla Benhabib, *Situating the Self: Gender, Community and Postmodernism in Contemporary Ethics* (New York: Routledge, 1992).

14. William Shakespeare, "The Phoenix and Turtle," in *The Riverside Shakespeare*, 27. All subsequent quotations of the poem are from this edition and are cited parenthetically in the text.

15. Perhaps the most bewildering of these physicalized images of love's transformative powers is Antipholus of Syracuse's assertion that his love for Luciana has the power to turn him into his beloved: "Call thyself sister, sweet, for I am thee" (3.2.66).

16. Robert Abbot, *A Wedding Sermon Preached at Bentley in Darbyshire, upon Michaelmasse Day last past Anno Domini. 1607* (London: Roger Jackson, 1608), 47–48.

17. Barbara Freedman, "Egeon's Debt: Self-Division and Self-Redemption in *The Comedy of Errors*," *English Literary Renaissance* 10 (1980), has suggested that "[a]ccording to Adriana, there is no 'thyself,' no sense of identity separable from one's identification with others. Yet her language simultaneously acknowledges a self separable from her, just as the play acknowledges an Antipholus of Syracuse separate and different from Antipholus of Ephesus" (382). I would argue, however, that Adriana's substantive and rhetorical emphasis is on love's ability to compound,

rather than to efface, individual identity and that her vision of selfhood is therefore consistent.

18. C. L. Barber, "Shakespearian Comedy in *The Comedy of Errors*," *College English* 25 (1964), characterizes Adriana as a "domineering" shrew who indulges in fits of "self-defeating rage" and "frenz[ies] of rage" motivated by extreme jealousy (495). Antipholus of Ephesus also, of course, accuses his wife of being "shrewish" and of upbraiding him (see 3.1.2; 109–13).

19. See Aristotle, *The Politics of Aristotle*, ed. and trans. Ernest Barker (Oxford: Clarendon Press, 1946), 1–91. Jürgen Habermas's *The Structural Transformation of the Public Sphere*, trans. Thomas Burger (Cambridge, Mass.: MIT Press, 1989), has drawn the attention of philosophers and literary critics alike to the overwhelming influence on Western conceptions of "publicness" and "privateness" of a Greek model of civic life that locates the community's political and ethical center in the agora while understanding the *oikos* as the source of mere survival. For an insightful account of the influence of the Aristotelian concept of the household on both economic and moral thought, see William James Booth, *Households: On the Moral Architecture of the Economy* (Ithaca, N.Y.: Cornell University Press, 1993).

20. Camille Wells Slights, *Shakespeare's Comic Commonwealths* (Toronto: University of Toronto Press, 1993), 19.

Notes to Chapter 4/Cuder-Domínguez

1. S. J. Wiseman, *Aphra Behn* (London: Northcote House & the British Council, 1996), 8; Ros Ballaster, "The first Female Dramatists," in *Women and Literature in Britain 1500–1700*, ed. Helen Wilcox (Cambridge: Cambridge University Press, 1996), 286; Elin Diamond, "Gestus and Signature in Aphra Behn's *The Rover*," *English Literary History* 56 (1989): 520. On this topic see also Janet Todd, *The Sign of Angellica: Women, Writing, Fiction, 1660–1800* (New York: Columbia University Press, 1989); Jane Spencer, "'Deceit, Dissembling, all that's Woman': Comic Plot and Female Action in *The Feigned Courtesans*," in *Rereading Aphra Behn: History, Theory, Criticism*, ed. Heidi Hutner (Charlottesville, Va.: University Press of Virginia), 86–101; and Ann Thompson, "Women/'women' and the Stage," in Wilcox, ed., *Women and Literature in Britain 1500–1700*, 100–16.

2. Ballaster, "First Female Dramatists," 268. Susan J. Owen, *Restoration Theatre and Crisis* (Oxford: Clarendon, 1996), 158. For other examples of this approach, see Owen's "'Suspect my loyalty when I lose my virtue': Sexual Politics and Party in Aphra Behn's Plays of the Exclusion Crisis, 1678–83," *Restoration* 18 (1994): 37–47; Robert Markley, "'Be impudent, be saucy, forward, bold, touzing, and leud': the Politics of Masculine Sexuality and Feminine Desire in Behn's Tory Comedies,"

in *Cultural Readings of Restoration and Eighteenth-Century English Theater*, ed. J. Douglas Canfield and Deborah C. Payne (Athens: University of Georgia Press, 1995), 114–40; and Alison Shell, "Popish Plots: *The Feign'd Curtizans* in Context," in *Aphra Behn Studies*, ed. Janet Todd (Cambridge: Cambridge University Press, 1996), 30–49.

3. Lawrence Stone, *The Family, Sex, and Marriage in England, 1500–1800* (Harmondsworth: Penguin, 1977), 183.

4. On this issue in Behn, see Lynne Taetzsch, "Romantic Love Replaces Kinship Exchange in Aphra Behn's Restoration Drama," *Restoration* 17 (1993): 30–38. On the theme in Restoration drama in general, see Christopher Wheatley, "Romantic Love and Social Necessities: Reconsidering Justifications for Marriage in Restoration Comedy," *Restoration* 14 (1990): 58–70.

5. Stone, *Family, Sex, and Marriage*, 221.

6. See Ben Ross Schneider Jr., *The Ethos of Restoration Comedy* (Urbana, Ill.: University of Illinois Press, 1971), 59–64, for the Restoration comic hero's extravagance. Schneider identifies here the dichotomy of liberality/avarice at the heart of Restoration comedy. Even though his discussion applies almost exclusively to the male characters, it is wide-ranging and thorough.

7. Todd, *The Sign of Angellica*, 19.

8. Charles H. Hinnant, "Pleasure and the Political Economy of Consumption in Restoration Comedy," *Restoration* 19 (1995): 77–87.

9. All quotations from Aphra Behn, *The Rover and Other Plays*, ed. Jane Spencer (Oxford: Oxford University Press, 1995), hereafter cited by line number in the text.

10. David M. Sullivan, "The Female Will in Aphra Behn," *Women's Studies* 22 (1993): 335–47.

11. For a Bakhtinian approach to the signification of carnival in this comedy, see Linda R. Payne, "The Carnivalesque Regeneration of Corrupt Economies in *The Rover*," *Restoration* 22 (1998): 40–49.

12. Joseph F. Musser, "'Imposing Nought but Constancy in Love': Aphra Behn Snares *The Rover*," *Restoration* 3 (1979): 21; John Franceschina, "Shadow and Substance in Aphra Behn's *The Rover:* The Semiotics of Restoration Performance," *Restoration* 19 (1995): 33–34.

13. Paula R. Backscheider, *Spectacular Politics: Theatrical Power and Mass Culture in Early Modern England* (Baltimore: Johns Hopkins University Press, 1993), has noted that Behn often gives "familiar lines to unexpected characters in order to foreground women's common lot" (86). See also Payne, "Carnivalesque Regeneration," 45, and Nancy Copeland, "'Once a whore and ever'? Whore and Virgin in *The Rover* and Its Antecedents," *Restoration* 16 (1992): 24.

14. Dolors Altaba-Artal, "Aphra Behn's *The Feign'd Curtezans; or, A Night's Intrigue* from Calderón's *Casa con dos puertas mala es de*

guardar," *Restoration and Eighteenth-Century Theatre Research* 10 (1995): 29–43, has suggested Calderón as a probable Spanish source for this play.

15. Spencer, "Deceit, Dissembling," 95.

16. Diamond, "Gestus and Signature," 527–28.

17. Jacqueline Pearson, *The Prostituted Muse: Images of Women and Women Dramatists, 1642–1737* (New York: St. Martin's Press, 1988), 166.

18. Peggy Thompson suggests that this lack of deflowerment seems to be central to the happy ending of this plot. "Closure and Subversion in Aphra Behn's Comedies," in *Broken Boundaries: Women and Feminism in Restoration Drama*, ed. Katherine M. Quinsey (Lexington, Ky., University Press of Kentucky, 1996), 83. However, such is not the case in Behn's earlier comedy *The False Count* (1681).

19. Robert A. Erickson, "Lady Fulbank and the Poet's Dream in Behn's *Lucky Chance,"* in Quinsey, ed., *Broken Boundaries: Women and Feminism in Restoration Drama*, (Lexington, Ky.: University Press of Kentucky,1996), 89–110, concurs as to the empowerment of Lady Fulbank, though he analyses it rather under the light of the playwright's control over action, characters, and staging.

20. Warren Chernaik, *Sexual Freedom in Restoration Literature* (Cambridge: Cambridge University Press, 1995), 186.

21. Peggy Thompson, "Closure and Subversion," 85.

22. Antonia Fraser, *The Weaker Vessel: A Woman's Lot in 17th-Century England* (London: Mandarin, 1984), 97.

23. Aphra Behn, *The Widow Ranter*, from *Five Plays* (London: Methuen, 1990), 214. Citation is by page number.

24. This unconventionality is also hinted at in her name. The ranters were members of a radical Protestant sect who held that believers participated in a kind of holiness that put them beyond common distinctions of good and evil, thus challenging the very notion of sin. They were denounced as blasphemous under the Commonwealth.

25. Bchn, *The Widow Ranter*, 277.

26. Margarete Rubik, *Early Women Drmatists, 1550–1800* (London: Macmillan, 1998), 39.

27. Chernaik, *Sexual Freedom*, 195.

Notes to Chapter 5/Staub

1. Epigraph from "Homily on the State of Matrimony" (London, 1563), qtd. in *Daughters, Wives and Widows: Writings by Men about Women and Marriage in England, 1500–1640*, ed. Joan Larsen Klein (Chicago: University of Illinois Press, 1992), 17; T. E., *The Lawes Resolution of Women's Rights; or, The Lawes Provision for Women* (London: John Grove, 1632), 6. A portion of this paper was published as "'Matchlesse

Monsters of the Female Sex': Murderous Women in Early Modern England," in *Renaissance Papers* (1995): 109–24, and is reprinted here by kind permission of the Southeastern Renaissance Conference.

2. Unmarried women, on the other hand, did seem to have limited legal rights. According to Alan MacFarlane, *The Origins of English Individualism* (New York: Cambridge University Press, 1979), an unmarried woman could hold land, establish a contract or write a will and sue or be sued. Widows also had some measure of legality since they frequently inherited property when their husbands died.

3. Frances Dolan, *Dangerous Familiars: Representations of Domestic Crime in England, 1550–1700* (Ithaca, N.Y.: Cornell University Press, 1994), 28; Carol Z. Wiener, "Is a Spinster an Unmarried Woman?" *American Journal of Legal History* 20 (1976): 27–31; on the ambiguity of women's social place, see Susan Amussen, *An Ordered Society: Gender and Class in Early Modern England* (London: Blackwell, 1988), and David Underdown, "The Taming of the Scold: The Enforcement of Patriarchal Authority in Early Modern England," in *Order and Disorder in Early Modern England*, ed. A. Fletcher and J. Stevenson (Cambridge: Cambridge University Press, 1985), 116–36; Catherine Belsey, *The Subject of Tragedy: Identity and Difference in Renaissance Drama* (New York: Routledge, 1985), 130.

4. Robert Cleaver, qtd. in Linda Fitz, "'What Says the Married Woman?': Marriage Theory and Feminism in the English Renaissance," *Mosaic* 13 (1980): 5.

5. This is one of the primary arguments of Frances Dolan's invaluable study of the popular literature of the period, cited above.

6. Tessa Watt, *Cheap Print and Popular Piety, 1550–1660* (New York: Cambridge University Press, 1991), 3; on the literacy rate, see David Cressy, *Literacy and the Social Order* (New York: Cambridge University Press, 1980), 72.

7. See C. Dobb, "Henry Goodcole, Visitor of Newgate," *The Guildhall Miscellany* 4 (1955): 17–20. Peter Linebaugh suggests that the ordinary of Newgate stood to make even more by publishing these accounts. See "The Ordinary of Newgate and His Account," in *Crime in England, 1550–1800*, ed. J. S. Cockburn (Princeton, N.J.: Princeton University Press, 1977), 246–69.

8. I derived this number by looking at Hyder E. Rollins's *Analytical Index to the Ballad-Entries in the Registers of the Company of Stationers of London* published in *Studies in Philology* 21 (1924). Of the 56 entries Rollins indexes under various murder categories from 1569 to 1640, 17 treat husband murder, five infanticide, two the murder of husband and child, and only one the murder of a nonfamily member. While these numbers are not representative of actual cases, because several of the more notorious stories are retold over and over, they do give some

idea of the popular fascination with murderous women during the period. I took the suggestion for this analysis from Betty Travitsky, "Husband-Murder and Petty Treason in English Renaissance Tragedy," *Renaissance Drama* 21 (1990): 176.

9. T. E., *The Lawes Resolution of Women's Rights*, 4, 206. T. E. goes on to suggest the complexities of assigning culpability by pointing out those occasions when a wife is not accountable for felonious crimes: "And note, if a Feme Covert steale anything by cohertion of her husband, this is not felonie in her" (206); Margaret Doody, "'Those Eyes Are Made So Killing': Eighteenth Century Murderesses and the Law," *Princeton University Library Chronicle* 46 (1984): 58.

10. Actually, the penalty for husband murder was greater than that for wife murder. A woman found guilty of murdering her husband was considered guilty of petty treason, a far more serious crime than murder, and one punishable by burning at the stake. More commonly, murderers were hanged. For further discussion of petty treason, see Betty Travitsky, "Husband-Murder and Petty Treason in English Renaissance Tragedy," *Renaissance Drama* 21 (1990): 171–98, and Frances E. Dolan, "The Subordinate('s) Plot: Petty Treason and the Forms of Domestic Rebellion" *Shakespeare Quarterly* 43 (1992): 317–40.

11. Belsey, *Subject of Tragedy*, 190–91. See also Belsey for a more complete discussion of the contradiction concerning accountability.

12. Leon Radzinowicz, *A History of English Criminal Law* (London: Stevens & Sons, 1948), 628.

13. J. S. Cockburn, "The Nature and Incidence of Crime in England 1559–1625: A Preliminary Survey," in *Crime in England, 1550–1800*, ed. J. S.Cockburn (Princeton, N.J.: Princeton University Press, 1977), 57.

14. *Murther, Murther. Or, A Bloody Relation how Anne Hamton dweling in Westminster nigh London, by pouson murthered her dear husband* (London: Thomas Bates, 1641), 2. Page numbers cited hereafter in the text.

15. John Dod and Robert Cleaver, *A Godly Form of Household Government* (London: Thomas Man, 1614), qtd. in Kathleen M. Davies, "Continuity and Change in Literary Advice on Marriage," in *Marriage and Society*, ed. R. B. Outhwaite (New York: St. Martin's Press, 1981), 67. (Sometimes attributed to Roger Carr or Robert Cawdry. John Deacon also claims authorship of this work.)

16. The handling of household goods seems a particularly troublesome matter in the prescriptive literature. Gouge's list of wifely duties, for example, includes at least ten sections devoted to the wife's management of the family's material possessions. "Of wives particular Duties" in *Of Domesticall Duties* (London: William Bladen, 1622), rpt. in *The English Experience: Its Record in Early Printed Books Published in Facsimile* (Norwood, N.J.: Walter J. Johnson, 1976).

17. "Anti-housewife" is Diane Purkiss's term. See her "Women's Stories of Witchcraft: the House, the Body, the Child," *Gender and History* 7 (1995), 414.

18. *The Adultresses Funeral Day* (London: N. and I. Okes, 1635), sig. Bv. Henry Goodcole writes pamphlets on three types of transgressive women: *The Adultresses Funeral Day* on husband murder; *Natures Cruell Step-dames: or, matchlesse monsters of the female sex* (London: Francis Coules, 1637) on infanticide; and *The Wonderfull Discoverie of Elizabeth Sawyer, a Witch, late of Edmonton* on witchcraft (London: William Butler, 1621).

19. *Natures Cruell Step-dames*, n.p.

20. Belsey, *Subject of Tragedy*, 191.

21. Thomas Deloney, "The Lamentation of Master Pages Wife of Plimouth," in *The Roxburghe Ballads*, ed. Charles Hindley (London: Rieves and Turner, 1874), 2:191–92.

22. The murder of M. Page is told in *Sundrye Strange and inhumaine Murthers, lately committed* (London: Thomas Scarlet, 1591). On forced marriages, see Joan Larsen Klein, "Women and Marriage in Renaissance England: Male Perspectives," *Topic* 36 (1982): 23, 6.

23. William Heale, *An Apologie for Women, or An Apposition to Mr. Dr. G. his assertion . . . that it was lawfull for husbands to beate their wives* (Oxford: Joseph Barnes, 1609), 30. T. E. is more ambivalent, arguing first that it is permissible for a husband to beat his wife because "by the Law common" she "can have no action." Also, "Lawfull and reasonable correction appertains to the office of a husband." But in the very same paragraph, he points out that the woman can sue her husband for bodily damage if he hurts her (128). For discussions of wife beating during this period, see Susan Amussen, "'Being Stirred to Much Unquietness': Violence and Domestic Violence in Early Modern England," *Journal of Women's History* 6, no. 2 (1994): 70–89, and Margaret Hunt, "Wife Beating, Domesticity, and Women's Independence in Eighteenth-Century London," *Gender and History* 4 (1992): 10–33.

24. Husbands in this tract seem particularly unsympathetic and malicious. In another case that Henry Goodcole briefly recounts as a parallel to Alice's, he depicts a husband refusing the antidote his wife offers repentantly once he has been poisoned: "Nay thou Strumpet and murderesse, I will receive no helpe at all but I am resolvd to dye and leave the world, be it for no other cause but to have thee burnt at the stake for my death." In a strange way, the husband here snatches back sovereignty by not allowing the wife to save him and effectively killing himself by refusing the antidote, if we believe the confession here — and Goodcole intimates that we should not.

25. Such is also the case with Mary Goodenough, a destitute widow with two children. In a futile attempt to provide for her family she exchanges sexual favors with a neighbor in return for "necessary mainte-

nance." Soon becoming pregnant, she does nothing to save the baby's life when it is born and is found guilty of infanticide in 1692. The author of the pamphlet admonishes her neighbors for their negligence: "If her Modesty made her ashamed to beg, did not her meagre Look, her starved Children, her meanly furnish'd House and Table beg from you?" *Fair Warning to the Murderers of Infants Being an Account of the Trial . . . of Mary Goodenough* (London, 1692), 4.

26. From *The Trueth of the most wicked and secret murthering of John Brewen, Goldsmith of London, committed by his owne wife through the provocation of one John Parker* (London: John Kid, 1592; often attributed to Thomas Kyd), in *Illustrations of Early English Popular Literature*, ed. J. Payne Collier (New York: Benjamin Blom, 1966), 1:14.

27. Gilbert Dugdale's *A True Discourse of the Practises of Elizabeth Caldwell* (London, 1604). The pamphlet is oddly reminiscent of *A Cristal Glasse for Christian Women* in which Philip Stubbes eulogizes his dead wife Katherine as the perfect mirror of womanhood. While Mary Beth Rose, "Where are the Mothers in Shakespeare? Options for Gender Representation in the English Renaissance," *Shakespeare Quarterly* 42 (1991), has suggested that during the early modern period, the "best mother . . . is a dead mother" (307), Stubbes's treatise suggests that the only good wife is a dead wife.

28. Richard Watkins, *Newes from the Dead, or a True and Exact Narration of the Miraculous Delivery of Anne Greene* (Oxford: Thomas Robinson, 1651). There are at least five versions of this story. For a more detailed discussion of the narratives relating this event, see my "'A Wench Re-Woman'd': The Miraculous Recovery of Anne Greene," *Renaissance Papers* (1997): 100–12, and "'News from the Dead': The Strange Story of a Woman Who Gave Birth, Was Executed and Was Resurrected as a Virgin," in *The Single Woman in Medieval and Early Modern England: Her Life and Representation*, ed. Laurel Amtower and Dorothea Kehler (Tempe, Ariz.: Arizona Center for Medieval and Renaissance Studies, forthcoming).

29. Frances Dolan, "'Gentlemen, I have one more thing to say': Women on Scaffolds in England, 1563–1680," *Modern Philology* 92 (1994): 171.

30. "The Source of *Arden of Faversham*," in *The Tragedy of Master Arden of Faversham*, ed. M. L. Wine (London: Methuen, 1973), 149.

31. *A Hellish Murder Committed by a French Midwife on the Body of her Husband* (London: Randal Taylor, 1688) (pages hereafter cited in text); *A Cabinet of Grief: Or, the French Midwife's Miserable Moan for the Barbarous Murther Committed upon the Body of her Husband* (London: [J.] Blare, 1688); *A Warning-Piece to All Married Men and Women. Being the Full Confession of Mary Hobry, the French Midwife* (London: George Croom, 1688), and "Epilogue to the French Midwife's Tragedy" (London: Randal Taylor, 1688), attributed by Wing to Elkanah Settle.

32. At one point, the narrative specifically associates the murder with her religion. The examiner asks her how she, "being of the Communion of the Church of Rome, came to throw the Quarters of her husband into the House of Office [privy] at the Savoy, which was a way to bring so great a Scandal upon the religion she professed, by laying the Murder at the Door of the Professors of that Religion?" (36).

33. Qtd. in Elizabeth Foyster, "A Laughing Matter?: Marital Discord and Gender Control in Seventeenth-Century England," *Rural History* 4 (1993), 13.

34. Adrian Wilson, *The Making of Man-Midwifery: Childbirth in England, 1660–1770* (Cambridge, Mass.: Harvard University Press, 1995), 26–31. According to Wilson, the time around the birth of the child inverted the normal order of the household. The lying-in month "belonged" to the mother; "what marriage had taken from her, the childbirth ritual temporarily restored" (29); Willoughby quoted in Wilson 30–31.

35. Dolan, *Dangerous Familiars*, 34; qtd. in Barbara J. Baines, "Effacing Rape in Early Modern Representation," *English Literary History* 65 (1998): 76. Baines's article provides a good overview of the complexities of rape law within the period and the ambiguities surrounding issues of consent.

36. T. E., *The Lawes Resolution*, 390. It is true that women were given more agency in rape cases as the seventeenth century progressed and the courts began to focus more on the issue of consent and changed the definition of the crime. Matthew Hale, *The History of the Pleas of the Crown*, qtd. in Miranda Chaytor, "Husband(ry): Narratives of Rape in the Seventeenth Century," *Gender and History* 7 (1995), for instance, redefined rape as "the carnal knowledge of any woman above the age of ten years against her will, and of a woman-child under the age of ten years with or against her will" (395). Ironically, once the law began focusing on consent, it simultaneously gave women agency and turned the fault back on them. Questions of the victim's innocence then became paramount (396). For additional discussion of consent, see Baines, "Effacing Rape."

37. Dolan, *Dangerous Familiars*, 34–35.

Notes to Chapter 6/Dubrow

1. I cite *The Riverside Shakespeare*, ed. G. Blakemore Evans (Boston: Houghton Mifflin, 1974).

2. William Gouge, *Of Domesticall Duties* (London: William Bladen, 1622), 581. Subsequent citations of this book will appear in parentheses within the text.

3. The most comprehensive study of death rates and the problems of studying them is E. A. Wrigley and R. S. Schofield, *The Population History of England 1541–1871: A Reconstruction* (Cambridge: Cambridge

University Press, 1981). On differing rates of remarriage, see esp. Vivien Brodsky, "Widows in Late Elizabethan London: Remarriage, Economic Opportunity and Family Orientation," in *The World We Have Gained: Histories of Population and Social Structure*, ed. Lloyd Bonfield, Richard M. Smith, Keith Wrightson (Oxford: Basil Blackwell, 1986), esp. 123–24. Also compare my essay "The Message from Marcade: Parental Death in Tudor and Stuart England," in *Attending to Women in Early Modern England*, ed. Betty S. Travitsky and Adele F. Seeff (Newark. N.J.: University of Delaware Press, 1994), which includes a preliminary exploration of a few of the ideas in this chapter.

4. On the odds of losing a parent, see esp. Ralph Houlbrooke, *The English Family 1450–1700* (London: Longman, 1984), chap. 4.

5. Francesco Petrarch, *Phisicke against Fortune*, trans. Thomas Twyne (London: Richard Watkyns, 1579), sig. Nviiiv; Lucy Hutchinson, *Memoirs of the Life of Colonel Hutchinson*, ed. James Sutherland (London: Oxford University Press, 1973), 24–25; Ilana Krausman Ben-Amos, *Adolescence and Youth in Early Modern England* (New Haven, Conn.: Yale University Press, 1994), 49–50.

6. See Marianne Novy's study, "Reading Adoption and Shakespeare," a version of her article in this volume. I am grateful to the author for making her work available to me before publication.

7. This process may be related to the decathectization of which Freud writes. His oeuvre includes many analyses of death and mourning, but his principal statement on decathectization and related issues is "Mourning and Melancholia," vol. 14, *The Standard Edition of the Complete Psychological Works of Sigmund Freud*, trans. James Strachey, 24 vols. (London: Hogarth Press, 1953–1974). Also see "Anxiety, Pain and Mourning," vol. 20, The Standard Edition, and letter #239 in *Letters of Sigmund Freud 1873–1939*, ed. Ernst L. Freud, trans. Tania and James Stern (London: Hogarth Press, 1970). For an analysis and criticism of his concept of decathectization, see my *Shakespeare and Domestic Loss: Forms of Deprivation, Mourning, and Recuperation* (Cambridge: Cambridge University Press, 1999), esp. 157–58.

8. Anthony Low, "*Hamlet* and the Ghost of Purgatory: Intimations of Killing the Father," *English Literary Renaissance* 29 (1999), 443–67. I thank the author for making his manuscript available to me prior to publication. Ralph Houlbrooke, "Death, Church, and Family in England Between the Late Fifteenth and the Early Eighteenth Centuries," in *Death, Ritual, and Bereavement*, ed. Ralph Houlbrooke (London: Routledge in association with the Social History Society of the United Kingdom, 1989), 36.

9. Joshua Scodel, *The English Poetic Epitaph: Commemoration and Conflict from Jonson to Wordsworth* (Ithaca, N.Y.: Cornell University Press, 1991), 21. On parental blessings as a form of intercession, see Bruce W. Young, "Ritual as an Instrument of Grace: Parental Blessings

in *Richard III, All's Well That Ends Well,* and *The Winter's Tale,"* in *True Rites and Maimed Rites: Ritual and Anti-Ritual in Shakespeare and His Age,* ed. Linda Woodbridge and Ralph Berry (Urbana, Ill.: University of Illinois Press, 1992), 170–73.

10. See Charles Carlton, *The Court of Orphans* (Leicester: Leicester University Press, 1974), 44.

11. For a useful overview of wardship, see H. E. Bell, *An Introduction to the History and Records of the Court of Wards and Liveries* (Cambridge: Cambridge University Press, 1953); Joel Hurstfield, *The Queen's Wards: Wardship and Marriage Under Elizabeth I,* 2nd ed. (London: Frank Cass, 1973). Exceptions to the neglect of this system by students of early modern literature include the brief but useful commentaries on wardship and inheritance in Lisa Jardine, *Still Harping on Daughters: Women and Drama in the Age of Shakespeare* (Sussex: Harvester Press, 1983), 80–84; Marilyn L. Williamson, *The Patriarchy of Shakespeare's Comedies* (Detroit, Mich.: Wayne State University Press, 1986), 61–64.

12. The ante mortem passing on of property is the central thesis of Lloyd Bonfield, "Normative Rules and Property Transmission: Reflections on the Link between Marriage and Inheritance in Early Modern England," in Bonfield et al., eds. *The World We Have Gained,* 155–76.

13. Hurstfield, *Queen's Wards,* chaps. 10, 12, 13.

14. Bell, *Court of Wards,* 115–16.

15. Richard Baxter, *Reliquiae Baxterianae* (London: T. Parkhurst et al., 1696), 12.

16. On the theatricality of death, see, e.g., Michael Cameron Andrews, *This Action of Our Death: The Performance of Death in English Renaissance Drama* (Newark, Del.: University of Delaware Press, 1989), 14–16.

17. On the presence of that myth see, for example, John Wilders, *The Lost Garden: A View of Shakespeare's English and Roman History Plays* (Totowa, N.J.: Rowman and Littlefield, 1978).

18. One of the best analyses of the connections between Richmond and Richard III is Barbara Hodgdon, *The End Crowns All: Closure and Contradiction in Shakespeare's History* (Princeton, N.J.: Princeton University Press, 1991), 113–15.

19. On his propensity for creating those divisions, see William B. Toole, "The Motif of Psychic Division in *Richard III,"* *Shakespeare Survey* 27 (1974): 21–32.

20. C. L. Barber and Richard P. Wheeler, *The Whole Journey: Shakespeare's Power of Development* (Berkeley: University of California Press, 1986), 3.

21. An early argument for the connection with the ballad appears in Sharon Turner, *The History of England During the Middle Ages* (London: Longman, Hurst, Rees, Orme, Brown and Green, 1825), 3:487. Also

compare David R. Carlson, "The Princes' Embrace in *Richard III*," *Shakespeare Quarterly* 41 (1990): 344 n. 2.

22. Spevack, *The Harvard Concordance to Shakespeare* (Cambridge, Mass.: Harvard University Press, 1973), s.v. "protect."

23. For a different but compatible view of rhetorical substitution, see Russ McDonald, "*Richard III* and the Tropes of Treachery," *Philological Quarterly* 68 (1989): 470–71. Marjorie B. Garber, *Dream in Shakespeare: From Metaphor to Metamorphosis* (New Haven, Conn.: Yale University Press, 1974), 23, and *Shakespeare's Ghost Writers: Literature as Uncanny Causality* (New York: Methuen, 1987), 36.

24. On Richard's propensity for delegating his evil deeds, see Robert Ornstein, *A Kingdom for a Stage: The Achievement of Shakespeare's History Plays* (Cambridge, Mass.: Harvard University Press, 1972), 66; R. Thomas Simone, *Shakespeare and "Lucrece": A Study of the Poem and Its Relation to the Plays* (Salzburg: Institut für Englische Sprache und Literatur, 1974), 113.

25. "Southern Baptists Declare Wife Should 'Submit' to Her Husband," *New York Times*, 10 June 1998, late edition, A1.

Notes to Chapter 7/Chamberlain

1. See *The Diaries of Anne Clifford* (Wolfeboro Falls, N.H.: Alan Sutton, 1991). For biographical accounts of Anne Clifford's life, see George C. Williamson, *Lady Anne Clifford, Countess of Dorset, Pembroke & Montgomery, 1590–1676: Her Life, Letters, and Work* (Kendal: T. Wilson, 1922); and Martin Holmes, *Proud Northern Lady: Lady Anne Clifford, 1590–1676* (Chichester: Phillimore, 1975).

2. This phrase is inscribed on the memorial Anne erected to her late mother Margaret in January 1654. Not only does it serve to memorialize her mother, but the inscription, by tracing her patrilineage, establishes in a quite visual and enduring form Anne's rightful claim to the lands and offices of her late father and thus the Cumberland estate.

3. Victor Turner, *The Anthropology of Performance* (New York: PAJ Publications, 1988).

4. On Thomas Stoner's will, see Keith Wrightson, *English Society, 1580–1680* (New Brunswick, N.J.: Rutgers University Press, 1982), 74; on monastic lands, see Jack Goody, *Development of the Family and Marriage in Europe* (Cambridge: Cambridge University Press, 1983), 127. Goody has suggested that as much as 20 to 30 percent of English land was owned by the Church in 1535, generating an annual revenue of £400,000. By comparison, crown lands are estimated to have generated only one-tenth of that amount. As he notes, "sometimes the King had to confiscate superfluous ecclesiastical wealth by the favourite medieval method of placing burdens on the land, such as military service, good, rents, or taxation" (115). With the dissolution of the monasteries during

the reign of Henry VIII, previously held monastic lands became available for purchase. For an extensive analysis of the estate of John Isham, see Mary E. Finch, *The Wealth of Five Northamptonshire Families 1540–1640*, publications of the Northamptonshire Record Society, vol. 19 (Oxford: Oxford University Press, 1966).

5. See Goody, *Development*, 155, and Cicely Howell, "Peasant Inheritance Customs in the Midlands, 1280–1700," in *Family and Inheritance*, ed. Jack Goody, Joan Thirsk and E. P. Thompson (Cambridge: Cambridge University Press, 1976). Goody has argued that primogeniture came increasingly to be practiced in the middle of the eleventh century as a means by which to curtail the widespread acquisition of estate lands by the Church: a practice which since the Middle Ages had contributed to the breakup of family estates. Church law, as Howell has noted, allowed for the free alienation of land, whereas customary law did not. The practice of primogeniture, whereby estates were entailed upon the eldest male child, discouraged the widespread alienation of land which had made the Church, in the words of Goody, "the largest landowner" in England. On "extreme pulverization," see John Day, "On the Status of Women in Medieval Sardinia," in *Women of the Medieval World*, ed. Julius Kirshner and Suzanne F. Wemple (Oxford: Blackwell, 1985), 306.

6. See Eileen Spring, *Law, Land and Family: Aristocratic Inheritance in England, 1300 to 1800* (Chapel Hill, N.C.: University of North Carolina Press, 1993), 10. This calculation is based upon existing demographics for a stationary early modern English society. Spring estimates that upwards of 40 percent of early modern English marriages failed to produce male heirs. Any daughters who survived to the age of majority thus had the potential to control a sizable percentage of landed estates in a country, ironically, which normally entailed lands in favor of male heirs. This figure is supported by Amy Louise Erickson, *Women and Property in Early Modern England* (London: Routledge, 1993), who suggests that "even if a son were born, he was unlikely to be of age at his father's death, so his inheritance 'wandered' to his mother" (5). *The Lawes Resolutions of Women's Rights: Or, The Lawes Provision for Woemen. A Methodicall Collection of Such Statutes and Customes, with the Cases, Opinions, Arguments and points of Learning in the Law, as doe properly concerne Women* (London: John Grove, 1632). James Holt, "Feudal Society and the Family in Early Medieval Europe: The Heiress and the Alien," in *Transactions of the Royal Historical Society*, 35 (1985): 3.

7. Lawrence Stone, *The Family, Sex and Marriage in England 1500–1800* (New York: Harper Torchbooks, 1977), 72. Much has been written on the plight of younger sons in early modern England, who, unlike daughters, were often left relatively unprovided for by their fathers. At his death in 1552, for instance, the widow of Sir William Fitzwilliam II provided for her two younger sons out of her jointure lands because their father had failed to make provision for them. Although some younger

sons, such as those of Sir John Spencer II, were amply endowed by their father, each receiving land as well as goods at his death, such provisions were not common in early modern England. To avoid alienating entailed lands which were to go to eldest sons, fathers had to rely on any savings they may have been able to accumulate from estate profits. Any land purchased during the course of estate owners' lifetimes not a part of original entails could also be used to endow younger sons, which proved the case with Sir John. On the plight of younger sons, see Finch, *Wealth*; Spring, *Law, Land*; and Erickson, *Women and Property.*

8. Finch, *Wealth*, 26, 60, 28, 127.

9. Ibid., 76–77. Sir Thomas Tresham, an avowed Catholic sympathizer, was assessed huge penalties beginning in 1581 for recusancy. According to Finch, Tresham paid just under £8,000 in fines over a 24-year period. This, coupled with the inability to secure long-term loans, ultimately led to the selling of outlying lands and the family's eventual extinction.

10. The £17,000 was the amount of the £20,000 settlement that Francis Clifford, Dorset and James I agreed upon for Anne Clifford's inheritance. In exchange for this partial settlement, Anne was required to sign off on the remaining £3,000 to relinquish her claim as heiress to the Clifford estate. Her refusal to do so resulted in her reclamation of the lands and offices of the estate at the deaths of the collateral male heirs. Alan Macfarlane, *Marriage and Love in England 1300–1840: Modes of Reproduction* (Oxford: Basil Blackwell, 1987), 269.

11. Finch, *Wealth*, 28.

12. Margaret Spufford, "Peasant Inheritance Customs and Land Distribution in Cambridgeshire from the Sixteenth to the Eighteenth Centuries," in *Family and Inheritance: Rural Society in Western Europe 1200–1800* (157).

13. Spring, *Law, Land*, 19. See Alan Macfarlane, *Marriage and Love in England 1300–1840* (Oxford: Blackwell, 1986), 274–75, on loss of patrilineal identity. It was for this reason that land was usually not part of the marriage portion. An early modern English husband, as Macfarlane has noted, could not alienate lands brought by his wife to the marriage unless it was explicitly transferred to him or unless he obtained his wife's consent. The husband did, however, have unrestricted use of the land and its profits during the term of coverture. For a balanced discussion of heiresses and the disposition of estate lands, see Erickson, *Women and Property*, and Spring. On alternate patronyms, see Lawrence Stone and Jeanne C. Fawtier Stone, *An Open Elite? England 1540–1880* (Oxford: Oxford University Press, 1984), 82–83. They note how some sons-in-law after about 1690 were required to assume their wives' surnames as a condition of marriage to preserve patrilineal identity. Although lands and titles might pass through heirs general to their husbands, these "fictive" tail males gave the illusion of uninterrupted patrilineal descent.

On Agnes Bussy, see Finch, *Wealth*, 141. In fact, Agnes Bussy's claim as heiress, not unlike that of Anne Clifford, was contested by her paternal uncle. When her father died in 1542, Agnes succeeded as sole heiress to her father's estate. Henry Bussy, her father's brother, immediately challenged his niece's claim, citing an ancient entail which granted the estate only to male heirs. When her uncle died, a male cousin, John Bussy, also challenged Agnes's right to inherit.

14. All *King Lear* citations are from *The Norton Shakespeare*, ed. Stephen Greenblatt et al. (New York: Norton, 1997).

15. *The Norton Shakespeare* includes both the Q1 and the F versions of the *King Lear* text, which show an interesting variation of the exchange between Kent and Gloucester. The Q1 text reads as "in the division of the kingdoms," whereas the F text reads as "in the division of the kingdom." Such a difference has serious ramifications for our understanding of Lear's opening action. The division of separate kingdoms would, I believe, carry less weight than that of a fully united one.

16. The Q1 text reads "equalities," whereas the F text reads "qualities."

17. Samuel Johnson, *Johnson on Shakespeare: Essays and Notes* (London: H. Milford, 1908; rpt., Oxford: Oxford University Press, 1929), 84.

18. For a good discussion of the espousal in early modern England, see David Cressy, *Birth, Marriage and Death: Ritual, Religion, and the Life-Cycle in Tudor and Stuart England* (Oxford: Oxford University Press, 1997).

19. Stanley Cavell, *Disowning Knowledge in Six Plays of Shakespeare* (Cambridge: Cambridge University Press, 1987), 70; Kathleen McLuskie, "The Patriarchal Bard: Feminist Criticism and *King Lear*," in *William Shakespeare: King Lear*, ed. Kiernan Ryan (New York: St. Martin's Press, 1992), 55.

20. Turner, *Anthropology*, 34.

21. This point is clearly established in a number of Shakespeare's sources. In Geoffrey of Monmouth's *Historia Regum Britanniae* (1135), for example, Leir bequeaths his kingdom as dowry among his three daughters, Gonorilla, Regan and Cordeilla because "male issue was denied to him" (448). In another principal source of the play, Holinshed's *The Chronicles of England, Scotland, and Ireland* (1587), Leir "had by his wife three daughters without other issue" (453), a circumstance which likewise results in the naming of female heirs. See *Shakespeare and His Sources*, ed. Joseph Satin (Boston: Houghton, 1966).

22. Turner, *Anthropology*, 22 (page references cited hereafter in the text); Stone and Stone, *Open Elite*, 85.

23. Cavell, *Disowning Knowledge*, 68.

24. See Erickson, *Women and Property*, 95, who has noted the connection between the marriage portion and the bride's perceived sexual

honor. As she argues, "the unspoken assumption . . . is that without dowries poor women would be unable to marry and therefore forced into prostitution."

25. Gayle Whittier, "Cordelia as Prince: Gender and Language in *King Lear*," *Exemplaria* 1 (1989), 374.

26. Ian Kirby, "The Passing of King Lear," *Shakespeare Survey* 41 (1988): 155.

27. John Roland Dove and Peter Gamble, "'Our Darker Purpose': The Division Scene in *King Lear*," *Neuphilologische Mitteilungen* 70 (1969): 312; Goody, *Development*, 257; Margaret Cavendish (Duchess of Newcastle) CCXI *Sociable Letters written by the Thrice Noble, Illustrious, and Excellent Princess, The Lady Marchioness of Newcastle* (London: William Wilson, 1664); Cressy, *Birth, Marriage*, 27.

28. See Macfarlane, *Marriage and Love*, 274–75. A husband's control of his wife's inheritance lands was a cloudy issue in early modern England. Although, as MacFarlane has noted, a husband could not legally dispose of his wife's land unless the land were explicitly transferred to him at the time of the marriage, he did retain virtually unrestricted use of it. Moreover, coercion, even abuse of his wife to obtain her "consent" to dispose of her legally-protected rights seems likely. The case of Anne Clifford again is illustrative here. Her husband, Richard Sackville, the third Earl of Dorset, undertook extreme measures to convince his yet unyielding wife to give up the Clifford lands.

29. Pierre Bourdieu, *Outline of a Theory of Practice*, trans. Richard Nice, Cambridge Studies in Social and Cultural Anthropology (Cambridge: Cambridge University Press, 1977), 54, 30; Whittier, "Cordelia as Prince," 374; Barbara C. Millard, "Virago with a Soft Voice: Cordelia's Tragic Rebellion in *King Lear*," *Philological Quarterly* 68 (1989): 148.

30. See Cavell, *Disowning Knowledge*, and Boose, "The Father and the Bride in Shakespeare," *PMLA* 97 (1982): 325–47. See also Dove and Gamble, "Our Darker Purpose," 316.

31. Turner, *Anthropology*, 46; Leonard Tennenhouse, "The Theatre of Punishment," in Ryan, ed., *William Shakespeare*, 71.

32. See Barbara Kiefer Lewalski, *Writing Women in Jacobean England* (Cambridge, Mass.: Harvard University Press, 1993), 130. In later life, Anne Clifford became a generous advocate for women and the poor, founding two almshouses for destitute widows.

33. See Geoffrey of Monmouth, *Historia Regum Britanniae*, 452, and Raphael Holinshed, *The Chronicles of England, Scotland, and Ireland*, 455. In Monmouth's *Historia*, Cordeilla "overwhelmed with grief at the loss of her kingdom . . . slew herself." A comparable, if more heroic fate is met by Holinshed's Cordeilla. While in prison, "she took such grief being a woman of a manly courage, and despairing to recover liberty,

there she slew herself." In both cases, it is collateral male authority which challenges and decisively defeats weak female rule to recover patrilineal descent.

34. Millard, "Virago," 143.

Notes to Chapter 8/Novy

1. See Lawrence Stone, *The Family, Sex, and Marriage in England 1500–1800* (New York: Harper and Row, 1977); Keith Wrightson, *English Society 1580–1680* (London: Hutchinson, 1982); Linda Pollock, *Forgotten Children: Parent-Child Relations from 1500–1900* (Cambridge: Cambridge University Press, 1983).

2. Beatrice Gottlieb, *The Family in the Western World from the Black Death to the Industrial Age* (New York: Oxford University Press, 1993), 145, 160. Gottlieb claims that apprenticeship often began around seven, but Ilana Krausman Ben-Amos finds that children were more commonly apprenticed at ten, 12, or even older (though younger children could be boarded out for schooling, outbreaks of plague, poverty or parental death). See her *Adolescence and Youth in Early Modern England* (New Haven, Conn.: Yale University Press, 1994), 54–64. Her view on apprentices' age is supported by Paul Griffith, *Youth and Authority: Formative Experiences in England 1560–1640* (Oxford: Clarendon Press, 1996), 33.

3. On the early modern lack of adoption laws, see Jack Goody, *The Development of the Family and Marriage in Europe* (New York: Cambridge University Press, 1983), 73.

4. An earlier and much shorter version of this essay appeared as "Multiple Parenting in *Pericles*," in *Pericles: Critical Essays*, ed. David Skeele (New York: Garland, 2000).

5. *The Tempest* deals with some of the same issues, but Caliban is treated as a servant rather than as a foster child, and no relative of his appears.

6. While noting that such plots in literature "predicate that the biological parents are superior to the adoptive ones," Barbara Estrin, *The Raven and the Lark: Lost Children in Literature of the English Renaissance* (Lewisburg, Va.: Bucknell University Press, 1985), also suggests that "the good of art appears in the adoptive sections where the supremacy of inheritance is superseded by the idealization of the replacement" (14).

7. See, for example, the discussion of the conflicting views of Aristotle, Hippocrates, and Galen in Thomas Laqueur, *Making Sex: Body and Gender from the Greeks to Freud* (Cambridge: Harvard University Press, 1990), 25–43, and his explanation on 55–57 of how the encyclopedist Isidore of Seville, still influential during the Renaissance, simultaneously holds "that only men have sperma, that only women have sperma, and that both have sperma" (55). See also Janet Adelman,

"Making Defect Perfection: Shakespeare and the One-Sex Model," in *Enacting Gender on the Renaissance Stage*, ed. Viviana Comensoli and Anne Russell (Urbana, Ill.: University of Illinois Press, 1999), 23–52, and François Jacob, *The Logic of Life: A History of Heredity*, trans. Betty E. Spillman (1983; rpt. Princeton, N.J.: Princeton University Press, 1993). Use of the term "blood" for biological kinship comes from the ancient belief that "seeds," whether male or female, are refined blood; see Laqueur, *Making Sex*, 38. But also see Aristotle's belief that the fetus feeds on menstrual blood, which accounts for the resemblance of children to their mothers, in Ian Maclean, *The Renaissance Notion of Woman* (Cambridge: Cambridge University Press, 1980), 37. For a classic, influential text on another dimension of belief in "blood," the natural love of parents for their children, combined with a description of how Nature uses women's blood to feed the seed, see Plutarch, "On Affection for Offspring," in *Moralia*, trans. W. C. Helmbold (Cambridge, Mass.: Harvard University Press, 1970), 6:343–53. For still other Renaissance notions of "blood," see Gail Kern Paster, *The Body Embarrassed: Drama and the Disciplines of Shame in Early Modern England* (Ithaca, N.Y.: Cornell University Press, 1993), 64–112.

8. Children's differences from their parents were sometimes explained as the influence of the maternal imagination. See Clara Pinto-Correia, *The Ovary of Eve: Egg and Sperm and Preformation* (Chicago: University of Chicago Press, 1997), 128–30. For other explanations related to the condition of both parents at conception, see Paster, *The Body Embarrassed*, 167–72.

9. For the early modern comparison of teachers to gardeners, see Rebecca Bushnell, *A Culture of Teaching: Early Modern Humanism in Theory and Practice* (Ithaca, N.Y.: Cornell University Press, 1996), 73–116. On the influence of wet nurses, see Valerie Fildes, *Breasts, Bottles, and Babies: A History of Infant Feeding* (Edinburgh: Edinburgh University Press, 1986), 168–78. See also Pastor, *Body Embarrassed*, 197–201, on early modern wet nursing and its transformation in drama.

10. *Pericles* 4.1.25, in *William Shakespeare: The Complete Works*, 4th ed., ed. David Bevington (New York: Harper Collins, 1992). Cited hereafter in the text by line number.

11. Carol Thomas Neely, *Broken Nuptials in Shakespeare's Plays* (New Haven, Conn.: Yale University Press, 1985), 202.

12. F. D. Hoeniger notes that Pericles's role as music teacher is emphasized in the sources. "Introduction," *Pericles*, ed. Hoeniger (London: Methuen, 1963), lxxviii.

13. Susan Baker, "Personating Persons: Rethinking Shakespearean Disguises," *Shakespeare Quarterly* 43 (1992): 312. Baker is the first to offer such a reading, to my knowledge.

14. Compare the way that Shakespeare, in adding to his historical source for *King John* developed the speculation about the bastard's

relation to his father, King Richard, by including a discussion of their physical resemblance; see Phyllis Rackin, *Stages of History: Shakespeare's English Chronicles* (Ithaca, N.Y.: Cornell University Press, 1990), 187–90.

15. Anne Barton, "*As You Like It* and *Twelfth Night*: Shakespeare's Sense of an Ending," in *Shakespearian Comedy*, Stratford-upon-Avon Studies 14, ed. D. J. Palmer and Malcolm Bradbury (New York: Crane, Russak, 1972), 176.

16. From the early example in Greek tragedies, such as *The Libation Bearers*, recognition scenes have often contained a prolonged questioning which heightens emotions by suspending the recognition in time. See my "Recognition Scenes and Their Thematic Significance in Shakespeare's Romantic Comedies" (Ph.D. diss., Yale University, 1973), 9.

17. Terence Cave, *Recognitions: A Study in Poetics* (Oxford: Clarendon Press, 1988), 289.

18. As Janet Adelman, *Suffocating Mothers: Fantasies of Maternal Origin in Shakespeare's Plays, "Hamlet" to "The Tempest"* (New York: Routledge, 1992), points out, they also rearticulate, benignly, "the deadly mergers of the beginning — the collapse of the mother, wife, and daughter in Antiochus's daughter's body and the attendant collapse of Pericles's masculine identity" (197).

19. I have commented on this imagery further in *Love's Argument: Gender Relations in Shakespeare* (Chapel Hill, N.C.: University of North Carolina Press, 1984), 178–79, where I note that recognition scenes in Shakespeare's comedies generally have less physical imagery.

20. Adelman, *Suffocating Mothers*, 197–98.

21. Ann Thompson, "Cymbeline's Other Endings," in *The Appropriation of Shakespeare: Post-Renaissance Reconstructions of the Works and the Myth*, ed. Jean Marsden (New York: St. Martin's, 1992), 207–08. Thompson also has some fun with reviewers' habits of "counting the number of separate explanations or revelations." She has "found totals of 14, 24 and just about every number in between" (204).

22. John Boswell, *The Kindness of Strangers: The Abandonment of Children in Western Europe from Late Antiquity to the Renaissance* (New York: Vintage, 1988). Such a requirement is also mentioned in a number of newly discovered private adoption contracts in early modern France. See Kristin Elizabeth Gager, *Blood Ties and Fictive Ties: Adoption and Family Life in Early Modern France* (Princeton, N.J.: Princeton University Press, 1996), 101–02.

23. In the ninth century *Apollonius of Tyre*, Marina's original has a little more to say to the dying nurse who reveals her ancestry: "[I]f by any chance any such thing had happened to me before you revealed this to me, I should have been absolutely ignorant of my ancestry and birth." See Elizabeth Archibald, *Apollonius of Tyre: Medieval and Renaissance Themes and Variations* (Bury-St. Edmunds: C. S. Brewer, 1991), 145.

24. On that prejudice, see Stephen Collins, "'Reason, Nature, and Order': The Stepfamily in English Renaissance Thought," *Renaissance Studies* 13 (1999): 312–24; see Neely, *Broken Nuptials*, 174, on the desexualization and sanctification of mothers in the romances through real and mock deaths. Shaw is cited from Thompson, "Other Endings."

25. See Adelman, *Suffocating Mothers*, 9–10 and passim, for a detailed analysis of the varying roles of mothers and fantasies about mothers in Shakespeare's works. Hermione and Thaisa are less idealized early in the play than after they reappear. Only two other plays include mother-daughter relationships — *Romeo and Juliet* and *Merry Wives of Windsor*. In both those plays, relations are rather cool and distant, to tragic effect in *Romeo and Juliet*.

26. Paster, *Body Embarrassed*, 179.

27. Collins, "Reason, Nature, and Order," 320–21. On polarization in views of women, see, for example, Mary Beth Rose, *The Expense of Spirit: Love and Sexuality in English Renaissance Drama* (Ithaca, N.Y.: Cornell University Press, 1988), 4–5.

28. Compare the presence of the idealized mothers Ceres and Juno in the masque of *The Tempest*.

29. Doreen Delvecchio and Antony Hammond provide a list of examples in their "Introduction" to *Pericles, Prince of Tyre* (Cambridge: Cambridge University Press, 1998), 47–49. See also Neely, *Broken Nuptials*, 191–92, and Novy, *Love's Argument*, 171–74.

30. For an interpretation of the cross-gendered imagery emphasizing male nurturance, see Novy, *Love's Argument*, 174; for the view that it involves male appropriation of female procreative power that excludes women, see Adelman, *Suffocating Mothers*, 197–98, a reading that also emphasizes the repression of sexuality, and Marilyn Williamson, *The Patriarchy of Shakespeare's Comedies* (Detroit, Mich.: Wayne State University Press, 1986), 165.

31. Lori Humphrey Newcomb discusses *Pandosto*, the source of *Winter's Tale*, in relation to the widespread institution of adolescent service in "The Romance of Service: The Simple History of *Pandosto*'s Servant Readers," in *Framing Elizabethan Fictions: Contemporary Approaches to Early Modern Narrative Prose*, ed. Constance Relihan (Kent, Ohio: Kent State University Press, 1996), 117–39. Newcomb generously provided me with a prepublication copy of this essay.

32. Paster, *Body Embarrassed*, 273.

33. Heather Dubrow, *Shakespeare and Domestic Loss: Forms of Deprivation, Mourning, and Recuperation* (Cambridge: Cambridge University Press, 1999), 161–62. She generously provided me with a prepublication copy of her chapter on the early death of parents. An earlier version of this discussion appears in her essay, "The Message from Marcade: Parental Death in Tudor and Stuart England," in *Attending to Women in Early Modern England*, ed. Betty S. Travitsky and Adele

F. Seeff (Newark, Del.: University of Delaware Press, 1994), 147–67, esp. 157.

34. Gottlieb, *Family in the Western World*, 133. Frances E. Dolan, *Dangerous Familiars: Representations of Domestic Crime in England 1550–1700* (Ithaca, N.Y.: Cornell University Press, 1994), has argued that *Winter's Tale* in particular is a displaced, aestheticized resolution of anxiety about infanticide (168). This issue is even more relevant to *Pericles*.

35. Paster, *Body Embarrassed*, 276.

36. See Adelman's chapter "Masculine Authority and the Maternal Body: The Return to Origins in the Romances," in *Suffocating Mothers*, 199–219. Meredith Skura, "Interpreting Posthumus' Dream from Above and Below: Families, Psychoanalysis and Literary Critics," in *Representing Shakespeare: New Psychoanalytic Essays*, ed. Murray Schwartz and Coppelia Kahn (Baltimore: Johns Hopkins University Press, 1980), notes that "Posthumus cannot find his parents in the flesh; he must find the idea of his parents. . . . [He] must make what he can of the past, recreate his family in his dreams" (215).

37. Dubrow, *Shakespeare and Domestic Loss*, makes an analogous comment about the relationship of stepparenting to role-playing (170).

38. Daniele Barbar, *Italian Relations* (1551), in *How They Lived*, ed. Molly Harrison and O. M. Royston (Oxford: Blackwell, 1963), 2:267–68. Gottlieb, *The Family in the Western World*, includes this comment and notes that criticism of the custom of fostering eventually developed in England, beginning with William Penn. She argues that "some people were genuinely puzzled by why they were doing what was expected" (161, 162). There were a few cases of infanticidal nursing, mostly of illegitimate children. See Keith Wrighton, "Infanticide in Earlier Seventeenth-Century England," *Local Population Studies* 15 (1975): 10–22. In this context, Dionyza's words, "Nurses are not the fates, / To foster it, nor ever to preserve" (4.3.14–15), echo ominously. Thanks to Frances Dolan for sending me a copy of this article.

39. Hoeniger, "Introduction," xxv.

40. Hoeniger notes that "There are few plays by Shakespeare for which as much evidence is available to testify to their popularity on the stage during the early decades of the seventeenth century" (lxvi–lxvii).

Notes to Chapter 9/Busse

1. William Shakespeare, *Measure for Measure*, in *The Riverside Shakespeare*, ed. G. Blakemore Evans (Boston: Houghton Mifflin, 1974), 545–86. All citations to Shakespeare are from this edition and are cited hereafter in the text.

2. See the notes for *Measure for Measure* 3.2.5–6 in *The Riverside Shakespeare*, 568, 2058, n. 2, in *The Norton Shakespeare*, ed. Stephen

Greenblatt (New York: Norton, 1997), 2021–90. E. Pearlman invokes the same lines from *Measure for Measure* at the beginning of her discussion of Shakespeare and usury to point to the "strangely askew raveling of sex and economics." "Shakespeare, Freud, and the Two Usuries, or, Money's a Meddler," *English Literary Renaissance* 2 (1972): 217. Pearlman raises similar questions to mine but quickly moves her discussion in a different direction, for her interests lie less in early modern cultural perceptions and practices concerning children than in the psychological "link between children and money" (227).

3. Charles Gibbon, *A Work Worth the Reading. Wherein is contayned, fiue profitable and pithy Questions, very expedient, aswell for Parents to perceive howe to bestowe their Children in marriage, and to dispose their goods at their death: as for all other Persons to receive great profit by the rest of the matters herein expressed* (London: Henry Kyrkham, 1591), 42. For consistency's sake, I have regularized, as much as possible, early modern spellings from Gibbon's work as well as the other treatises and laws quoted in this article.

4. Cohen, *Norton*, interprets this as an attempt on Shakespeare's part to "smuggle in a defense of economic behavior often felt to be destructive of tradition," yet perceives the connection of children and usury to be a metaphor without any powerful material grounding (1918).

5. Legal and religious approaches to usury in the early modern period rarely identified the Aristotelian depiction of money breeding in their attempts to regulate the practice. However, as Carl F. Taeusch, "The Concept of 'Usury' The History of an Idea," *Journal of the History of Ideas* 3 (1942): 291–318, argues, the metaphoric power of this image historically surpassed the actual practices concerning usury: "the Aristotelian concept of usury was more influential in determining medieval thought on the subject than were the preceding centuries of a more realistic development in the Roman Law, or of actual behavior" (295). For a discussion of the legal and religious development of usury laws see Taeusch; Benjamin Nelson, *The Idea of Usury: From Tribal Brotherhood to Universal Otherhood*, 2nd ed. (Chicago: University of Chicago Press, 1969); and John T. Noonan, *The Scholastic Analysis of Usury* (Cambridge, Mass.: Harvard University Press, 1957). For early modern religious responses to usury, see Helen C. White, *Social Criticism in Popular Religious Literature of the Sixteenth Century* (New York: Macmillan, 1944), 189–223, and Charles H. George, "English Calvinist Opinion on Usury, 1600–1640," *Journal of the History of Ideas* 18 (1957): 455–74.

6. Aristotle, *The Politics*, ed. Stephen Everson (Cambridge: Cambridge University Press, 1988), 15; on Aquinas, see Norman Jones, *God and the Moneylenders: Usury and Law in Early Modern England* (Oxford: Blackwell, 1989), 9. For a discussion of the distinctions in Aquinas's use of Aristotle see Noonan, *Scholastic Analysis*, 51–53. Ann Louise Kibbie, "Monstrous Generation: The Birth of Capital in Defoe's *Moll Flanders*

and *Roxana*," *PMLA* 110 (1995): 1027–28; E. Pearlman, "Shakespeare, Freud, and the Two Usuries, or, Money's a Meddler," *English Literary Renaissance* 2 (1972): 218.

7. References throughout this article are to the following texts: John Lyly, *A Pleasant Conceited Comedy Called Mother Bombie* and *Love's Metamorphosis* in *The Plays of John Lyly*, ed. Carter A. Daniel (Lewisburg, Pa.: Bucknell University Press, 1988); John Stockwood, *A Bartholomew Fairing for Parentes, to bestow upon their sonnes and daughters, and for one friend to give unto another* (London: John Harrison, 1589); Henrie Smith, *A Preparative to Marriage. The summe whereof was spoken at a contract, and inlarged after. Whereunto is annexed a Treatise of the Lord's Supper: and another of Usurie* (London: Thomas Man, 1591).

8. C. John Sommerville links this increasing concern for children's moral status to the rise of the Puritan movement in *The Discovery of Childhood in Puritan England* (Athens, Ga.: University of Georgia Press, 1992).

9. Jones, *God and the Moneylenders*, 48–63.

10. At first glance the composition of Smith's treatise suggests that there is little connection between children and usury. Each of the three main topics, marriage, the lord's supper, and usury, are separated by individual title pages that suggest that each section is an autonomous work. However, the content of these sections suggests that there is a theme driving the collation of these texts.

11. Ilana Krausman Ben-Amos, *Adolescence and Youth in Early Modern England* (New Haven, Conn.: Yale University Press, 1994), suggests that "since one third of the population of early modern England was under the age of 15" (40) in a society that valued labor, children were most likely working and performing simple tasks at a young age.

12. Ivy Pinchbeck and Margaret Hewitt, *Children in English Society, Volume I: From Tudor Times to the Eighteenth Century* (Toronto: University of Toronto Press, 1969); for a discussion of the Court of Wards, see 58–74, and Joel Hurstfeld, *The Queen's Wards: Wardship and Marriage Under Elizabeth I* (London: Frank Cass, 1973). For a discussion of the Courts of Orphans, see Pinchbeck and Hewitt, 81–90; all citations to follow hereafter in the text.

13. According to Pinchbeck and Hewitt, *Children*, 79–81, in some cases the guardian could gain direct control of the orphan's estate only if a security was paid to the City Chamber. Although many towns had provisions for their citizens' orphans I am, for the sake of brevity, focusing my discussion on London's Court of Orphans.

14. For a detailed analysis of the Poor Law's legislation about children, see Pinchbeck and Hewitt's chapters, "The Vagrant and Delinquent Child" and "The Succourless Poor Child," esp. 126–46.

15. Great Britain, Public Record Office, *Calendar of State Papers, Foreign Series, of the Reign of Edward VI, 1547–1553* (Nendeln: Kraus Reprint, 1979). Hereafter cited in text by regnal year and chapter.

16. John Stockwood, *A Bartholomew Fairing For Parentes*, 22. Hereafter cited in the text by page number.

17. Charles Gibbon, *A Work Worth the Reading*. Hereafter cited in the text by page number.

18. Although this statement appears in the next section of the treatise, "Whether the Father may lawfully disinherit his first borne," I have included it here because it is clearly a continuation of the argument Philogus introduces at the beginning of the treatise.

19. References to Lyly's plays will be limited to act and scene.

20. Lyly's play *Gallathea* also considers the issue of whether parents' concern for their children can be detrimental to society. Unlike his position in *Mother Bombie*, however, Lyly seems to come out in support of these "overnatural" and hence loving parents.

21. See G. K. Hunter, *John Lyly: The Humanist as Courtier* (Cambridge, Mass.: Harvard University Press, 1962), 220–29, for a discussion of how wit "becomes the motive of the plot" in *Mother Bombie*.

22. Interestingly, Protea hypocritically accuses and criticizes the merchant for participating in usurious transactions, claiming that he has acquired his social position as a member of the gentry through the profits of usurious transactions (3.2). Protea may also be participating in such practices, but she is aware of the social stigma the designation of usurer places on an individual.

23. See Patricia Fumerton, *Cultural Aesthetics: Renaissance Literature and the Practice of Social Ornament* (Chicago: University of Chicago Press, 1991), 173–87, and Joyce Oldham Appleby, *Economic Thought and Ideology in Seventeenth-Century England* (Princeton, N.J.: Princeton University Press, 1978).

24. Peter Stallybrass and Allon White, *The Politics and Poetics of Transgression* (London: Methuen, 1986), 27–79.

25. This quote, from Stockwood, *A Bartholomew Fairing*, 49, 59, which links the pig to the fair, is strangely appropriate, for it is soon followed by a discussion that examines the use of pigs to represent children.

Notes to Chapter 10/Potter

1. Geffrey Whitney, *A Choice of Emblemes and Other Devises*, English Experience 161 (Leyden, 1586; Amsterdam: Theatrum Orbis Terrarum, 1969), 155.

2. Quotations from Juan Luis Vives's works are cited in the text using the following abbreviations:

REW: *Vives and the Renascence Education of Women*, ed. Foster Watson, Educational Classics (London: Edward Arnold, 1912).

D: *Tudor School-Boy Life: The Dialogues of Juan Luis Vives*, ed. and trans. Foster Watson (London: Frank Cass, 1970).

3. Quotations from the works of Desiderius Erasmus are cited in the text using the following abbreviations:

DPI: *De pueris statim ac liberaliter institutendis declamatio* (1529), trans. Beert C. Verstraete, *Collected Works of Erasmus, Literary and Educational Writings 4*, ed. J. K. Sowards (Toronto: University of Toronto Press, 1985).
C: *The Colloquies of Erasmus*, trans. Craig R. Thompson (Chicago: University of Chicago Press, 1965).
TT: *Tudor Translations of the Colloquies of Erasmus* (1536–1584), ed. Dickie A. Spurgeon (New York: Scholars' Facsimiles and Reprints, 1972).

4. *Richard Mulcaster: Positions Concerning the Training Up of Children* (1581), ed. William Barker (Toronto: University of Toronto Press, 1994), 175.12–14. Quotations from the work of Maturin Corderius are cited in the text using the following abbreviation:

P: *Pueriles confabulatiunculae* (1617), trans. John Brinsley (1614), ed. R. C. Alston, English Linguistics 1500–1800, no. 269 (Menston: Scolar, 1971).

5. Robert Burton, *The Anatomy of Melancholy* (1621), ed. Floyd Dell and Paul Jordan-Smith (New York: Tudor, 1938), 285–86; William Kempe, printed in Craig R. Thompson, *Schools in Tudor England* (Washington, D.C.: Folger Shakespeare Library, 1958), pl. 12.

6. D. W. Sylvester, *Educational Documents 800–1816* (London: Methuen, 1970), 113.

7. Walter J. Ong, "Latin Language Study as a Renaissance Puberty Rite," *Studies in Philology* 56 (1959): 107; Bon Record: Records and Reminiscences of Aberdeen Grammar School from the earliest times by many writers, ed. H. F. Morland Simpson (Edinburgh: Ballantyne Press, 1906), 107.

8. For the Tudor homily, see "Homily on the State of Matrimony," ed. Ian Lancashire, *Renaissance Electronic Texts* 1.2, online, University of Toronto, Internet, 25th Feb. 1999, 2:18, line 375. (http://www.library.utoronto.ca/utel/ret/ret.html); see also *The Catechism of Thomas Becon with Other Pieces Written by him in the Reign of King Edward the Sixth (1560–64)* (Cambridge: Cambridge University Press, 1844), 338; Vives quote from *Vives: On Education, a Translation of the "De Tradendis Disciplinis" of Juan Luis Vives*, ed. and trans. Foster Watson (Cambridge: Cambridge University Press, 1912), 179; Erasmus qtd. in T. W. Baldwin, *William Shakspere's Small Latine & Lesse Greeke* (Urbana, Ill.: University of Illinois Press, 1944), 2.241; on Alcibiades, see Philip A. Stadter, introduction to "Alcibiades" by Plutarch, in *Greek Lives: A Selection of Nine Greek Lives*, trans. Robin Waterfield (Oxford:

Oxford University Press, 1998) 218–19. Alcibiades was renowned for his bisexual promiscuity, and Erasmus may be suggesting this should be a feature of the debate.

9. Reprinted in Nicholas Orme, *Education and Society in Medieval and Renaissance England* (London: Hambledon, 1989), 139.

10. Rebecca Bushnell, *A Culture of Teaching: Early Modern Humanism in Theory and Practice* (Ithaca, N.Y.: Cornell University Press, 1996), 40.

11. "Nice Wanton,'" *The Tudor Interludes Nice Wanton and Impatient Poverty*, ed. Leonard Tennenhouse, The Renaissance Imagination, vol. 10 (New York: Garland, 1984). Quotations are cited in the text by line number.

12. Greg Walker, *The Politics of Performance in Early Renaissance Drama* (Cambridge: Cambridge University Press, 1998), appendix 2, 234–35; Michael Shapiro, *Children of the Revels: The Boy Companies of Shakespeare's Time and Their Plays* (New York: Columbia University Press, 1977), 152. See also Walker, *The Politics of Performance*, 234–35; on statutes at King Edward VI's school, see R. H. Harris et al. *A History of Norwich School* (Norwich: N.p., 1991), 46.

13. Mulcaster, *Positions*, 270.29–33.

14. Thomas Elyot, *The Book named The governor* (1531), ed. S. E. Lehmberg (London: Dent, 1962), 20; Sir Henry Sidney qtd. in *A History of Shrewsbury School 1552–1952*, ed. J. Basil Oldham (Oxford: Basil Blackwell, 1952), 314–15. Sir Henry's letter may, in fact, have contributed more to perpetuating the problem than dispelling it, as this letter was published and publicly circulated in 1591 as an exemplum of a very godly letter to a son.

15. Ursula Potter, "The naming of Holofernes in *Love's Labour's Lost*," *English Language Notes* 38 (December 2000): 13–26.

16. "Misogonus," in *Six Anonymous Plays*, ed. John S. Farmer (London: Early English Drama Society, 1906), 140.

17. Mulcaster, *Positions*, 277.34–279.6.

18. Linda Woodbridge, *Women and the English Renaissance: Literature and the Nature of Womankind, 1540–1620* (Brighton: Harvester Press, 1984), 290, 127.

19. Harrison qtd. in Frederick J. Furnivall, ed., *The Babees Book*, Early English Text Society o.s. 32 (London: 1868), xxiv. By blaming women first, Harrison indicates that mothers were usually the decision making parent in relation to schooling, although this may be a rhetorical tactic for indirectly critiquing fathers.

20. On Kirkwall schoolmasters, see William P. L. Thomson, *Kirkwall Grammar School from Sang School to Comprehensive* (The Orkney Islands Council, 1976), 14; on Aberdeen, see H. F. Morland Simpson, *Bon Record: Records and Reminiscences of Aberdeen Grammar School from the earliest times by many writers* (Edinburgh: Ballantyne, 1906),

313–14; on Guildford, see D. M. Sturley, *The Royal Grammar School Guildford* (N.d.: N.p., 1980), 90; and on Almondbury, see Taylor Dyson, *Almondbury and Its Ancient School* (Huddersfield: The Advertiser Press, 1926), 20–21.

21. *July and Julian*, ed. F. P. Wilson (Oxford: Oxford University Press, 1955). Quotations are cited within the text by line number.

22. John M. Ward, *Music for Elizabethan Lutes* (Oxford: Clarendon Press, 1992), 1.16–21.

23. Reprinted in *Educational Documents 800–1816*, ed. D. W. Sylvester (London: Methuen, 1970), 114.

24. Erasmus, *De ratione studii*, trans. Brian McGregor, in *Collected Works of Erasmus, Literary and Educational Writings 2*, ed. Craig R. Thompson (Toronto: University of Toronto Press, 1978), 687–89.

25. "The World and the Child," *A Select Collection of Old English Plays*, rev. and enlarged by W. Carew Hazlitt, 4th ed. (London: Reeves and Turner, 1874), 1:247.

26. "The Court and Country?" and Ruthin School statutes rpt. in Sylvester, *Educational Documents*, 142–43, 112.

27. The Black Bill was a paper on which the names of transgressing students were entered for due punishment. See John Brinsley, *Ludus Literarius* (1612), ed. E. T. Campagnac, *Ludus Literarius or The Grammar Schoole* (Liverpool: Liverpool University Press, 1917), 287. Quote from Dyson, *Almondbury*, 21.

28. Ralph A. Houlbrooke, *The English Family 1450–1700* (London: Longman, 1984), 141. Houlbrooke cites Jeremy Taylor (1616–1667).

29. Letter qtd. in T. H. Vail Motter, *The School Drama in England* (London: Longman, 1929), 107; on mothers' bribes, see Edith Rowland, ed., *A Pedagogue's Commonplace Book* (London: Dent, 1924), 46. Compare *The School of Infancy* (1654), which encourages better relations between child and master by suggesting that parents send gifts to the schoolmaster and that the schoolmaster also give small presents to the child, for which the parents should compensate him. John Amos Comenius, *The School of Infancy*, ed. Ernest M. Eller (Chapel Hill, N.C.: University of North Carolina Press, 1956), 121.

30. Becon, *A New Catechism*, 343; *The Tragedy of Othello, the Moor of Venice*, ed. Anne Barton, in *The Riverside Shakespeare*, gen. ed. G. Blakemore Evans (Boston: Houghton, 1974) 1.3.147.

31. Beatrice White, ed., *The Vulgaria Of John Stanbridge and the Vulgaria of Robert Whittinton*, Early English Text Society o.s. 187 (London: Kegan Paul, 1932), 87–88.

32. William Hormon, *Vulgaria* (1519), The English Experience, no. 745 (Amsterdam: Theatrum Orbis Terrarum, 1975), 142. There is no suggestion of irony in the Latin or in the *vulgaria* context.

33. Becon, *A New Catechism*, 343.

34. Desiderius Erasmus, *De recta latini graecique sermonis pronun-*

tiatione dialogus (1528), trans. Maurice Pope, in *Collected Works of Erasmus, Literary and Educational Writings 4*, ed. J. K. Sowards (Toronto: University of Toronto Press, 1985), 391.

35. Brinsley, *Ludus Literarius*, 37–40.

36. Edward Pudsey's Commonplace Book, MS Eng. poet D.3, The Bodleian Library, Oxford, 14.

37. Henry Peacham, *The Complete Gentleman* (London, 1622; Amsterdam: Da Capo Press, 1968), 34.

38. John Lyly, *Mother Bombie*, ed. Kathleen M. Lea (Oxford: Oxford University Press, 1948), 1.3.316–19; *The Second Maiden's Tragedy*, ed. Anne Lancashire (Manchester: Manchester University Press, 1978) 1.1.167.

Selected Bibliography

Abbott, Mary. *Family Ties: English Families 1540–1920.* London: Routledge, 1993.

Amtower, Laurel, and Dorothea Kehler, eds. *The Single Woman in Medieval and Early Modern England: Her Life and Representation.* forthcoming from Arizona Center for Medieval and Renaissance Studies.

Amussen, Susan Dwyer. *An Ordered Society: Family and Village in England, 1560–1725.* New York: Blackwell, 1988.

———. "'Being Stirred to Much Unquietness': Violence and Domestic Violence in Early Modern England." *Journal of Women's History* 6 (1994): 70–85.

Amussen, Susan Dwyer, and Adele F. Seeff. *Attending to Early Modern Women.* Newark, Del.: University of Delaware Press, 1998.

Ariès, Philippe. *Centuries of Childhood: A Social History of Family Life.* New York: Knopf, 1962.

Ariès, Philippe, and Georges Duby. *A History of Private Life.* 5 vols. Cambridge, Mass.: Belknap Press of Harvard University Press, 1987–91.

Ben-Amos, Ilana Krausman. *Adolescence and Youth in Early Modern England.* New Haven, Conn.: Yale University Press, 1994.

Boswell, John. *The Kindness of Strangers: The Abandonment of Children in Western Europe from Late Antiquity to the Renaissance.* New York: Vintage, 1988.

Brodsky, Vivien. "Widows in Late Elizabethan London: Remarriage, Economic Opportunity and Family Orientation." In *The World We Have Gained: Histories of Population and Social Structure,* ed. Lloyd Bonfield, Richard M. Smith, and Keith Wrightson. Oxford: Basil Blackwell, 1986.

Burt, Richard, and John Michael Archer. *Enclosure Acts: Sexuality, Property, and Culture in Early Modern England*. Ithaca, N.Y.: Cornell University Press, 1994.

Carlson, Eric Josef. *Marriage and the English Reformation*. Cambridge, Mass.: Blackwell, 1994.

Carlton, Charles. *The Court of Orphans*. Leicester: Leicester University Press, 1974.

Clark, Alice. *Working Life of Women in the Seventeenth Century*. London: Routledge, 1919. Rpt. New York, N.Y.: A.M. Kelley, 1968.

Crawford, Patricia, and Laura Gowing. *Women's Worlds in Seventeenth-Century England: A Sourcebook*. London: Routledge, 2000.

Cressy, David. *Birth, Marriage and Death: Ritual, Religion, and the Life-Cycle in Tudor and Stuart England*. Oxford: Oxford University Press, 1997.

Davis, Natalie Zemon. *Society and Culture in Early Modern France: Eight Essays*. Stanford, Calif.: Stanford University Press, 1975.

Dolan, Frances. *Dangerous Familiars: Representations of Domestic Crime in England, 1550–1700*. Ithaca, N.Y.: Cornell University Press, 1994.

Dubrow, Heather. *A Happier Eden: The Politics of Marriage in the Stuart Epithalamium*. Ithaca, N.Y.: Cornell University Press, 1991.

———. "The Message from Marcade: Parental Death in Tudor and Stuart England." In *Attending to Women in Early Modern England*, ed. Betty S. Travitsky and Adele F. Seeff. Newark, Del.: University of Delaware Press, 1994.

———. *Shakespeare and Domestic Loss: Forms of Deprivation, Mourning, and Recuperation*. Cambridge: Cambridge Univ. Press, 1999.

Earle, Peter. "The Female Labour Market in London in the Late Seventeenth and Early Eighteenth Centuries." *Economic History Review*, 2nd ser., 42 (1989): 328–53.

Erickson, Amy Louise. *Women and Property in Early Modern England*. London: Routledge, 1993.

Ezell, Margaret. *The Patriarch's Wife: Literary Evidence and the History of the Family*. Chapel Hill, N.C.: University of North Carolina Press, 1987.

Ferguson, Margaret W. "A Room Not Their Own: Renaissance Women as Readers and Writers." In *The Comparative Perspective on Literature: Approaches to Theory and Practice*, ed. Clayton Koelb and Susan Noakes, 93–116. Ithaca: Cornell University Press, 1988.

Ferguson, Margaret W., Maureen Quilligan, and Nancy J. Vickers, eds. *Rewriting the Renaissance: The Discourses of Sexual Difference in Early Modern Europe*. Chicago: University of Chicago Press, 1986.

Fildes, Valerie. *Breasts, Bottles, and Babies: A History of Infant Feeding*. Edinburgh: Edinburgh University Press, 1986.

Fletcher, Anthony, and John Stevenson. *Order and Disorder in Early Modern England*. Cambridge: Cambridge University Press, 1985.

Foyster, Elizabeth. "A Laughing Matter? Marital Discord and Gender Control in Seventeenth-Century England." *Rural History* 4, no. 1 (1993): 5–21.

Fraser, Antonia. *The Weaker Vessel: Woman's Lot in Seventeenth-Century England*. London: Weidenfeld and Nicolson, 1984.

Friedman, Alice T. *House and Household in Elizabethan England: Wollaton Hall and the Willoughby Family*. Chicago: University of Chicago Press, 1989.

Fumerton, Patricia, and Simon Hunt, eds. *Renaissance Culture and the Everyday*. Philadelphia: University of Pennsylvania Press, 1999.

Garber, Marjorie. *Vested Interests: Cross-Dressing and Cultural Anxiety*. New York: Routledge, 1992.

Girouard, Mark. *A Country House Companion*. New Haven, Conn.: Yale University Press, 1987.

———. *Hardwick Hall*. London: National Trust, 1989.

———. *Life in the English Country House: A Social and Architectural History*. New Haven, Conn.: Yale University Press, 1978.

———. *Robert Smythson and the Elizabethan Country House*. New Haven and London: Yale University Press, 1983.

———. *Town and Country*. New Haven, Conn.: Yale University Press, 1992.

Goldberg, Jonathan. *Desiring Women Writing*. Stanford, Calif.: Stanford University Press, 1997.

Goody, Jack. *Development of the Family and Marriage in Europe*. Cambridge: Cambridge University Press, 1983.

Goody, Jack, Joan Thirsk, and E. P. Thompson. *Family and Inheritance: Rural Society in Western Europe, 1200–1800*. Cambridge: Cambridge University Press, 1976.

Gottlieb, Beatrice. *The Family in the Western World from the Black Death to the Industrial Age*. New York: Oxford University Press, 1993.

Griffiths, Paul. *Youth and Authority: Formative Experiences in England,*

1560–1640. Oxford: Clarendon Press; Oxford and New York: Oxford University Press, 1996.

Griffiths, Paul, Adam Fox, and Steve Hindle. *The Experience of Authority in Early Modern England.* New York: St. Martin's Press, 1996.

Hall, Kim F. "Reading What Isn't There: 'Black' Studies in Early Modern England." *Stanford Humanities Review* 3 (1993): 23–33.

———. *Things of Darkness: Economies of Race and Gender in Early Modern England*. Ithaca, N.Y.: Cornell University Press, 1995.

Heal, Felicity. *Hospitality in Early Modern England*. Oxford: Clarendon Press, 1990.

Heal, Felicity, and Clive Holmes. *The Gentry in England and Wales, 1500–1700*. Basingstoke, England: Macmillan, 1994.

Helgerson, Richard. *Adulterous Alliances: Home, State, and History in Early Modern European Drama and Painting*. Chicago: University of Chicago Press, 2000.

Holt, James. "Feudal Society and the Family in Early Medieval England: iv. The Heiress and the Alien." *Transactions of the Royal Historical Society*, 5th ser. 35 (1985): 1–28.

Houlbrooke, Ralph A., ed. *Death, Ritual, and Bereavement*. London: Routledge, 1989.

———. *The English Family, 1450–1700*. London: Longman, 1984.

Howard, Jean E. "The New Historicism in Renaissance Studies." *English Literary Renaissance* 16 (1986): 13–43.

Howard, Maurice. *The Early Tudor Country House: Architecture and Politics 1490–1550*. London: George Philip, 1987.

Hull, Suzanne. *Chaste, Silent, and Obedient: English Books for Women, 1475–1640*. San Marino, Calif.: Huntington Library, 1982.

———. *Women According to Men: The World of Tudor-Stuart Women*. Walnut Creek, Calif.: AltaMira Press, 1996.

Hurstfield, Joel. *The Queen's Wards: Wardship and Marriage Under Elizabeth I*. 2nd ed. London: Frank Cass, 1973.

Hutson, Lorna. *The Usurer's Daughter: Male Friendship and Fictions of Women in Sixteenth-Century England*. London: Routledge, 1994.

Ingram, Martin. *Church Courts, Sex and Marriage in England, 1570–1640*. Cambridge: Cambridge University Press, 1987.

Jardine, Lisa. *Still Harping on Daughters: Women and Drama in the Age of Shakespeare*. Brighton: Harvester Press and Barnes and Noble, 1983.

Kelly-Gadol, Joan. "The Social Relations of the Sexes: Methodological Implications of Women's History." *Signs* 1 (1976): 809–24.

Kelso, Ruth. *Doctrine for the Lady of the Renaissance.* Urbana, Ill.: University of Illinois Press, 1956.

Klein, Joan Larsen, ed. *Daughters, Wives, and Widows: Writings by Men about Women and Marriage in England, 1500–1640.* Urbana, Ill.: University of Illinois Press, 1992.

Lamb, Mary Ellen. "The Cooke Sisters: Attitudes Toward Learned Women in the Renaissance." In *Silent But For the Word: Tudor Women as Patrons, Translators, and Writers of Religious Works,* ed. Margaret Patterson Hannay. 107–25. Kent, Ohio: Kent State University Press, 1985.

Leventen, Carol. "Patrimony and Patriarchy in *The Merchant of Venice.*" In *The Matter of Difference: Materialist Feminist Criticism of Shakespeare,* ed. Valerie Wayne. New York: Harvester Wheatsheaf, 1991.

Levine, David. *Family Formation in an Age of Nascent Capitalism.* New York: Academic Press, 1977.

Lewalski, Barbara Kiefer. *Writing Women in Jacobean England.* Cambridge: Cambridge University Press, 1993.

Macfarlane, Alan. *Marriage and Love in England: Modes of Reproduction, 1300–1840.* New York: Blackwell, 1986.

———. *The Origins of English Individualism.* New York: Cambridge University Press, 1979.

Mendelson, Sara, and Patricia Crawford. *Women in Early Modern England.* Oxford: Oxford University Press, 1998.

Mertes, Kate. *The English Noble Household 1250–1600: Good Governance and Politic Rule.* Oxford: Blackwell, 1988.

Miller, Naomi J., and Noami Yavney, eds. *Maternal Measures: Figuring Caregiving in the Early Modern Period.* Aldershot, England: Ashgate Press, 2000.

O'Day, Rosemary. *The Family and Family Relationships, 1500–1900: England, France, and the United States of America.* London: Macmillan, 1994.

Orgel, Stephen. *Impersonations: The Performance of Gender in Shakespeare's England.* Cambridge: Cambridge University Press, 1996.

Orlin, Lena Cowen. *Private Matters and Public Culture in Post-Reformation England.* Ithaca, N.Y.: Cornell University Press, 1994.

Outhwaite, R. B., ed. *Marriage and Society: Studies in the Social History of Marriage.* New York: St. Martin's Press, 1981.

Parker, Patricia. *Literary Fat Ladies: Rhetoric, Gender, Property*. London: Methuen, 1987.

Pinchbeck, Ivy, and Margaret Hewitt. *Children in English Society. Vol. 1, From Tudor Times to the Eighteenth Century*. Toronto: Toronto University Press, 1969.

Pollock, Linda. *Forgotten Children: Parent-Child Relations from 1500–1900*. Cambridge: Cambridge University Press, 1983.

Prior, Mary. *Women in English Society, 1500–1800*. London: Methuen, 1985.

Purkiss, Diane. *The Witch in History: Early Modern and Twentieth-Century Representations*. London: Routledge, 1996.

Raber, Karen L. "Murderous Mothers and the Family/State Analogy in Classical and Renaissance Drama." *Comparative Literature Studies* 37 (2000): 298–320.

Schultz, James A. *The Knowledge of Childhood in the German Middle Ages, 1100–1350*. Philadelphia: University of Pennsylvania Press, 1995.

Shammas, Carole. "The Domestic Environment in Early Modern England and America." *Journal of Social History* 14 (1980): 1–24.

———. *The Pre-Industrial Consumer in England and America*. Oxford: Clarendon Press, 1990.

Sharpe, J. A. *Early Modern England: A Social History 1550–1760*. 2nd ed. New York: Arnold, 1987.

Sharpe, Pamela. *Women's Work: The English Experience 1650–1914*. London: Arnold: Oxford University Press, 1998.

Sommerville, C. John. *The Discovery of Childhood in Puritan England*. Athens, Ga.: University of Georgia Press, 1992.

Spring, Eileen. *Law, Land and Family: Aristocratic Inheritance in England, 1300 to 1800*. Chapel Hill, N.C.: University of North Carolina Press, 1993.

Stallybrass, Peter. "Patriarchal Territories: The Body Enclosed." In *Rewriting the Renaissance: the Discourses of Sexual Difference in Early Modern Europe*, ed. Margaret Ferguson, Maureen Quilligan, and Nancy Vickers, 123–42. Chicago: University of Chicago Press, 1986.

———. "The World Turned Upside Down: Inversion, Gender, and the State." In *The Matter of Difference: Materialist Feminist Criticism of Shakespeare*, ed. Valerie Wayne, 201–20. Brighton: Harvester Press, 1991.

Stone, Lawrence. *Broken Lives: Separation and Divorce in England, 1660–1857*. Oxford: Oxford University Press, 1993.

———. *The Family, Sex and Marriage in England, 1500–1800*. New York: Harper & Row, 1977.

———. *Road to Divorce: England 1530–1987*. Oxford: Oxford University Press, 1990.

———. *Uncertain Unions: Marriage in England 1660–1753*. Oxford: Oxford University Press, 1992.

Summerson, John. *Architecture in Britain 1530–1830*. Rev. 7th ed. Harmondsworth: Penguin, 1986.

Thirsk, Joan, John Chartres, and David Hey. *English Rural Society, 1500–1800: Essays in Honor of Joan Thirsk*. Cambridge: Cambridge University Press, 1990.

Thomson, Gladys Scott. *Life in a Noble Household, 1641–1700*. New York: Alfred A. Knopf, 1937.

Underdown, David. *Revel, Riot, and Rebellion: Popular Politics and Culture in England 1603–1660*. Oxford: Oxford University Press, 1985.

Wiesner, Merry E. *Women and Gender in Early Modern Europe*. Cambridge: Cambridge University Press, 1993.

Wiltenburg, Joy. *Disorderly Women and Female Power in the Street Literature of Early Modern England and Germany*. Charlottesville, Va.: University Press of Virginia, 1992.

Woolf, Virginia. *A Room of One's Own*. London: Hogarth Press, 1929.

———. *Three Guineas*. London: Hogarth Press, 1938.

Wrightson, Keith. *English Society, 1580–1680*. New Brunswick, N.J.: Rutgers University Press, 1982.

———. "Infanticide in Earlier Seventeenth-Century England." *Local Population Studies* 15 (1975): 10–22.

About the Contributors

CLAIRE M. BUSSE is assistant professor of English at La Salle University. She is currently working on a book about children in the early modern stage.

STEPHANIE CHAMBERLAIN is assistant professor of English at Southeast Missouri State University, where she teaches Shakespeare and Renaissance literature. Her work on early modern marriage appears in the *Ben Jonson Journal*. She is currently working on a study of clandestine marriage as represented on the Shakespearean stage.

PILAR CUDER-DOMÍNGUEZ is associate professor at the University of Huelva, Spain, where she teaches courses on English literature, women's writing in English, and postcolonial literature. She is currently engaged in a research project on Restoration women writers, including an edition of the dramatic works of Catherine Cockburn Trotter.

HEATHER DUBROW, Tighe-Evans professor and John Bascom professor at the University of Wisconsin-Madison, is the author of five scholarly books. The most recent is *Shakespeare and Domestic Loss: Forms of Deprivation, Mourning, and Recuperation*. Her other publications include a coedited collection of essays, numerous articles on early modern literature and pedagogy, and two chapbooks of poetry.

Kari Boyd McBride is assistant professor of women's studies at the University of Arizona, where she teaches courses in feminist theories and early modern literature and culture. Recent publications include *Country House Discourse in Early Modern England: A Cultural Study of Landscape and Legitimacy*.

Marianne Novy is professor of English and women's studies at the University of Pittsburgh. She has written *Love's Argument: Gender Relations in Shakespeare* and *Engaging with Shakespeare: Responses of George Eliot and Other Women Novelists*, and has edited *Women's Re-Visions of Shakespeare, Cross-Cultural Performances, Transforming Shakespeare*, and *Imagining Adoption*. She is writing a book on literary representations of adoption.

Ursula Potter was awarded a PhD from the University of Sydney in 2001 for a thesis on *Pedagogy and Parenting in English Drama 1560–1610* that explores these issues through an analysis of Tudor school texts, school records, and sixteenth century writings on education. She has previously published on the schoolmaster, Holofernes, in *Love's Labour's Lost*, and has a book chapter forthcoming on greensickness, the disease of virgins, in *Romeo and Juliet*, as well as an article on Patient Griselda as political allegory for Anne Boleyn in a 1560s play. She is an honorary associate in the School of English, Art History, Film and Media at the University of Sydney.

Sid Ray teaches Shakespeare, early modern literature, and women's and gender studies at Pace University, where she is associate professor of English. She has just completed a book on marriage and monarchy in early modern texts and is currently coediting a collection of essays on medieval and early modern heroes in film.

Jessica Slights is assistant professor of English at Acadia University in Wolfville, Nova Scotia. She has published on various aspects of Shakespearean drama in *Studies in English Literature, Studies in Philology*, and *English Studies in Canada*. She has recently completed a book-length study of the everyday in Shakespeare's comedies.

Katharine Capshaw Smith is assistant professor at Florida International University where she teaches African-American literature, ethnic American writers, children's literature, and women's studies. Her articles on race and gender have appeared in *The Southern Quarterly, Ariel, Children's Literature, The Lion and the Unicorn*, and other academic journals.

Susan Staub is professor of English at Appalachian State University. She has published articles on various aspects of Renaissance prose and poetry. This essay is part of a larger study of women and domestic violence in seventeenth century street literature. Her current research focuses on motherhood in Shakespeare.

Index